THEY SAY THE WIND IS RED

THEY SAY THE WIND IS RED

The Alabama Choctaw—
Lost in Their Own Land

JACQUELINE ANDERSON MATTE

FOREWORD BY VINE DELORIA JR.

NEWSOUTH BOOKS

Montgomery

Newsouth Books
105 S. Court Street
Montgomery, AL 36104

Copyright © 2002, 2018 by Jacqueline A. Matte.
All rights reserved under International and Pan-American Copyright
Conventions. Published in the United States by NewSouth Books, a division of
NewSouth, Inc., Montgomery, Alabama.

Library of Congress Cataloging-in-Publication Data

ISBN: 978-1-58838-079-1 (trade paper)
ISBN: 978-1-60306-247-3 (ebook)

An earlier edition of this book with the same title was printed in 1999 by
Greenberry Publishing Company with the ISBN 0-926291-04-01. The present
volume was re-edited and contains additional content.

Design by Randall Williams
Printed in the United States of America

The painting on the front cover, *Choctaw Belle* by Phillip Romer, is used with
the permission of and by the courtesy of the Reeves Center, Washington and Lee
University, Lexington, Virginia.

To the Elders

CONTENTS

FOREWORD

BY VINE DELORIA JR.

ARELESS HISTORIANS have not done well by American Indians or their general readers. Failing to use original sources and shamelessly using each other's footnotes and fantasies, they have created a homogenous history around a thinly disguised theme of manifest destiny. In such accounts, the struggles of real people are never made clear, and nowhere is this practice more insidious than in the treatment of eastern Indians. Believing that Andrew Jackson's Removal Act was the final event in the story of the Indian nations east of the Mississippi, they move quickly to the Oregon Trail and the conflicts with the colorful and romantic Plains Indians, convincing themselves that no further attention should be paid to the eastern Indians.

Actually, removal begins when the Indian nations of the Ohio Confederacy, after the treaty of Greenville, ceded large tracts of land including some sites critical to domination of the fur trade in the Illinois-Indiana-Ohio area. Removal then shifted briefly to a small band of Cherokees and some miscellaneous parties of Creeks, Delawares, and Choctaws who moved into Texas in an effort to escape the relentless advance of the Europeans. By the 1830 passage of the Removal Act, many southeastern tribes had begun to look anxiously at western lands and, aside from extinguishing the few remaining tracts of land owned by Potawatomi families in Indiana, the eastern region was pretty much cleared of formal Indian groups. The 1830s Removal treaties then formally removed the bulk of people willing to immigrate and loyal to their governments.

But from Virginia to the Texas border, there were hundreds of small villages of Indian people who did not remove to the West. Many of

the smallest groups were simply not in the way of white settlement,
living as they did in obscure bays and alongside rivers where the land
was unsuited to the commercial growing of cotton, indigo, and sugar
cane. These tribal groups had been self-sufficient before the coming of
the white man and many retained their traditional way of life into the
twentieth century. Indian nations such as the Tunica, the Chitimacha,
Houma, Apalachicola, and many villages of Cherokees, Choctaws, Creeks,
Seminoles and Chickasaws were simply left to fend for themselves. They
had not, as a rule, been party to the tedious negotiations with the federal
government and saw no reason to burden themselves with the stifling
bureaucracy that it represented.

Over the decades some of these groups sought and received federal
recognition as Indian nations for whom the United States had a respon-
sibility. During John Collier's term as commissioner of Indian Affairs,
anthropologists were sent to various communities in the Southeast to
determine whether the inhabitants were Indians and if they should be
allowed to organize under the Indian Reorganization Act. An apocryphal
tradition relates that these scholars measured the heads of the people in
Robeson County, North Carolina, and those individuals who matched
the average measurements of the Blackfeet Indians in Montana were
declared to be Tuscaroras and received benefits and land under the Re-
settlement Act. Obviously federal recognition was not the rigorous task it
is today. In fact nearly one hundred Indian communities have been given
federal status in the past century, many with no more than a simple bill
sponsored by a local congressman who listened sympathetically to their
story. Today, the federal acknowledgement process is confused, unfair,
and riddled with inconsistencies. Much of the confusion is due to the
insistence that Indian communities meet criteria which, if it had been
applied in the past, would have disqualified the vast majority of presently
recognized Indian groups.

The MOWA Choctaws have a typical profile for southeastern Indians.
Their credentials are solid and the historical data that identifies them as
Indians extends back to the days when they were integral villages in the
Choctaw Nation. Few people realize that not all Indians were removed

when the Army marched the nations to the West. Indeed, the fragmentation of the Five Civilized Tribes before, during, and after Removal makes the MOWA history a fascinating story of persistence and survival but certainly does not eliminate them from the groups of people that should rightfully be recognized as Indians. That they were once called "Cajuns" by local whites is merely a symptom of the tri-racial problems in the American South from the very beginning of settlement.

The MOWA are and have always been a self-governing community following ancestral traditions and not accommodating themselves to the rigid institutional organization that the majority of the Indian nations adopted. Traditional ways, the MOWA rightly feel, are more precise and enable the community to meet the needs of its people whereas the institutional process serves only those who fit into rigidly defined categories of assistance. Thus the political and social profile of the MOWA does not always fit into the neat and narrow categories required by the federal acknowledgment process. So the MOWA need help in interpreting their traditional ways in a format that institutional minds can understand.

If you like this book, and there is certainly enough food for deep thought here, why not write your senators and congressman and ask them to give the MOWA Choctaws a hand and let's get this recognition problem solved once and for all.

VINE DELORIA JR. *is a Standing Rock Sioux and professor emeritus at the University of Colorado in Boulder, where he taught history, law, religious studies, and political science. He is one of the most outspoken figures and significant voices in Native American affairs. His works promote Native American cultural nationalism and a greater understanding of Native American history and philosophy.*

Acknowledgments

THIS BOOK could not have been written without the stories told by the elders, without whose prodigious memories the stories handed down by their elders would now be lost. I have recorded their oral histories here, using their own words to reflect each individual's cadence or speech pattern in hopes the voices will be "heard" by our readers.

The elders include: Sancer Byrd, Bootsie Joe Byrd, Lessie Mae Byrd, Mary Byrd, Ressie Byrd, Albert Chastang, Abb Cole, Jane Davis, "Tall" Sancer Davis, Alice Echols, Guy Fields, Spencer Fields, Charles Lofton, Camilla Reed, Ida Reed, Mary Reed, Mauvilla Reed, Ruth Reed, Van Early Reed, William Reed, Clasbee Rivers, Josephine Rivers, Ola Irene Rivers, Price Rivers, Rosie Byrd Rivers, Ruth Shepard, Daisy Jane Snow, Dinah Snow, Ella Snow, Ella Taylor, Leon Taylor, Mary Taylor, Annie "Shomo" Weaver, Bennett Weaver, Chandler Weaver, Gallasneed Weaver, Lee Weaver, Mary Ann Weaver, Richard Weaver, Roosevelt Weaver, Willard "Bud" Weaver, Woodie Weaver, and Delia White.

MY ASSOCIATION WITH THE MOWA Choctaw began in 1980 when I was writing *History of Washington County: The First County in Alabama*. I contacted Chief Framon Weaver because I wanted to include the story of the MOWA. Tribal members appreciated this and furnished much helpful information.

After that book was published in 1982, Chief Weaver asked if I would help research the tribe's history as part of an ongoing Federal Acknowledgment Petition project. I thought this would be intriguing, and it was, but it also turned out to be quite a challenge. Local genealogist Doris Jordan Brown was hired to help compile MOWA ancestor charts; her work and friendship have been invaluable. Several anthropologists worked on this project in the 1980s, and I want to especially recognize the contributions of Susan Greenbaum, Ph.D., University of South Florida, Margaret Searcy, M.A., University of Alabama, and Samuel J. Wells, Ph.D., University of Southern Mississippi. After several submissions of petitions and rejections for not meeting the BIA/BAR requirements, Richard W. Stoffle, Ph.D., University of Arizona, was hired in 1996 to do a neutral third-party review. He brought a fresh approach to our project with insight gained from twenty-plus years of experience working with sixty American Indian tribes and participating in two prior Federal Acknowledgment Petitions. In addition, he did extensive field research among rural communities located in southern Mississippi, about sixty miles west of the MOWA Choctaw lands. His contribution—looking at the MOWA as a group rather than as individual families, as had been done by researchers for the Bureau of Indian Affairs-Branch of Acknowledgment and Research (BIA/BAR)—confirmed our research. We are grateful for Dr. Stoffle's help and his professionalism.

Many thanks go to the MOWA who volunteered their time and hospitality to the researchers. Special recognition and thanks are due the liaisons (or "go-betweens"), Peter A. Rivers, Reva Lee Reed, and the late Mary Taylor, who went with the "outsiders" from house to house interviewing the elders. Our car became mired in muddy ruts and in sandbeds as we hunted for cemeteries so that we could record births and deaths. Dust, dirt, and mildew greeted us in the basements of county courthouses where we searched through land records, estate papers, and deed books. We visited libraries and archives in Alabama, Florida, Georgia, Mississippi, Oklahoma, and Washington, D.C. We appreciate the patience of all the librarians and archivists who helped us. The Administration for Native Americans, a division of the Department of Health and Human Services, partially funded the initial research. After the submission of the first petition in 1988, volunteers continued the research through 1996 to meet the criteria established by the BIA/BAR.

During one summer, I photographed old pictures, some of which are included in this volume. The Ethnic Studies Division of the W. Stanley Hoole Special Collections Library at the University of Alabama funded this project. The negatives of more than two hundred pictures of the MOWA are deposited there.

A number of my historian friends were kind enough to read my manuscript and offer advice. I thank Virginia Van der Veer Hamilton, Leah Rawls Atkins, Virginia Pounds Brown, and Jay Higginbotham for their suggestions and encouragement. I am especially grateful to Stewart Rafert, author of *The Miami Indians of Indiana: A Persistent People, 1654–1994*, a story of Native Americans who sought federal acknowledgment and were rejected. I met Stewart when we served on a grants-review panel for the Administration for Native Americans in Washington, D.C. We compared stories and commiserated on the futility of trying to satisfy the BIA/BAR requirements for federal acknowledgment. He read my manuscript and made invaluable suggestions for reorganization and revision. Three other friends read the manuscript, each of whom offered a different perspective: Milton Brown, film producer of *Indian Blood*; Darla Fields Graves, former director of the Alabama Indian Affairs Commission; and Sam Hill, attorney and professor of Indian law at Cumberland Law School. Thank you.

I am grateful to Joey Brackner, state folklorist with the Alabama State Council on the Arts, who directed me to the "Choctaw Belle" portrait. He said this painting would be perfect on the cover. He was right.

In 1990, I met Vine Deloria, Jr., when we both testified as expert witnesses in Congress before the U.S. Senate Committee on Indian Affairs. Subsequently he graciously agreed to write a foreword for the revised edition of *They Say the Wind Is Red*. The comments of the foremost advocate of this generation for Native American rights are valued and appreciated.

W. Richard West, director of the Smithsonian Institution's National Museum of American Indians is a long-time friend and classmate of Laretta Weaver. He visited the Rivers Church where the Rev. Gallasneed Weaver was pastor for more than thirty years. Chief Longhair Taylor also knew Dr. West as a schoolmate at Bacone College. All of us appreciate Dr. West's enthusiastic endorsement of our book.

Also, I express my gratitude to my cousin Mary Ann Wells, author of many books, among which *Native Land: Mississippi, 1540–1798* and

Searching for Red Eagle: A Personal Journey into the Spirit World of Native America qualify her as an expert on Southeastern Indians for refining my work; and to Jennifer Horne, writer and editor, who at the time of this writing worked as associate editor for *Alabama Heritage* magazine.

My husband Jack supported my research, provided airline tickets to Washington when I went there to testify before congressional committees, and put up with my long summer visits with the MOWA. He refers to this work as my search "for the Holy Grail," which unfortunately too accurately describes the quest for federal recognition. I continue to be grateful for his encouragement and understanding.

The original edition of *They Say the Wind Is Red* sold out. Suzanne La Rosa and Randall Williams of NewSouth Books then agreed to republish it. Randall has smoothed out the rough spots and improved the book overall. He suggested that I bring the book's final chapter, the epilogue, up to date, which gave me the opportunity to share where the MOWA Choctaw stand now, as of 2002. I also added to the present edition a short resource guide on Southeastern Indian Genealogy.

THEY SAY THE WIND IS RED

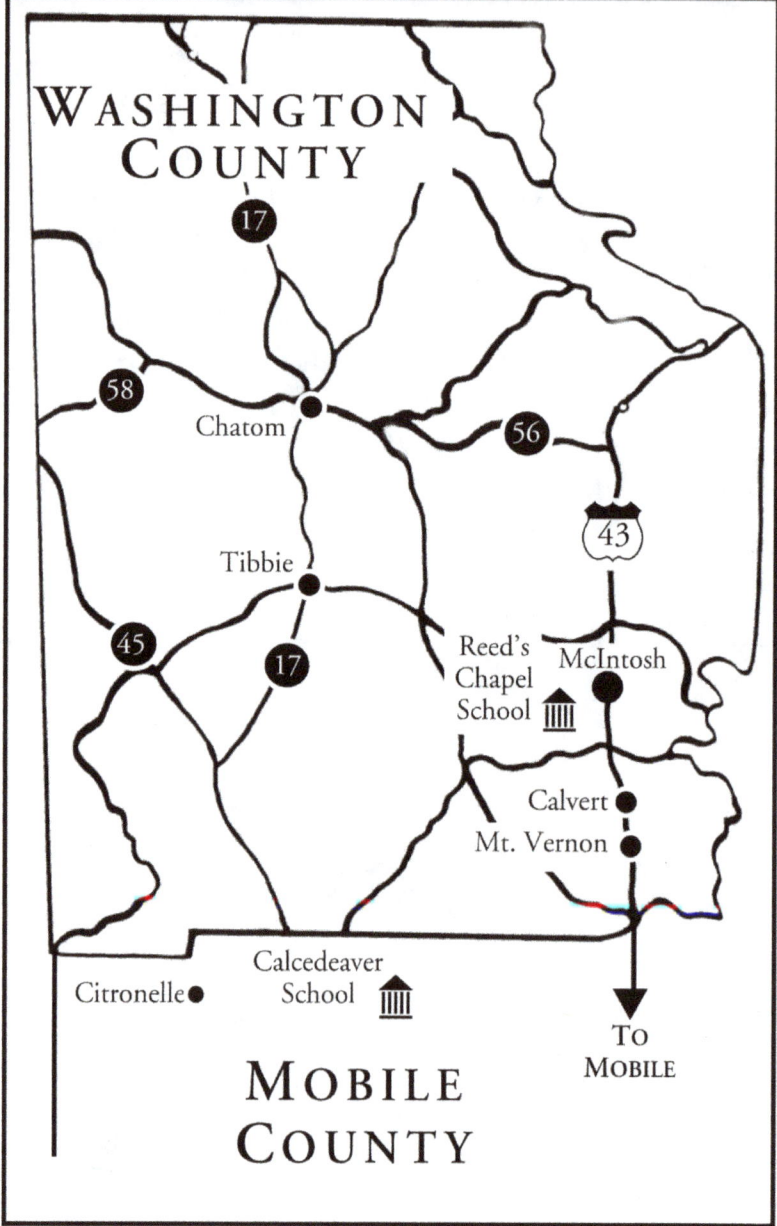

MOWA LANDS

WASHINGTON COUNTY

17

58

Chatom

56

43

Tibbie

45

17

Reed's
Chapel
School

McIntosh

Calvert

Mt. Vernon

Citronelle

Calcedeaver
School

MOBILE COUNTY

To
Mobile

1

INTRODUCTION

WHILE VISITING CITRONELLE in southwest Alabama in 1934, Carl Carmer, author of *Stars Fell on Alabama*, observed that some of the local inhabitants were neither whites nor blacks and asked his host, "What's your theory of the origin of these people?"

"I can tell you as good a one as the next man. Which one do you want to hear?"

"Doesn't anybody know?"

"Try asking around, just for fun."

So, for two days, Carmer asked around.

> "Long time ago wasn't no folks on them sand flats . . . Them Cajans sprung up right out'n the ground. Some say they come from animals—coons and foxes and suchlike—but that ain't right. Just sprung up out'n the ground."[1]

Tellingly, Carmer's story reflects Choctaw origin legends that say that the Choctaw emerged from a hole in the huge mound, *Nanih Waiya*. The common theme of these legends is that the Choctaw were "created in the center of the mound by the Great Spirit and that they crawled through a hole or cave to the surface."[2]

The mislabeling of the ancestors of today's MOWA Choctaw as so-called "Cajans" apparently began in the 1880s with a local state senator, L. W. McRae.[3] He called his constituents "Cajuns"[4] under the mistaken assumption that they were somehow related to the Louisianians of Acadian descent. Although the MOWA Choctaw vehemently repudiated this misconception, the term stuck, mainly because it served to demarcate their group from the surrounding black and white populations. In 1924, the MOWAs' origins grabbed the attention of politicians again, as well as that of anthropologists, sociologists, and journalists, with publicity surrounding the murder trial of an Indian who had shot the deputy sheriff of Mobile County—his partner in selling moonshine whiskey. Because of the publicity, Governor William W. Brandon ordered a report to determine the circumstances that led to a business arrangement between this nonliterate Indian and the officer of the law who betrayed him. Following that report, many news articles and studies were published, each presenting a brief discussion of MOWA origins. These accounts are all similar, and one might assume that their redundancy implied validity. However, each succeeding author had simply echoed the ones before. Little historical research was ever done. "No one knows where those people came from" was a recurrent observation about the Choctaws living in the southwest corner of Alabama. Scanty and questionable data was merely embellished with speculation. All the accounts were written, like earlier chronicles of history, from a white point of view.

The people who are now known as the MOWA Choctaw have always asserted that they were the descendants of historical Indians who remained in Alabama after the 1830s. In fact, most but not all Southeastern Indians were moved in the 1830s from their homelands to inhospitable lands west of the Mississippi River, lands already claimed by western Indians. Southeastern Indians did not want to leave, but were coerced into ceding land by promises of fair treatment and good land to be held in perpetuity. Mixed-blood leaders, bribed with land reserves and generous annuities, encouraged their tribespeople to comply. But many still refused to leave. Fragments of small bands, families, and individuals remained in isolated places—caves, mountains, and swamps—hunting, fishing, and living off the land. Some worked as day laborers for farmers or owners of pine forests. Landowners, needing farm labor and turpentine workers, helped hide them by passing them off as slaves, threatening to expose them as Indians if they tried to leave without working out their indebtedness for food and housing.

Thus, the MOWAs' ancestors remained isolated in the swamps and forests of south Alabama and were virtually unnoticed as being different from other frontier families until after Reconstruction. Then, as the laws and customs of segregation supplanted those of slavery, everyone who was not "pure white" was identified as black. Black and white were the only legally recognized racial/social classifications. Because Indians in south Alabama fit neither category, they were labeled "Cajuns." While their Indian identity was submerged, they remained separate from Southern society, constrained subjectively by their fear and suspicion of white men and restrained objectively by the racial stratification of the postbellum South.

Some critics have argued that the Choctaw of south Alabama lost their lands in an 1805 treaty[5]; however, in 1830 they still lived on their traditional lands, thus having *de facto* if not *de jure* ownership. Whether or not the south Alabama Choctaw legally owned their lands in 1830, they existed as an Indian community.[6] "Since 1830, the Choctaw who remained have been left to follow their own inclination, the greater part of them wandering not only through Mississippi, but generally in Louisiana and the southern part of Alabama, deriving a precarious subsistence by hunting and fishing in swamps," wrote William Armstrong in 1847.[7]

Today's MOWA include descendants of the Six Towns Choctaw. The Six Towns District (comprised of six villages) was in the southeastern district of the Choctaw Nation. The Choctaw, one of the southern tribes of Muskhogean stock, lived west of the Tombigbee and Mobile rivers. Remnants of the Six Towns Choctaw remained northwest of the city of Mobile, in swamps and pine barrens, in their original homeland.[8] Today's tribe, who have officially named themselves the MOWA Choctaw, are descendants of not only the Six Towns Choctaw, but also of the ancient peoples known as the Tohomé, Naniaba, and Mobilian, all of whom historically had villages in the modern MOWA country.[9] These separate peoples were lumped in with the Choctaw by the English for treaty purposes, a policy the Americans followed. Their descendants continue today not only as a recognizable community of Indians in Alabama, but also as a group aggressively seeking restoration of full federal status as an Indian tribe.

While the terms "American Indian" or "Native American" are widely used and considered "politically correct," the MOWA refer to themselves simply as "Indians"; therefore, that term is used in this history.

MOWA, of course, refers to the geographic area of the Choctaw homeland in north *Mo*bile County and south *Wa*shington County. This descriptive term was selected by the MOWA themselves.

2

Known and Unknowable Ancestors

1800–1813

"During the year 1812 Tecumsi sent his prophet on a visit to all the southern tribes. He passed through the Chahta [Choctaw] nation, called a meeting at several places, where he made speeches and prophesied against the American people, predicting the downfall of the government of the United States, the utter destruction of the white people and the repossession of the whole continent by the red people. . . . The prophet went to the Six Towns where he was met by Apushimataha [Pushmataha], who told him . . . that his predictions were false, and that he must absent himself from the Chahta country. . . . His prophecies had, however, been favorably received by some of the Chahtas, and forty-five families of them went over and fought with the Muskogees against the whites. Apushimataha, with a brigade of Chahtas, joined the United States army and was of much assistance to them in the Creek war. As soon as the war had ended Apushimataha hunted up and put to the sword all he could of his traitor countrymen. Most of them, however, escaped, running into the marshy country near Mobile, Ala., where they remain to this day."

— Gideon Lincecum, 1861[1]

I N THE EARLY PART of the nineteenth century, white settlers who emigrated into the territory now forming the southeastern United States found it occupied by tribes of Indians who had lived there for centuries. The Creek, Cherokee, Chickasaw, and Choctaw Indians saw the land they inhabited become an object of desire as settlers passed through to make new homes in the Mississippi Territory. In 1798 the newly formed United States established the Mississippi Territory (later the states of Mississippi and Alabama). Spain still claimed Mobile and the land below the thirty-first parallel (the present Alabama-Florida state line) according to the terms of the Pinckney Treaty made in 1795. Inevitably, this interest in the homeland of southeastern Indians caused contention, conflict, and the eventual forced removal of the tribes to Indian Territory in what is now Oklahoma.

During this era of disruption and dislocation, few written records were left of the ancestral families of the south Alabama Choctaw. Most of their names are unknowable, but some are known because their stories were handed down from generation to generation. Also, several ancestors were involved in treaty making and others traded at the Choctaw Trading House, so their names are recorded. Others are unrecorded in government records but their presence is documented in accounts by travelers and in oral history. Altogether, these people, known and unknowable, are the ancestors of the MOWA Choctaw.

Almost from the time of its establishment, the United States government worked to take control of Indian homelands from native inhabitants and began negotiating a series of treaties to accomplish that goal. Under President Thomas Jefferson, a cynical campaign increased the pressure on the southern Indians to relinquish their lands. The history of reluctant land cessions convinced Jefferson that a speedier method of gaining Indian lands was needed. He approved a plan that called for establishing trading houses or "factories," luring the Indians into contracting enormous debts, then forcing the chiefs into ceding their tribal lands so as to settle the accounts with honor. Indians were encouraged to purchase supplies from a factory on credit and pay for them at an unspecified future date with deerskins and furs. Buying on credit became common, and these factories offered unlimited credit to encourage large debt.[2]

As credit purchases escalated, Indian agents were instructed to offer debt liquidation in exchange for land cessions. Jefferson stated this government objective in correspondence with William Henry Harrison on

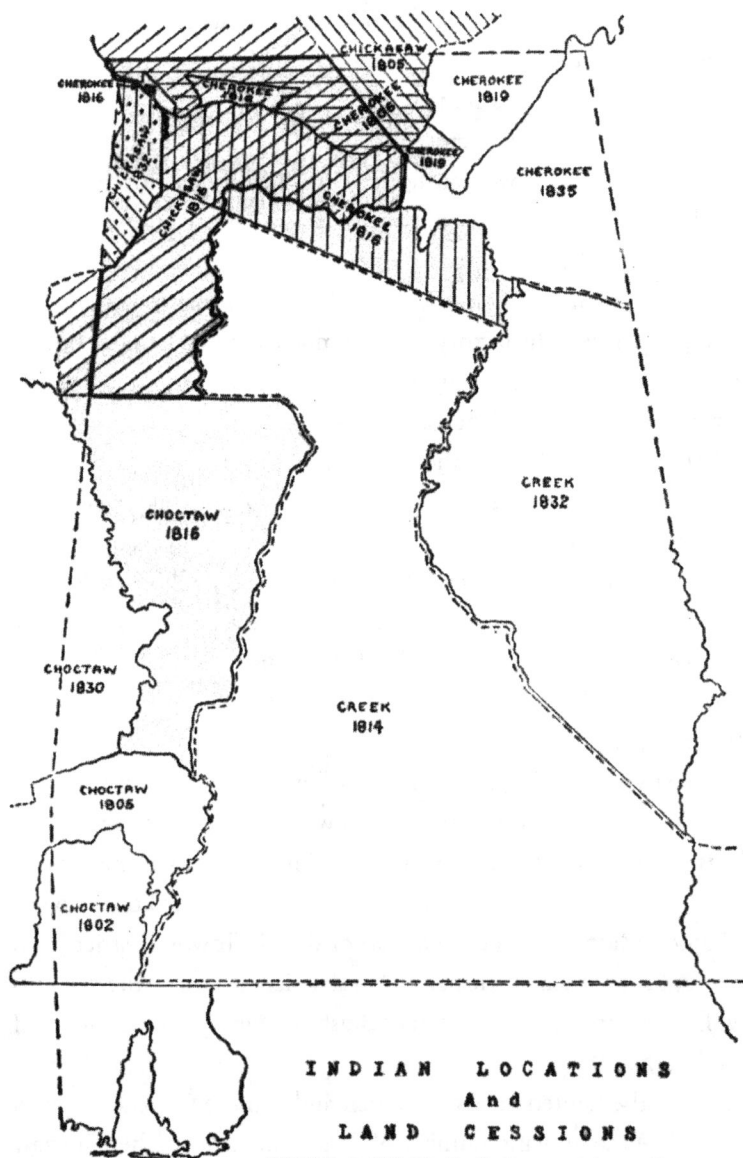

INDIAN LOCATIONS
And
LAND CESSIONS

ACCORDING TO 18ᵀᴴ ANNUAL REPORT OF THE BUREAU OF ETHNOLOGY

This map depicts the conflicting tribal claims to lands in Alabama in the early 1800s. The dates of the various cessions indicate the gradual acquisition by the U.S. government of all Indian lands in the state.

February 27, 1803, when he wrote: "We shall push our trading houses, and be glad to see . . . [the Indians] run in debt, because we observe that when these debts get beyond what the individual can pay they become willing to lop off by a cession of lands."[3]

Plans to open two new factories in the Mississippi Territory for the Choctaw and Chickasaw were authorized in 1802. The site for the Choctaw Trading House was St. Stephens, in Washington County. Located on the Tombigbee River close to its junction with the Alabama River, on the east-west Indian trail from the Lower Creek territory to Natchez on the Mississippi River, the factory could compete for all the trade coming down the rivers, plus all the trails converging toward Mobile.[4]

Payment of land for debt gained large Choctaw cessions for the United States stretching from the Mobile River in Alabama to the Pearl River in Mississippi. Between 1800 and 1830, the federal government approached the Choctaw forty times to negotiate land cessions. More than thirteen million acres were ceded.[5] In 1801 the Choctaw felt the effects of Jefferson's Indian policy when they were asked to sign a treaty ceding over two million acres of land. In return, the Choctaw were granted "two thousand dollars in goods and merchandise and three sets of blacksmith's tools."[6]

The next year, 1802, a treaty made at Fort Confederation provided for a complete delineation of the Choctaw Nation in accordance with the British treaty of 1765; this treaty carried no compensation.[7] One of the Choctaw chiefs who signed this treaty on behalf of the Lower Towns was "Poosha Mattahaw" (Pushmataha) of the Six Towns District, who lived near St. Stephens.[8] Turner Brashears signed and witnessed this treaty. Descendants of the Choctaw Brashears family are members of the modern MOWA Band.

In 1803, the United States again demanded more Choctaw land to accommodate the growing number of American settlers. The Choctaw signed the Treaty of Hobuckintopa (St. Stephens), ceding over eight hundred thousand acres of land lying above Mobile, in part to satisfy debts. General James Wilkinson gave the chiefs "as consideration in full for the above concession: fifteen pieces of strouds [cloth], three rifles, one hundred and fifty blankets, two hundred and fifty pounds of powder, two hundred and fifty pounds of lead, one bridle, one man's saddle, and one black silk handkerchief."[9] Choctaw chiefs signing for these goods were Pio Mingo, Pasa Mastubby Mingo, Tappena Oakchia, Tuskenung Cooche, Cussoonuckchia, and Pushapia, chiefs residing on the Tombigbee, near St. Stephens. Young Gaines, an interpreter who signed the treaty as a witness, had four children by Kalioka, a Choctaw woman. Their daughter, Rose Gaines, has many descendants among the MOWA Band.

Land acreage ceded in the previous treaties seems relatively small in comparison with the four million acres of the Treaty of Mount Dexter in 1805. Colonel Silas Dinsmoor, United States Agent to the Choctaw, negotiated the 1805 treaty in council with the chiefs. Mingo Homastubbee proposed that the nation dispose of some lands for the payment of debts due their traders and merchants. He had attended the council of the four nations where the Creek had relinquished all claim to the land in the fork of the Tombigbee and Alabama rivers, and he proposed that this land, which the Choctaw claimed as their territory, be sold.

Dinsmoor approved of Homastubbee's proposal but advised that an even larger tract of land be offered for sale, as this would not only enable the Choctaw to pay their debts, but would give them an annuity to supply necessaries and establish a fund to defray their contingent expenses. The eastern boundary was set "between the Creeks and Chaktaws on the ridge dividing the waters running into the Alabama from those running into the Tombigbee."[10] Though the land between the rivers (the forks) had been claimed by both Creek and Choctaw, "many of the fertile fields already rested in the hands of mixed bloods who claimed priority because of long-term occupancy. In many cases these 'squatters' were actually 'half-breeds,' and their kinsmen, residing there with the knowledge and permission of the Creek and Choctaw nations," wrote Samuel J. Wells.[11]

Also, Article IV of this treaty confirmed an earlier grant to John McGrew of fifteen hundred acres on the Tombigbee River above Hobuckintopa (St. Stephens). It "was in fact granted to the said McGrew by Opiomingo Hesnitta, and others, many years ago. This grant, made during British occupation, was confirmed in 1799 by Choctaw chiefs

Piamingo Hometah of Hobuckintopa and Poosha ma Stubbee of Okah Coppasa towns."[12] After Piamingo Hometah gave his land away, he and his band of Six Towns Choctaw lived on High Hill, at that time a relatively inaccessible, isolated area northwest of present day McIntosh, Alabama, where his descendants now live.[13]

While the Treaty of 1805 removed the Choctaw claim to land north of Mobile in south central Mississippi Territory,[14] it did not actually remove all Six Towns Choctaw. Six Towns inhabitants, unhappy with their loss of land, strengthened their alliance with the Spanish, who still occupied land south of the 31st parallel (West Florida). The Spanish also saw the 1805 treaty as a threat to their political strength.[15] Captain Shamburgh, United States commander of Fort Stoddert (present day Mount Vernon, Alabama), located at the boundary line between Spanish territory and the Mississippi Territory, reported:

> "an Indian informs me that the chiefs of the six towns have sent word to Mr. [Samuel] Mitchell, the Indian Agent, that he must tell Mr. [John] McKee, lately appointed an Agent for the six towns—that they wanted no beloved man [agent] in their Towns—those rascals you must know sir have always been attached to the Spaniards."[16]

The Spanish furnished the Six Towns with military supplies in 1805, with the aim of taking territory north to Tennessee. The Six Towns Choctaw raided the area and drove eleven hundred head of cattle across the boundary line into Spanish Territory.

The Six Towns had little regard for boundary lines whether international or individual. They allied themselves with the country that offered them the best deal for trade and protection.[17] Eventually, the majority were won over to the American side by the increased efforts of the United States government to trade fairly with Indians by establishing trading posts with reputable agents to protect Indians from unscrupulous traders. Only licensed traders, Indians, or spouses of Indians were allowed to trade by the Americans.[18]

The principal factor (agent) at the Choctaw Trading House at St.

Stephens, George S. Gaines, was appointed in May 1805. A native of Virginia, he was a nephew and son-in-law of Young Gaines and was greatly loved and trusted by the Choctaw.[19] His account books show who traded, who received pay as interpreters, and what goods were traded.[20] Customers and employees were identified according to tribal affiliation and occupation.

Known ancestors of modern MOWA Choctaw—Hoosha Hooma; Young Gaines, interpreter; Charles Frazer, interpreter; Mingo Pushmataha; General William Colbert, Chickasaw—bartered bear oil, kegs of honey, beeswax, bacon, groundnuts, kegs of tobacco, and a variety of furs and deerskins for the cloth, iron tools, arms and ammunition, and plows kept in stock by the federal government. White settlers sold fodder, salt, and wood. Also, George S. Gaines reported that "hunters of the Creek settlement at the falls of the Black Warrior came frequently to trade and I had occasional visits from Creeks residing beyond the Alabama River."[21] St. Stephens, established by the Spanish as Fort San Esteban in 1789 and now headquarters for Choctaw trade and a newly established federal land office, became a brawling frontier town at the crossroads of the Mississippi Territory.

Increasingly, Americans demanded more land and "squatted" without title or permission on Indian land. Although the Choctaw, Creek, and Cherokee had ceded small areas of land around Mobile and Huntsville to the United States, Indians still held most of Alabama and in general meant to keep their lands. But they were eventually coerced into granting the American government the right to maintain horse paths on which pioneers would be allowed to travel peaceably. One path, the Federal Road, led through the immense Creek lands stretching through Georgia westward through Alabama along the Alabama River to St. Stephens on the Tombigbee River. Another led through Chickasaw lands from Muscle Shoals on the Tennessee River to St. Stephens. Soon, white families, horse-drawn carts, cattle, hogs, and horses were threading their way through Indian territory. Horse paths had become highways of settlement.

The Federal Road, with its constant stream of settlers, was a major source of irritation to the Creek Indians as it divided the Creek Nation.

The traditional Upper Creek nation experienced a religious awakening, similar in strength and focus to that of the tribes of the Old Northwest under Tenskwatawa, the Shawnee Prophet who embraced traditional beliefs, and his brother Tecumseh, who was an experienced military and political leader.[22] The Upper Creek rejected European-American influences and embraced the belief of common Indian ownership of the land, while the Lower Creek, who early on were closely associated with whites near the coast, gradually became more assimilated. In 1812 Tecumseh and his prophets came south with the goal of uniting all southern tribes against the whites. With his message of unity, Tecumseh fueled the religious awakening of the Upper Creek.[23] Beginning as a religious or civil war between the Upper and Lower Creek Indians, the Creek War in Alabama became a part of the War of 1812. United States General Andrew Jackson led the American militia against the Upper Creek faction known as the "Red Sticks."[24]

Although leaders of the Cherokee, Chickasaw, and Choctaw refused Tecumseh's plea to form an Indian confederacy, forty-five Choctaw warriors and their families embraced Tecumseh's message and joined the Upper Creek, according to Gideon Lincecum.[25] Choctaw chief Pushmataha and other Choctaw leaders vigorously supported the Americans and condemned the Choctaw who opposed their decision.[26] United States agent George S. Gaines recorded in his Day Book: "pd. Cholutubbee for bringing a letter express from the principal chief of the middle Choctaws to the agent of the Choctaw Trading House at St. Stephens advising him of the determination of the Choctaw's Council to put any of their people to death who might dare to join the Creek in a war against the U.S., Aug. 15, 1813."[27]

Today, Pushmataha is seen by MOWA descendants of the forty-five Six Towns families as a traitor to his people for fighting against fellow Indians. Pushmataha joined General Jackson with a large number of his warriors—two hundred Six Towns were sent to Mobile; four hundred assembled at Mount Vernon, and one hundred thirty-six served at Fort St. Stephens. Jackson's aide-de-camp ordered that, "They are to be mustered into service on the same footing, in the same numbers and with the same proportion of officers and non-commissioned officers, as the regular troops of the U.S."[28] Encouraged by the British, but meagerly supplied by the Spanish at Pensacola, the Upper Creek Red Sticks fought against great odds—nontraditional Creek, Choctaw, Chickasaw, Cherokee, American militia—and lost. Refugees from the war, mostly women and children, homeless and hungry, fled to places of safety in the forests. There they joined the now-homeless Choctaw families from Six Towns who had fought against the Americans.

Caught up in the passions of their time, whites, Indians, blacks, and mixed-bloods fought and died during the Creek War. Ironically the Red Sticks, in rising up against white settlements on their borders, hastened the loss of their entire domain. The only Indians who signed the Treaty of Fort Jackson, ceding some twenty million acres of land to the United States, were "the friendly" Creeks who were allied with the Americans. Ultimately the Creek War was the turning point in the destruction of all southern tribes.

3

DISAFFECTED CHOCTAW

— THE 'LOST TRIBE'

1813–1830

*"It does not matter who the swamp belongs to. No one lives on it,
nor does any white man ever go into it. It is all marsh or water, except an occasional dry spot of elevated ground. On these little islands
we have our houses and live very comfortably and out of the way
of the rest of the world. We have our canoes, and fish and hunt for
ducks and other water fowls during the winter, and in the summer
we move out of the marshy country into the pine woods lying between here and New Orleans. There it is dry and healthy and game
is very plentiful. We shall never go back to the Chata people again."*
— LEADER OF DISAFFECTED CHOCTAW, 1824[1]

A FTER THE WAR OF 1812 was officially over and the Treaty of
Fort Jackson signed, pioneers flocked to the former Creek lands
in large numbers. By the time the Alabama Territory was formed
in 1817, when Mississippi became a state, the non-Indian population
had increased more than 1,000 percent[2] (Indians were not counted in
U.S. censuses).

The forty-five Choctaw families who had joined the Upper Creek
against the Americans remained in the vicinity of south Alabama. Two
accounts written within the first decade after the Creek War describe
how the ancestors of the MOWA survived during this era of rapid development. In 1819, James L. Cathcart was an agent appointed by the

U.S. Navy to locate and reserve for naval purposes public lands along the coast of the Gulf of Mexico. Cathcart kept a journal. His entry for March 31, 1819, from Mobile, reads:

> The steam boat being detained until tomorrow in consequence of the last gale, we had an opportunity to view the Choctaw village about 1½ miles from the town (if it may be so called). Their huts are the work of an hour, composed of a few forked sticks with others placed across & partially covered with bark on three sides & open on the front, & are not sufficient to shelter them from the elements. Their furniture consists of a pot to boil their corn & a wooden platter to eat it from, a small barrel to bring water in & a gourd shell to drink out of. They sleep on the ground wrapt up in a filthy blanket with a stone for their pillow which, with a few cords made of deerskin & a few who have a rifle or gun of some sort, is the whole bulk of their worldly possessions. They are without exception the most abject of the human race, & yet, those miserable beings have both ambition & vanity & aim at distinction amongst themselves. Frequently you will see both male & female daubed all over with soot & painted with patches of a vermillion colour on their cheeks & round their eyes & their heads decorated with feathers, pieces of tin & other ornaments. The men sometimes hunt, but more frequently are seen following their females who are loaded with firewood, & often with a young child sitting on the top of their load with another at the breast & leading a third, while their lazy husbands saunter unconcerned behind them waiting until the poor creatures dispose of their load & then inhumanly deprive them of their hard earned trifle & regale themselves with rum & leave their wives and children to suffer with hunger. Some few have petticoats, which they procure from the inhabitants, but the children are all naked, & I have seen some stout girls as naked as they were born. It is necessary, however, to observe that the Choctaws who are in the vicinity of Mobile are outlaws & banished from their tribe for various misdemeanors . . .[3]

In 1824, Gideon Lincecum reported:

Soon after the death of Apushimataha [Pushmataha], I was down at Mobile, where I met with the leader of the fugitive Chata . . . when I told them that Apushimataha was dead, they made plans to go home . . . nearly a hundred of them dressed in their Chata costumes went about the streets of Mobile singing and collecting money for their trip . . . they sang and walked the street all day. I saw them when it was nearly night; the leader held up his sack showing me that it was nearly full. The next day I saw all the men, leader and all, in town drunk. The leader said to me that he made more money yesterday than he could have made in the Chata country in a lifetime, and laughed heartily. He said also that his people were all rich and doing well. The women carried fat pine and sold it in town every day and the men hunted and sold a good deal of venison and a great many ducks and fish at good prices, and that they were rich, better off for clothes and provisions than any of the Chata in the nation . . .[4]

Choctaw legends claim that from time immemorial the Choctaw had hunted and camped near Twenty-seven-mile Bluff on the Mobile River-Cedar Creek area, from below Mt. Vernon south to Cold Creek in Mobile County. During French occupation, Indian land was granted to French settlers. Chastang's Bluff, settled first by the French, was later occupied during the time of Spanish rule by a Creole colony descended from Dr. John Chastang.[5]

The homeless Choctaw camped in this area where refugees from the Creek War joined them. Dr. Chastang died in 1813 and left his vast holdings to his "beloved worthy friend and companion, Louison, a free negro woman (who has resided with me for twenty years past and has been my sole attendant in health and particularly so in sickness)" and then to their mixed blood children, called Creoles.[6] A story in a Baldwin County Historical Society Quarterly described the family — "Jacque [John] Chastang took refuge in the deep swamps near Stockton when the English took over Mobile. With his Indian-black wife he lived apart from the outside world."[7] Descendants of John Chastang and Louison appear in censuses variously as white, Creole, colored, Indian, mulatto, other, and black. Jerome Chastang—son of Cecile Weatherford (described below) and Edward Saustiene Chastang, son of John Chastang—is the ancestor of today's MOWA Chastangs.

Today the MOWA tell the legendary story of Cecile's mother, a refugee of the Creek War, "the Indian woman who swam the river with her baby on her back." The story of her heroic escape from the embattled Fort Mims has been has been told through the generations. Fort Mims, a hastily erected fort around the home of Samuel Mims, an Indian countryman (a Euro-American married to an Indian woman), was located at Tensaw Lake on the lower Alabama near a channel called the Cut-Off, which served as a route across Nannahubba Island to the Tombigbee and Mobile rivers. Historians cite the Fort Mims Massacre as a key event that set off the Creek War. Amidst increasing hostilities between white settlers and the Red Stick Creek faction, several hundred American settlers, slaves, and families of mixed blood ancestry had sought protection in the crude fort. On August 30, 1813, a party of Red Sticks led by Chief Red Eagle (William Weatherford) attacked and overran the fort. As many as five hundred settlers, including women and children, were killed. As news of the massacre spread through the Territory, it increased the efforts of those like General Andrew Jackson who wanted to drive out all Indians remaining in what is present-day Alabama.

Some of Cecile Weatherford's many descendants, including Sancer Byrd, Ola Irene Rivers, Rosie Rivers, Emma Johnston, and Ruth Shepard relate the essential details of Cecile's mother's story: Her name was Nancy Fisher. Her baby's name was Cecile. Cecile's daddy was William Weatherford, a Creek warrior. Grandma Tiny was Cecile's daughter.[8] Historians have been unable to document this tradition, although records do show a Nancy Fisher (alias Oaks) who was crudely identified by Colonel Gilbert C. Russell, a U.S. officer who served in the Creek War, as a "half-breed strumpet entitled to not one tit."[9] Accounts of other people fleeing from the Battle of Fort Mims to safety on the Choctaw side of the river can be found in *The Creek War of 1813–14* by H. S. Halbert and T. H. Ball. The exact number and all the names of those who escaped were never fully determined.[10]

Family stories, documented by government and church records, indi-cate that Cecile Weatherford first married Saustiene Chastang who was born at Twenty-seven-mile Bluff, the first site of Mobile on the Mobile River. They had two children, Jerome and James, who were born at Fort Stoddert, located on the northeast side of present-day Mt. Vernon.[11] Cecile then married Dave Weaver and had at least ten more children, some of whom were born at Cold Creek and others near Mt. Vernon: Thomas, Lorinda, Ellen "Tiny" Bretina, David Crockett, Emma, Eliza Jane, Mathilda, Albert, Alfred, and George W.[12] Perhaps Nancy Fisher, mother of Cecile, eventually married Philip Chastang because in 1847, Philip left his land to his wife, Nancy, and after her death, to her grand-daughter, Fotenay Weaver.[13] One of the witnesses to this will was William Byrd, son of Anna Weaver and Lemuel Byrd, refugee Cherokee-Creek from Georgia.

The Weaver-Byrd extended family was one of many fleeing from General Andrew Jackson's continuing war on Indians in Alabama and Georgia who found shelter with the homeless south Alabama Choctaw.[14] In the late 1820s, Georgia Creek streamed onto the lands of their Ala-bama kin. Some seven thousand arrived in 1827 alone, "many of them skeletons and their bones almost worn through the skin."[15] Crossing the Chattahoochee River at Fort Mitchell, near the Creek town of Coweta, they reached the Tallapoosa River, then the Alabama River, which they followed south, some settling near Creek families in Monroe County, others going into the swamps between the rivers above Mobile.

Lemuel Byrd, his wife, Anna Weaver, and her brothers, Dave and Jim Weaver, joined this community of refugee Choctaw sometime between 1820 and 1830. Their mother, Linney Weaver, and their sister Edy, who married Joel Rivers, a Methodist minister from Virginia, stayed with him at Claiborne in Monroe County.[16] This family came to Alabama as part of the exodus of Creek and Cherokee who fled Georgia during the Florida (Seminole) Wars. Lemuel Byrd was a private in the American army and served in a Cherokee regiment near the Flint River on the frontier of Georgia. He enlisted in Putnam County, Georgia, in Captain William Avera's Company, under Brigadier General Thomas Glasscock,

Tom Weaver and Virginia Byrd Weaver, second-generation ancestors of today's MOWA Choctaw.

Above left, Percy Weaver, son of Tom and Virginia Byrd Weaver; right, his wife, "Mama" Frankie Weaver; above right, Clifford Weaver, grandson of Cecile Weatherford and Dave Weaver.

was mustered into service at headquarters at Fort Hawkins by General Edmund P. Gaines in November 1817, and was discharged in February 1818. He married Anna Weaver in Greene County, Georgia, on April 19, 1819.[17]

Sancer Byrd, a lineal descendant of Lemuel and Anna Byrd, said,

> Pappy Lem fought with General Jackson. His daddy was Irish and his mother was Cherokee. He was tall, big jointed and had a red beard. Folks called him Captain Red Byrd. He said they came to Alabama hoping to find his uncle Slim Byrd, who was tall and one-eyed with five or six children; said they never did find him. They stopped first at Claiborne on the Alabama River, then at Oven Bluffs, below Jackson on the Tombigbee River. They came on down the river. They lived for a while at Mobile, at the Indian camps down on Dog River then the [yellow] fever got so bad, they started dying. They all had to leave, so they moved up to Kunsly below Mt. Vernon. Kunsly is where the graveyard is near Fort Stoddert. Pappy Lem bought a place down there. He had six boys; fever killed two of them and they are buried down there. Fever struck them there and they moved to Movico[18] where Pappy Lem bought a piece of land [in 1836]—right over here where we are now.[19] While they were in Movico, one of Pappy's boys, Jim Byrd, had a shooting scrape with his uncle, old man Jim Weaver, and got killed. This is when the Weavers split up. Old man Jim Weaver's bunch went to Washington County. That left Bill, Lem, and Wash.[20]

The eldest son, William "Bill" T. Byrd, married Betsy Gibson, a Six Towns Choctaw descendant of Elitubbee (Chief Tom Gibson). They had six children. Dave Weaver and Cecile Weatherford and their children moved with Lemuel Byrd to a higher elevation called The Level, an area about three-quarters of a mile square, four miles west of Calvert on Red Fox Road. Edward S. Stone, author of *The History of Calvert*, says, "About two or three miles farther west [of Calvert] was an area known as 'The Choctaw Camp.' Here the Choctaw mingled with the local citizens."[21]

They found work nearby, building the wall for the federal arsenal at Mt. Vernon.

Sancer Byrd continues:

"Pappy Lem said when they moved up here to the Level there was nothing but wild things here then, wolves. You couldn't tote no fresh meat from one house to another; wolves would take it away from you. Pappy said one old man tried it anyway. He had a sharp hatchet with him. The wolves came after him, he backed up in a big hollow tree, and he fought them all night at that tree. Said next day, there was more dead wolves and foots around that tree than he ever saw. When a wolf would stick his foot in the hollow tree, the old man would chop it off. But when daylight come, the wolves went on back to their den. The old man got out of the tree and carried that meat on to them children, where he was going. Pappy helped build the wall at Searcy [Mt. Vernon Barracks], where the soldiers stayed. He hauled

Sancer Byrd told the stories handed down generation-to-generation of "Pappy" Lemuel Byrd who "fought with General Jackson." Sancer married Mae Lofton; his parents were Annie Lee and Clifton Byrd; his sisters were Rosie Byrd, who married Crockett Rivers, and Ola Irene Byrd.

clay for the government, four mules to the wagon. He made bricks for the wall down there."[22]

The wall built in 1836 at the Mt. Vernon Arsenal was one mile long, ten feet high and two feet thick. Searcy Hospital Institution for the Insane, was later established at this site.[23]

When Jim Weaver (brother of Dave and Anna) was banished to Washington County for killing his nephew Jim Byrd, he joined another refugee family who lived on High Hill. High Hill was the domain of Piamingo Hometah's band, a group of Six Towns Choctaw known to have been fiercely opposed to the treaties of 1802 and 1805 between the Choctaw Nation and the United States, and who challenged the U.S. surveyors who ran the boundary line which separated Six Towns territory from the Choctaw Nation. Piamingo Hometah, Chief of Hobuckintopa, who had lived near St. Stephens on the Tombigbee River, is remembered as Chief Homa by his descendants, who said, "he gave his land away." While this family relationship cannot be documented by written records, this story survived through Piamingo Hometah's grandson, Henry "Doc" Eaton. Young Henry lived with his Choctaw family on High Hill in relative peace until he was about ten years old. Then everything changed. Roosevelt Weaver explained,

"Doc Eaton got lost when the white people were taking this country. His people would run and flee and hide. He thought white people were going to kill him. He was fleeing for his life and had to hide to live. His father was killed and thrown in the river. They chopped up his mother and stuffed her in a gopher hole. He lived in a cave. He was ten or twelve years old when the Daughertys got him and made a flunky out of him. Sometimes, he stayed with first one family and then another. He made 'hummocks' [brush shelters] in the woods, hunted, fished, and trapped. He talked Choctaw; he was a full-blooded Choctaw.[24] He was an old man when I was a little boy seven or eight years old. He come to our house and drank coffee. Doc homesteaded on High Hill, but lost his land."[25]

Viney Reed Taylor, daughter of Henry "Doc" Eaton, grandson of Piamingo Hometah.

Doc Eaton's grandson, Leon Taylor, adds to this story:

"My mother, Viney, told me about her father, Doc Eaton. She spoke Choctaw and said that Doc built huts to live in. They were about eight by ten feet with upright poles covered with cane and brush. He would tie the top together with bear grass to hold it together. He also used bear grass to hang meat to smoke it. He built *kuk boos* out of rocks or out of wood high as his waist and filled it up with dirt. Then he would make a fire on top and hang a pot on a stick to cook. He would roast his corn with the shuck on or roast potatoes in ashes. He trapped, hunted, and lived on wild meat. Folks said he could tell them what traps had something in it before he got there, like a prophet, a 'seer' or fortuneteller. People were superstitious about him. They didn't want him to pray on them or 'put the finger on them.' He was like a medicine man; that's why he was called "Doc." He could tell people things they wanted to know and could cure people. Irvin McRae, state [Alabama] representative, tried to get my mother to take us to Philadelphia, Mississippi, around 1930. McRae told mother that he knew she was Choctaw, but she wouldn't go. She wanted to stay where she was. She tried to teach us Choctaw, but none of us wanted to learn it. She could sing songs in Choctaw and told a lot of stories."[26]

Leon Taylor married Ella Weaver and had eleven children. Their son, Wilford "Longhair" Taylor, a direct lineal descendant of Choctaw chief Piamingo Hometah, was elected Chief of the MOWA Choctaw in 1995.

The High Hill area is referred to as Caretta or "where the Carettas live," indicating a wild place. Although the origin of this nickname is lost in time, it possibly came from the Creek town of Coweta (also spelled Kawita, Caouritas) located near Fort Mitchell on the Chattahoochee River boundary between Georgia and Alabama. Coweta was called the "bloody town" by William Bartram on his travels in 1775.[27] This settlement also became the home of Jim Weaver and his wife, Marguerite "Peggy" Parnell (who was described as having blond hair and blue eyes), when Jim was forced to leave Mobile County after the family feud. Peggy's guardian, James Johnston, purchased property in this settlement in 1836.[28]

Jim Weaver and Peggy Parnell had nine children. Their children, grandchildren, and great-grandchildren who lived in this High Hill enclave are nicknamed "Carettas."[29]

One other known ancestor of the MOWA, Kalioka, mentioned earlier, was the daughter of a Choctaw chief. Kalioka had four children

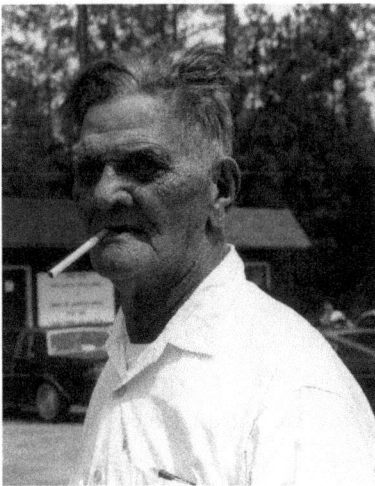

Left, Roosevelt Weaver, son of Dorsey Weaver and Caroline "Callie" Sullivan; right, Leon Taylor, son of Viney Taylor.

Left, Ella Weaver, wife of Leon Taylor; above, Dorsey Weaver, son of Taylor Weaver, grandson of Jim Weaver who settled on High Hill in 1836.

by Young Gaines, an early settler who came into the Mobile area in the 1780s. Gaines received Spanish land grants and ran large herds of cattle freely on Indian land.[30] He also had a white family, which included a daughter, Ann, who married George S. Gaines, an agent at the Choctaw Trading House. George Gaines said in his reminiscences,

> "My father in law sent us a drove of cattle. A few days after they reached us, a second grade chief . . . complained that strangers had driven a great number of cattle on his lands and asked if I knew about it. I told Hopia-skitteena (Little Leader) that my wife [Ann] was a daughter of Young Gaines, and the old gentleman had sent the cattle to me. He replied, 'It is all right then. I know Young Gaines. He is a good

and sensible man, I will see that your cattle eat my grass in safety.'"[31]

As a white inhabitant of the Mississippi Territory, Young Gaines signed petitions to Congress and served jury duty; as an Indian countryman, he witnessed treaties and was a paid interpreter for the Choctaw Trading House at St. Stephens where he sold corn, cowhides, and beef.[32]

Of the four children born to Kalioka and Young Gaines, more is known of Rose, the eldest daughter who stayed in the Mississippi Territory, than of their sons, Jerry and Isaac, who went west with their mother. Ann (daughter of the Indian wife, not the white daughter who married George), the youngest, died at an early age.[33] A story appeared in the *Birmingham News-Age Herald* when a cache of gold was found in 1933 near Young Gaines's home, about twenty miles west of the Alabama state line, in McLain, Mississippi: "Young Gaines married the daughter of a Choctaw Indian chieftain; Mississippi folk thrilled over finding [a] hidden cask of gold coins left by Choctaw. They gave all their gold and silver to Gaines, who buried it all in five separate piles and then mapped the exact locations."[34] While the name of the chief's daughter was not mentioned in the article, many people believed it referred to Kalioka.[35] This is one of the many stories surrounding the ethnicity of Rose Gaines, who lived to be almost one hundred years old and became a controversial legend in Washington County.

Inconsistent census records indicate that Rose was born between 1775 and 1780.[36] Although it cannot be documented, she was said to be the Indian wife of George S. Gaines (who was married to her white half-sister Ann) and was with child when she became the wife of Daniel Reed, an employee of Young Gaines. Rose's children were Juda, Eliza, George, Matilda, Lucretia, Reuben, Emaline, and William.

Daniel Reed, evidently a trusted employee, worked for Young Gaines as a cattle drover. A notice in the local newspaper, *The Halcyon and Tombeckbe*, proclaimed: "Lost, a red Morocco Pocket book containing a Due bill on Mr. Young Gaines for $60; which I forewarn all persons from trading for the same. Daniel Reed. St. Stephens."[37] Daniel traveled between Spanish territory, the Choctaw Nation, and the Mississippi

Territory, driving cattle and conducting business for Gaines. Legend claims that when Daniel Reed saw Rose "he wanted her."

Stories of Daniel Reed's origins are many—Spanish, Mexican, and Portuguese. The most plausible and most often-repeated story is that he came with Young Gaines into the Mississippi Territory and was of "Portuguese" descent, a term commonly used during the early territorial days for any European/American who appeared slightly darker than the average Anglo-Saxon. Eighteenth-century Virginia records show that the Reed family of Portuguese descent migrated to Kentucky, Indiana, North Carolina, and Alabama.[38] Historically, they are listed as "free people of color" in official records. "Free people of color" or "free colored" or "mulatto" are generic descriptive terms used interchangeably in the 1830 and 1840 U.S. Censuses in the South to apply to "non-whites," both to those of African and to those of Native American ancestry who left the tribal environment to live in Euro-American society, who appeared brown to Anglo-American census takers.[39] For example, the 1830 federal census of Carroll County, Georgia lists Cherokee Indians with phonetically spelled names as "free colored persons."[40] The 1870 United States Census was the first to list Indians in the South as Indians.

Free people of color could own property; Indians could not. Mississippi Territorial records show Daniel Reed paying taxes in 1805, buying land in 1817, and relinquishing part of it in 1821, with no racial designation.[41] In 1818 he was identified as a "free person of color" when he sought emancipation for Rose by securing classification for her as a "free person of color."[42] Giving her, a mixed blood Choctaw, the status of a citizen who could own property ensured that she would not be sent west against her will.

Daniel Reed first purchased land in 1817 in the Hobson community located on the trail from St. Stephens west to Mississippi.[43] Then in 1836 he purchased land near the Alabama-Mississippi state line at Tibbie (Okatibbaha) and built a stand—inn and cowpens.[44] Rose and Daniel provided food and shelter for travelers and their livestock on the way to market in Mobile. Although Rose owned land and paid taxes after the death of Daniel in 1844, the "free person of color/mulatto" status was passed on to her descendants who became stigmatized under increasingly stringent segregation laws after the Civil War.[45]

Rose Gaines Reed's descendants were persecuted by local society and were prosecuted under a miscegenation law. Under this law, anyone of African descent within the third degree of lineage could be prosecuted for marrying a white person; Indian descent was irrelevant under this law. Coming from people designated as "free people of color," her descendants had to prove in court that they were Indian, not black. The question of whether Rose's mother was Indian was first addressed in 1882 in the context of a trial (where she was described in testimony as a "Choctaw squaw") for miscegenation by an alleged white man, John Goodman, who married Virginia "Jennie" Reed, one of Rose and Daniel Reed's granddaughters. The court found the defendants "Not Guilty."[46] The jury foreman in this case, G. W. Sullivan, testifying at age seventy-four in a later miscegenation case in 1920, repeated the testimony given in the 1882 case that Rose's hair was brought to court and that "it was one and a half to two feet long and straight. Her hair was not kinky."[47] He was allowed to repeat the testimony of Glovina Rush, an old settler, a contemporary of Rose Reed and George S. Gaines, who knew them both. Mrs. Rush had testified in 1882 that Rose Gaines said that her mother was Choctaw. It was Rose's children, Kalioka's grandchildren, who married descendants of the disaffected Choctaw, the so-called "Lost Tribe."

The Lost Tribe, both known and unknowable ancestors of the MOWA Choctaw, lived on public land, hunted, fished, and planted small gardens of corn and beans. They remained relatively secluded and self-sufficient during the early territorial period, but the mounting pressures of American migration forced more land cessions. Three more treaties were made between the United States and the Choctaw in 1816, 1820, and 1825 with the stated purpose to "promote the civilization of the Choctaw Indians, by the establishment of schools amongst them; to clarify boundary lines and provide reservations for those who desire to remain where they now reside."[48]

The official national policy of assimilation was intensified when the American Board of Commissioners for Foreign Missions, with the

*Daughter
and mother:
left, Lucy
Cole, youngest
daughter of
Eliza Reed
Pargado Cole,
right, who was
the daughter
of Rose Gaines
and Daniel
Reed and the
grand-daughter
of Kalioka and
Young Gaines.*

support of the United States government, sent Christian missionaries to live among all the southern tribes. To expedite the "civilization" process, missions with schools were established for the Cherokee, Chickasaw, and Choctaw. Among the several mission schools in the Choctaw Nation, the easternmost, Emmaus, was located on the east side of Buckatunna Creek near the present dividing line between Mississippi and Alabama. The Reverend Alfred Wright spent time at various missions and Choctaw settlements. According to an 1824 mission report: "Mr. Wright has spent more than two-fifths of his Sabbaths from home; nine at Mayhew and Emmaus, and nine in the settlements in Washington Co., Ala. . . . In the settlements, he found the congregations respectable for numbers and attention to the Word."[49] Wright's work established the beginning

of Christian religion in what was to become the MOWA Choctaw community through George Reed, son of Rose, who became a preacher.
However, it did not influence the Choctaw to move away from their
homeland. The "civilizing" process of Christian religion and education,
introduced by the federal government to smooth the way west, had little
impact overall among the ancestors of the MOWA.[50]

In any case, assimilation as a national policy came to an end when
General Andrew Jackson became President Andrew Jackson. The new
national policy then became the complete removal of all Indians living
east of the Mississippi River. The disaffected Choctaw, hidden in the
swamps and thickets of southwest Alabama, remained where they were.
They were gradually joined by other Choctaw seeking to evade forced
removal to reservations in the West. The homeless thus found refuge
with their formerly outcast relatives, the disaffected, and together these
Choctaw formed the backbone of the community that would evolve into
the modern MOWA Band.

REFUGEES — SIX TOWNS CHOCTAW

1830–1890

"Brothers listen—you must now make a voluntary choice: remove—seek a home beyond the Mississippi, or else remain, where you are, under the laws of the state, and as good people endeavor to conform to them. No other alternative is presented."

— PRESIDENT ANDREW JACKSON, 1830.[1]

"Chishahoma called a Council to meet in the Spring of the year [1831]. At this meeting he spoke to them of their Country, and how dear it was to them. It was their own; it was the Country of the red-men given to them by their great father; they had sprung from it, and it was their mother. They had enjoyed it, until a few straggling white men, who had no lands or Country of their own had come among them and had begotten upon their lewd women a race of faithless half breeds who had bartered it for a land not adapted to their wants and comforts but destined to be their great burial ground. His mind was decided: he should meet his fate in the Country of his fathers, and when the Great Spirit recalled him his bones should rest in the bosom of his mother."

— TOKAHAJO[2]

ULTIMATELY, THE FEDERAL government forced almost all of the southeastern Indians to exchange their remaining lands for land in Indian Territory. Notwithstanding the fact that most Indians fiercely resisted leaving their ancestral homelands, Indian removal was established as a national policy with the election of Andrew Jackson as president in 1828 and passage of the Indian Removal Act of

1830.[3] The individual states quickly passed laws to ensure jurisdiction over Indians living within their borders. Among other things, these laws abolished tribal governments and made it a crime for a person to claim to be a chief of an Indian tribe.[4] These laws were intended to destroy what remained of the Choctaw, Creek, and Cherokee nations and to make it easier for incoming white settlers to take Indian lands.

President Jackson informed the Indians that the federal government was helpless to interfere with state laws. He told them their only option was to comply with removal or give up their Indian identity and become citizens of the states which had been established around them. A series of treaties then effectively removed the majority of the Indians east of the Mississippi, forcing them to leave forever the land where their ancestors had lived for hundreds or perhaps thousands of years.

With respect to the Choctaw, Jackson wrote a letter to the chiefs and appointed Secretary of War John H. Eaton and General John Coffee as Treaty Commissioners to deliver it. Jackson set forth the time, meeting place, and terms of a proposed treaty negotiation to be held in 1830 at Dancing Rabbit Creek in Mississippi.

The Choctaw were bitterly opposed to this treaty, under which their nation would be surrendering their lands to the federal government. According to Article 3 of the Treaty of Dancing Rabbit Creek, one-third of the Choctaw were to go west in 1831, with the rest to follow in two stages over the next two years. Indian Agent George S. Gaines reported that "This proposition acted as a bomb thrown among the Choctaw. It filled them with surprise, astonishment, excitement, grief and resentment. Not a single Choctaw favored the sale and cession of the lands of the tribe. It had not a solitary advocate among them."[5]

Agent Gaines was present at the treaty grounds at Dancing Rabbit Creek. He was ordered by the government to supply provisions for three thousand persons for a week, which he did with considerable effort. The supply of flour and corn meal was transported to the meeting place on Indian ponies because the Indians had no roads, only paths.

Chishahoma (Captain Red Post Oak), leader of the Six Towns Choctaw, attended the negotiations of the Treaty of Dancing Rabbit Creek, which lasted several days. When the treaty question was submitted to the assembled Choctaw and the majority voted against it, Chishahoma considered this action final, left the treaty ground with other leading chiefs, and started home. However, Secretary of War Eaton persuaded a small number of chiefs, mostly mixed-bloods, to remain. Through bribery and coercion, he obtained their signatures to the treaty. Even then it would not have been signed without the insertion of Article 14, which read:

> "Each Choctaw head of a family being desirous to remain and become a citizen of the States, shall be permitted to do so by signifying his intention to the Agent within six months from the ratification of this Treaty, and he or she shall thereupon be entitled to a reservation of one section of six hundred and forty acres of land to be bounded by sectional lines of survey. . . . If they reside upon said lands intended to become citizens of the States for five years after the ratification of this Treaty, in that case a grant in fee simple shall issue. . . . Persons who claim under this article shall not lose the privilege of a Choctaw citizen, but if they ever remove are not to be entitled to any portion of the Choctaw annuity."[6]

This relocation treaty between the Choctaw and the United States provided for an exchange of lands, guaranteed protection for the Indians, and specified annuities and other payments or services. It was signed September 27, 1830, at Dancing Rabbit Creek in Neshoba County, Mississippi.

When Chishahoma heard that a treaty had been made after he left the treaty grounds, he called a council of the Six Towns people and told them the treaty terms that had been proposed and now, by deception, had been imposed on them. He explained that a provision [Article 14] in the treaty allowed them to keep their lands if they registered within six months with U.S. Agent Colonel William Ward; otherwise they would be removed.

Nearly all the Six Towns people attended and discussed the matter in open council. All were opposed to the treaty and declared that they would not go west. They voted instead to stay and take land under the treaty. Then they discussed how they were to apply and get their names registered with Colonel Ward.

Using small sticks was the official Choctaw method of tribal enumeration. A stick about six to eight inches long represented the head of a family and was called the family stick. Male children over ten years of age were represented by smaller sticks for each, attached by string to the family stick. Female children over ten years of age were represented by notches cut in the middle of the family stick, and younger children, whether male or female, by notches cut in the family stick at one end. Adopted children were included in the same manner.[7]

In preparation for registration with Colonel Ward, a leading man was appointed from each town to supervise preparation of these sticks and to see that they corresponded with the numbers and ages of the children. The leading men were: Chishahoma for Chinakbi Town; Mahubbee for Okatalaia Town; Elitubbee for Killistamaha Town (English Town);[8] Tokahadjo for Tala Town; Malachubbee for Nashwaiya Town; and Shikopanowa for Bishkun Town.

The completed sticks were handed over to Chishahoma and Toboka, a man of prodigious memory, to take to Colonel Ward at the agency in Oktibbeha County about 120 miles north. It was not unusual to find an old-time Choctaw (like Toboka) who was thoroughly familiar with the name, age, and sex of every member of his clan or tribe.[9]

The sticks were tied up in six bundles, one for each town; the six bundles were then tied up into one large bundle, larger than could be grasped with both hands. When the two tribal representatives arrived at the agency, Chishahoma explained to Colonel Ward that he had come to register himself and his people for land as provided in the treaty. Colonel Ward told him that he would register them and began writing down names as Chishahoma gave them. After registering some fifty names, Ward got up, took a drink of whiskey and pushed the book aside. He told Chishahoma that was enough and that Chishahoma must come again. The bundle of sticks was left with

Colonel Ward, who promised to write them all down.

Several months later, Chishahoma and Toboka returned to the agency to finish the registration. On the way, Chishahoma learned from two Indians he met that Colonel Ward had not registered all his people and that the agent's book containing the names of the Six Towns Indians who had been registered had been destroyed. On receiving this information Chishahoma and Toboka prepared from memory a new bundle of sticks. When Chishahoma reached the agency he reminded Colonel Ward that he had been there before and had not got all his people registered; that he had come again and brought sticks to represent them, and that he wanted them all to be put down. Colonel Ward said there were too many people registered already, and if he wanted land he should go west of the Mississippi where there was plenty of it. Colonel Ward then took the bundle of sticks and threw them away.[10]

Indian agent Colonel William Ward, described in DeRosier's *Removal of the Choctaw Indians* as "an arbitrary, tyrannical, and insulting bully,"[11] allowed only sixty-nine heads of family to remain in Mississippi in token compliance with Article 14. Chishahoma's people, ancestors of the modern MOWA Choctaw who eventually sought refuge with the disaffected Choctaw in Alabama, were never registered despite their determined attempts. The Choctaw of the Southeastern district, in full council through their headmen, including Chishahoma, announced their unalterable intention not to remove west; the band of Chishahoma determined likewise; but they, too, were soon to be uprooted and forced out.

A census of the Choctaw was necessary before removal could begin. William Armstrong, the U.S. agent who was appointed for this task, enumerated 17,963 Indians.[12] They were to be removed by thirds, overland to Vicksburg, Mississippi, and then by boat to Arkansas. Funds obtained from the sale of Choctaw land were to be used for transportation and provisions. Difficult traveling conditions, inclement weather, disease, and insufficient supplies dogged the emigrants on their trek to the West. In 1834, when the War Department terminated its formal removal operations, an estimated six thousand Choctaw remained east of the Mississippi River.[13]

White citizens of Alabama and Mississippi were determined to rid their states of all American Indians and continued to move onto Indian land. Public sales of Indian lands began even before the survey of the claims was completed. The Indians were left landless and destitute, but unremoved.

During the Creek uprising of 1836, brought on by desperate circumstances—fraud, land loss, starvation—white people of Alabama and Mississippi demanded that the remaining Choctaw be removed so they would not become involved in the disorder; orders were given for their removal, but no action was taken.[14] Instead, Secretary of War Eaton called several hundred homeless, wandering Choctaw warriors into service for six months against the Creek and ordered the immediate removal of the whole Creek tribe as a military measure.[15] The governor of Alabama issued a proclamation that all Indians who did not aid in quelling the uprising would be treated as enemies. The Choctaw once again fought on the side of the Americans, evidently believing they would be allowed to stay.

The hundreds of Choctaw who had made application under Article 14 of the Dancing Rabbit Creek Treaty and had done all that was required of them to keep their homes were defeated in their claims by the negligence of the United States. Several times, the Choctaw made application to the federal government to regain their rights, but they were easy prey for unscrupulous land speculators, who defrauded them at every turn. Based on the unfulfilled treaty provisions, the government made several efforts to settle the claims and remove the remaining Choctaw west.

Proceedings implemented in 1838, 1842, 1845, and 1855 to determine rightful claimants were for the most part unsuccessful and tainted with fraud. In these investigations, depositions were taken from village leaders who listed from memory the names of their people who wished to exercise the five year homestead provision that had been promised to them. One of these village leaders was Elitubbee, alias Tom Gibson, a full blood Choctaw, who spoke for the Killistamaha (English Town) clan of the Six Towns. Elitubbee testified on June 20, 1844, and provided the list of 107 phonetically spelled names (unless English names appear with phonetically spelled Choctaw names, as in the case of Elitubbee, identities of individuals are unknowable) of the heads of Choctaw families as of the date of the Treaty of Dancing Rabbit Creek. These were the Choctaw families whose enumeration had been taken to the dishonest agent William Ward by Chishahoma and Toboka.[16]

(Records generated by these investigations were used in 1881 by the Choctaw Nation of Indians (Oklahoma) who brought the "Net Proceeds" case against the United States in the Court of Claims and won almost three million dollars, "most of which was spent to reimburse the lawyers who fought the case through the courts."[17] The 1,240-page document of the proceedings to settle the Choctaw claims includes depositions, testimony from witnesses, lists of claimants, correspondence, record books, journals, claims, instructions, and reports.[18] This report clearly shows that the Six Towns Choctaw attempted to sign up for reservations in their homeland, but were not allowed to do so.)

From time to time orders were given to organize the Choctaw who remained east of the Mississippi for removal, but due to inconsistent and negligent administration, little was done to implement removal, a pattern that continued up to the outbreak of the Civil War in 1860. The ancestors of today's MOWA Choctaw avoided removal policies by quietly remaining where they had lived for decades, hunting, fishing, and gardening in settlements in the swamps and pine barrens north of Mobile.

Exploiting their hidden status, these families (perhaps three hundred to four hundred people) maintained their separate culture through intermarriage. Their numbers were increased when remnant bands of Choctaw from Mississippi, who were not enrolled according to the terms of the 1830 Treaty of Dancing Rabbit Creek, joined them because the United States Government, through its agents, failed to fulfill the terms of this treaty.

Those who then remained became victims of one of the most flagrant episodes of fraud, intimidation, and speculation in American history.[19] Charles Hudson, author of *The Southeastern Indians*, wrote,

"Some of them settled around Mobile and others worked on plantations in the cotton fields, but most of them wandered about the countryside where unscrupulous men stripped them of virtually everything they possessed."[20]

Remnants of the Six Towns Choctaw who came to Mobile sought relief from government agents whose schemes to defraud them of their land and later, of their scrip (certificates for land) stripped them of all their possessions. Another fraudulent scheme, perpetrated by agents who contracted with the U.S. government to emigrate the Choctaws west, was to promise them that they would escort them for half of their "Indian money"; for the other half, they would bring them back, sign them up under different names and emigrate them again. This moneymaking scheme was in addition to funds the government paid the contractor for "furnishing" (providing food and transportation) the Indians on the trail west.[21]

The dispossessed Six Towns Choctaw joined the Indian community north of Mobile. For the next quarter-century they periodically sought help from the federal government through government agents, lawyers, and local citizens. Correspondence between 1832 and 1860 describes the hardships they endured and provides their phonetically spelled names and the names of individuals who helped them.

Government agents reported on the population, location, and living conditions of the remnant Choctaw. George S. Gaines, former U.S. Agent for the Choctaw Trading House and long-time friend of the Choctaw,[22] wrote to the Commissary General of Subsistence regarding a Resolution of the City of Mobile in relation to the removal of the Indians from the city:

"Mobile, 30th June 1832 —A great number of Chaktaw Indians for many years past have resided within the corporate limits of this city during the winters and spring months, and many families remaining through the summer, to the annoyance of the citizens . . . from the Sixtowns and Chickasawhay towns every winter . . ."[23]

The Mobile Resolution stated that "it is expedient at as early a period as possible to procure the removal of the Indians from the corporate limits of the city of Mobile. And that in order to carry into effect such removal permanently they (the Indians) ought to be removed by the Government of the U. States."[24]

George S. Gaines, who was subsequently hired as Commissioner to remove the Choctaw, reports on September 22, 1844, that

"the least enlightened and most helpless of the nation have been left to the mercy of the pioneer settlers, who flocked into the ceded country soon after the ratification of the treaty, bringing with them no sympathies for the poor defenseless Indians who still have to be removed West . . . the southeastern Indians known as the Six Towns [are] under the influence of Capts. Oaklahbee and Post Oak. Their agent and attorney is Col. John Johnson, Sr. and their number about 2000. The Bay Indians as they are now called from their residence on the sea coast have also filed claim under the 14th article of the Treaty of Dancing Rabbit Creek, were principally of the Six Towns, originally now numbering 200 and although they have their own agents and attorneys, I class with the Six Towns, under the influence of Col. Johnson, altogether about 2200."[25]

On November 9, 1845, William Armstrong, Acting Superintendent for the Choctaw, reported from Jackson, Mississippi, that

"nothing has been done towards emigration of the Choctaw [from Mississippi]…the setting in of the cold weather will cause them to wander off, some to the swamps in pursuit of game, others to Mobile and other towns on the coast, in which case it will be impossible to collect them again till spring."[26]

Armstrong wrote again on November 26, 1845 from Garlandsville, Mississippi,

"I arrived in this place, expecting to meet the Six Towns in council. It was expected that upwards of 2000 would be present, . . . yet less than one-third have assembled. Those chiefs who are present say that their people are scattered over a wide extent of country, some of them being 200 miles off when the council was called . . . The Indians are to a great extent under the influence of their attorneys or agents, who appear to be in favor of their removal . . . Their own individual feelings, so far as I have been able to judge, are decidedly adverse to emigration."[27]

As years passed, small groups of Choctaw were moved west by the government; others emigrated at their own expense with promises of reimbursement when they reached Indian Territory. However, the Six Towns, camped with their long-lost Alabama relatives, the "disaffected" Choctaw, asked the government to allow them to select their own emigrator to take them west if they had to leave their homeland and not to assign any more fraudulent agents who were trying to cheat them out of their "Indian money." On December 6, 1849, Henry Chamberlain, an attorney in Mobile,[28] wrote on behalf of the Choctaw a letter from "One Hundred Red Men" from Mobile to George S. Gaines, who was then in Washington, D.C.:

"We, about one hundred of the principal men from a remnant of the Choctaw Tribe of Indians residing at and about Jasper and Newton counties in the State of Mississippi, respectfully represent—That we have been hereunto requested by the entire remnant of our tribe living in the counties aforesaid consisting of about 800 persons, to come to Mobile where we now are, and make known to you, who have always been our friend, our complaints, and we petition you to intercede yourself with the government of the U. States in our behalf.

"Our tribe has been woefully imposed upon of late. We have had our habitations torn down and burned, our fences destroyed, cattle turned into our fields, and we have ourselves been scourged, manacled, fettered & otherwise personally abused—until by abuse, exposure & want of sustenance some of our best men have died. These are the acts of those persons who profess to be the agents of the government to procure our removal to the State of Arkansas & who cheat us out of all they can by the use of fraud, duplicity, and even violence.

"We have become tired of this treatment & wish you to procure for us some better protection from the government. We desire that an agent of our own appointing may be recognized by the government as their agent to protect us and procure our removal upon fair and equitable terms, & that all other persons may be strictly inhibited from interfering in any manner whatever with the treatment of our tribe, or with the property or possessions they have.

"We have been long acquainted with Mr. William Fisher[29] a creole of Mobile, who has been our friend, understands our language & wants. We also know well Mr. Russell W. Lewis of Mobile, who also understands our language well. These persons have no interest in the lands where we live, & we believe they would be agents equally faithful to the government and to us. —We pray that they may be appointed as such.

"We trust we will be pardoned for calling upon you to add another to the many obligations we are already under. —Please do something for us during your present visit to Washington City. We subscribe ourselves One Hundred Red Men, in behalf of Eight Hundred of our tribe."[30]

William Fisher was the son of William Fisher, Sr., who owned extensive property northwest of Mobile, land near the Tensaw River originally purchased from the Apalatchee Indians, and an island on the east side of the Tensaw River, opposite to the Middle River.[31] This is the area where the disaffected Choctaw subsisted. According to oral history, William Fisher, Sr., had an Indian family in addition to his Creole family. His home near present-day Spring Hill Avenue in Mobile was the meeting place for Choctaw and government Indian agents.

From March 15, 1851, to August 17, 1852, twenty-two letters describe fraudulent actions of government agents, desolation, deprivation, and requests for their trusted friend William Fisher to be appointed agent. Choctaw leaders, speaking for their people living in south Alabama, asked leading citizens of Mobile, including the mayor, to write to the United States government asking that they receive the land or money due them. On December 10, 1851, John Seawall, mayor of Mobile, wrote to John Bragg, House of Representatives, Washington, D.C., enclosing a petition from 119 Choctaw. No English names, only Choctaw names, were to be found among the 119 signatures, a list that includes seventy men and forty-nine women (four of them orphan girls). Felix Andry (a Creole married to Nancy, a Choctaw woman), who prepared the petition, certified that "I did commit the signatures of the Choctaw Indians to writing as found in this and the foregoing pages and that they were done and executed by their marks in proper position by each Indian and witnessed by my person." This list of phonetically spelled Choctaw names and signatures on the letters is significant because it reflects traditional name use by MOWA ancestors who were rejecting relocation in order to fight for traditional lands or for their choice of an agent—in short, the right to choose their own destiny. Their action parallels that of other Indian groups who stayed in the South, for example the Cherokee in North Carolina and the Seminole in Florida. [See Appendix A, Hand-written Petition.]

Bragg forwarded the petition and correspondence to Luke Lea, Commissioner of Indian Affairs, on December 29, with his own letter explaining that Mayor Seawall's letter is

"in reference to a remnant of Choctaw Indians still remaining in South Alabama. Accompanying his letter you will find a Petition from these Indians asking for the appointment of William Fisher of Mobile Co., as a special agent selected by themselves to attend to such relations as may exist between them and the Gov't. In addition to the testimony furnished as to Wm. Fisher's character, I can say that I know him well. That he is an intelligent & *honest Creole* & has the confidence of the Indians to a degree far beyond that of any other man in Alabama or nation. Indeed he was brought up among them, knows them all and speaks their language."[32]

The U.S. government did nothing to relieve the situation, so on August 17, 1852, the Choctaw asked the Mayor of Mobile to write a letter again on their behalf, this time to President Millard Filmore. This petition included:

> "We, a remnant of the Tribe of Indians called Choctaw residing in Southern Alabama and near Mobile would respectfully bring to your notice, the frauds which are attempted to be practiced on us, to deprive us of our property and just rights by real or pretended agents of the Government. . . . We are informed that a Mr. [H. L.] Martin has just gone to Washington to secure for us the moneys due us by the Government, this is without our knowledge or consent. We have been assembled once at Mobile, and Mr. Jack [John] Johnson, a Mr. [James H.] Bowman and Mr. [F. S.] Hunt, agent or clerk for Bowman, offered to give us $20, $15 and 45 for the scrip [certificate for land] of each Indian and child. They refused to give us scrip, and endeavored by bribes to induce us to settle with them, stating that the scrip was theirs . . . There are over four hundred of us here who have been thus ill treated and who are kept in ignorance and suspense as to our claims. We are unwilling to have anything to do with these men who come to us as the pretended agents of the Government. We prefer to receive our money through our own agent and we want the whole, not $5 in 100 or even less . . . We do not wish to be robbed and we know a plan is now laid to cheat us out of our money and right. We do not wish to emigrate but to remain where we are and become citizens."

The above petition was signed (with x marks next to their names) in behalf of all the Indians of South Alabama of the Choctaw Nation by:

Holli ta nau tubee
Hou cha
Ila tam be
Me ha
August 17, 1852[33]

The next several letters refer to Choctaw returning from the West and wandering across Louisiana, Mississippi, and Alabama with the agent complaining that there is nothing he can do to stop them; and letters from the Choctaw who reside in Mobile complaining about the fraudulent government agents and again requesting their own agent, William Fisher.

Finally, on January 20, 1854, William Fisher requested an appointment for himself to be agent for the removal of the Choctaw "in and about Mobile."[34] On February 24, the *Mobile Advertiser* announced, "About 50 Choctaw Indians left our city on the steamer *Oregon* for New Orleans on their way to Arkansas. A large crowd of those remaining in our neighborhood collected on the wharf to see them off...." [35] Then on July 1, "a large delegation of about 100 Choctaw Indians, left this city yesterday on the steamer *Oregon* for a home in the far west, under the charge of Mr. William Fisher . . ."[36]

In September of that year, William Fisher and large bands of Choctaw Indians were reported "passing through Hot Springs, Arkansas, on their return to the states of Mississippi and Alabama—and that there is some fraud going on against the government."[37]

Then in 1855 Commissioner of Indian Affairs George W. Manypenny instructed Agent Douglas H. Cooper to take a census of the Choctaw remaining east of the Mississippi River. Cooper traveled from town to town throughout Mississippi, Alabama, and Louisiana looking for remnant groups of Choctaw. On May 3, 1856 he reported that he remained "a few days to see a party of Choctaw, who ran off from me when here before, (under the false idea that I had come to tie them & put them on a boat & take them to Arkansas)."[38]

Cooper finished his census in 1856. The original, handwritten "Census Roll of Choctaw Families, residing East of the Mississippi River and in the States of Mississippi, Louisiana and Alabama," lists the residence of the Six Towns Clan as "Jasper and Newton Counties, Miss., and Mobile, Ala., with 129 men, 191 women, 194 children, or 96 families."[39] When this census was transcribed from handwritten copy to print, "Mobile, Ala." was omitted, thus dooming the Alabama Choctaw to oblivion in the historical record. [See Appendix B, Handwritten 1856 Census.]

No further forced westward emigration of Choctaw Indians took place. To a series of petitions written in 1859 by citizens of Alabama and Mississippi requesting that all Choctaw Indians be moved west, the federal government replied that "the government has no intention to make any further removal of Choctaws."[40] And on September 3, 1860, to an inquiry in respect to the appointment of a Special Agent for the emigration of Choctaw Indians, Acting Commissioner of Indian Affairs Charles E. Mix replied "that no such agent has been appointed by the Department."[41]

DURING THE THIRTY YEARS between the Treaty of Dancing Rabbit Creek and the outbreak of the Civil War, world travelers interested in the "children of the forest" published rather romanticized accounts of the Choctaw but also recorded their numbers and where and how they lived. Charles Lanman, author of *Adventures in the Wilds*, published in 1856, commented that "the number of Indians who spend much of their time in Mobile, but who live in the neighboring pine woods, is estimated at 1,000."[42] Mobile historian Caldwell Delaney describes the picturesque Indian camp in the days before the Civil War:

> "Choctaws had camped there since the time of Bienville, and when the nation moved west those who occupied the old camp site chose to remain even though they knew that they must soon die out. The women raised vegetables, which they sold on the streets of Mobile but the men remained proud and haughty and would not do any manual labor. They hunted and the game they killed was also sold by the women in the markets. The girls of the tribe gathered lightwood knots and sold them in bundles. They called these bundles 'chumpa' for 'chumps,' and they were very successful in selling, since everybody used lightwood for kindling. They walked very quietly and never spoke unless they were selling, so people often did not know the girls were near until they heard the soft question, 'Chumpa?' whispered in their ears. Stories are told of Chumpa Girls who would even go upstairs and wake up people who were in bed, to try to sell them chumpa. Visitors

were always interested in them, and many artists passing through Mobile painted them, saying they were the most beautiful Indian girls to be found in the South at that time."[43]

One of these artists, Frederica Bremer, included sketches of the Choctaw in *The Homes of the New World: Impressions of American (1849–1851)*.[44] Bavarian-born artist Phillip Romer painted a portrait of a young woman in 1850 as a romantic and exotic subject, which he named *Choctaw Belle*.[45] The Choctaw dressed in their best finery when they came into town, and they gave Mobile a romantic frontier appearance even at the height of the cotton boom when it had become an elegant and sophisticated city.

Eventually, some Choctaw left the Mobile area and joined their relatives in Jasper and Newton counties, Mississippi; they are ancestors of the Philadelphia Choctaw. Others, ancestors of the MOWA Choctaw, stayed in their homeland in Alabama. They had refused removal despite great pressure and great hardship, but further dissolution occurred with the outbreak of the Civil War.

Beginning in 1862, the Confederate States of America recruited Choctaw men into service. A recruiting camp was established in Mobile at the foot of Stone Street adjoining the grounds occupied by Spann's Battalion of White Mounted Cavalry. S. G. Spann advertised in the *Mobile Advertiser and Register*, from May 8 to July 10—

"A Chance for Active Service. The Secretary of War has authorized me to enlist all the Indians east of the Mississippi River into the service of the Confederate States, as Scouts. In addition to the Indians, I will receive all white male citizens, who are good marksmen. To each member, Fifty Dollars Bounty, clothes, arms, camp equipage &c: furnished. The weapons shall be Enfield Rifles. For further information address me at Mobile, Ala. (Signed) S. G. Spann, Comm'ing Choctaw Forces."[46]

Spann's Battalion of Mounted Scouts was formed by authority of the

Frederica Bremer's 1851 sketch, "Choctas Indians"; courtesy of Marion Viccars, Special Collections, West Florida University, Pensacola.

Secretary of War under the immediate auspices of General Dabney H. Maury, Commander of the Department of the Gulf. The Mobile Camp filled up rapidly under the personal charge of Lieutenant Robert Welch, of Marion, Alabama, and Captain R. [Russell W.] Lewis, of Dekalb County, Mississippi. One recruit, Eahantatubbee, also known as Jack Amos, acted as interpreter for Major Spann and kept him informed about problems that arose with the Choctaw. Again, an unscrupulous lawyer tried to take advantage as their "agent." Jack Amos "discovered that some mutterings and dissension prevailed among the women and noncombatant Indians. Further investigations led him to discover that Percy Walker, Esq., a prominent lawyer of the Mobile bar, had informed the noncombatants that the Indians were not liable to do Confederate service, and therefore exempt from conscription; and if they would pay him one dollar per capita, he would procure papers of exemption for the whole tribe for the war."[47] This incident was reported to General Maury, who stopped the scam.

Other than these fragments of information, little has been found on the Choctaw recruitment camp in Mobile. After the Civil War, the Choctaw continued to live in the Mobile area, a hidden community virtually unnoticed until their forest habitat became commercially desirable in the second half of the nineteenth century. The people who would become the MOWA Choctaw became almost invisible to the public except for a few references to them being seen by journalists. T. H. Ball in *Clarke County, Alabama and its Surroundings, 1540–1877* states in 1877 that Choctaws continued to visit Mobile and sell firewood.[48] James M. Glenn, Ph.D., who wrote "Indians Still Make Homes in South Alabama Counties: Familiar Figures in Small Towns," stated in 1889 that he had "seen members of the Choctaw tribes in upper Mobile County."[49] In the late 1930s, Frances Beverly, who wrote "The Red Man in Mobile History" for the Federal Writers Project, remembers the Choctaw coming into Mobile from the northern part of the county to sell firewood.[50] The Choctaw who remained were seen as oddities, a separate people, apart from Southern society.

The Reconstruction era brought additional stress to ancestors of the

MOWA—they were non-white in a biracial society where people were usually identified as either Black or White. Without a land base, the surviving Indian community underwent a process of enclavement, surrounded by black and white communities but part of neither.

5

The Green Wall—Homeland

1890–1920

"One time when we lived up at Caretta a big fowl flew down in the yard, big as a peacock. It was about this high [measured from ground to shoulder] with a head this big [measured about 12 inches with hands] wouldn't eat no corn. Eddie, my brother's child, asked my mother 'what is it?' Mama said 'I don't know.' Eddie said, 'I'm going to get a piece of wood and kill it.' He went to the porch to get a piece of wood and Mama said, 'No, don't kill it.' Then Eddie said 'I'm going to ask it "What in the name of God do you want?"' With that, that thing jumped up about this high [hand raised above head] and did everything but talk, 'Er, er, er, er!' That next day Eddie was in the woods and a big rattlesnake struck him in the britches leg. He had to jump a big log that had blown down and knocked it off from his britches. The snake didn't bite him all the way through. In Caretta, we believed that fowl was a warning."

— Mary Ann Weaver, 1986

FROM 1890 TO 1920, the Indian community that would evolve into the MOWA Choctaw changed many aspects of their material culture, as did every other American Indian tribe and immigrant group in the United States during this transition period. Since 1830, few people other than refugees from other Indian communities in the region have wanted to join what became the MOWA Choctaw community. From an Indian perspective the community was a way to hold onto a valued traditional way of life while living in a sacred place.

From the perspective of local non-Indians, the Choctaw community, the place where they lived, and the people themselves were marginal. In fact, over time a social wall was built around the Indian community. This wall limited where they could live, where they could work, whom they could marry, and what they could become. This wall restricted them to their forest region of refuge. This wall became, in the words of one modern-day elder, "like that wall in Berlin, Germany." Not made of stone but nonetheless effectively restricting the Indian community, this "green" wall would limit them to the forest and to what is today called wood work.

The modern concept of the American Indian did not officially exist in this post-Civil War society. For the next one hundred years, laws written in the South were for either whites or blacks. Anyone not identified as "pure white" was governed under civil regulations that applied to blacks; Indian identity was submerged. Thus American Indians living in the South became a group of people who officially did not exist.

The Indian community north of Mobile, however, persisted as a system of social relationships and shared cultural symbols. Major symbols of community cohesion and commitments to traditional lands are (1) Indian churches, (2) Indian schools, (3) Indian ceremonial gathering areas, (4) Indian cemeteries, and (5) Indian kin-based subdistricts.

Choctaw Indian churches began in the 1800s when Protestant Indian missionaries arrived. Two core communities developed around pioneer churches and their Indian leaders. In Mobile County, Lemuel Byrd and David Weaver furnished both tribal and religious direction. Together they constructed a log building around 1840 that became Byrd Church.[1] In Washington County, George Reed and Jim Weaver provided the leadership to build a log church at Reed's Chapel in the 1830s. Early Protestant missionary work probably had no better impact on acculturation than had earlier French and Spanish Catholic missionary efforts.

By 1830, the small number of Indian people who stayed in their ancestral homelands had to seek new adaptive strategies in an environment dominated by whites. As the result of the Dancing Rabbit Creek Treaty, the Choctaw lost their lands and were turned into squatters. The lands they held through squatting tended to be the wetter, poorer lands that white settlers did not desire for cotton growing, but these were also lands that were more desirable for Choctaw subsistence hunting, fishing, and gardening. Indian farming along the major rivers continued until the 1890s, but the best farming locations were continually encroached upon. Lacking a large population, diseases further reduced the Indian people who stayed. By 1890, the Eleventh United States Statistical Census reported: "The civilized (self-supporting) Indians of Alabama, counted in the general census, number 749, 338 males and 421 females, and are distributed as follows: Autauga County, 116; Escambia County, 173; Mobile County, 402; other counties with eight or less in each, 68. [These numbers reflect how many Indians the government counted, not necessarily the true Indian population.] The mode of life of these Indians is akin to that of their neighbors of small property. Among them are the descendants of Creek, Cherokee, Chickasaw, and Mobile Indians, more or less affected by white and negro blood."[2]

Reduced in numbers, and increasingly a dominated minority in their own homeland, the forerunners of the MOWA Choctaw made new alliances. The most important of these were the Protestant Indian missions. The Indian missions did not want to take land or power; rather, they wanted conversion. And conversion to non-Indian religion is an adaptive strategy that is well documented as being used when Indian communities are dominated by white culture. In some cases, the church becomes a central symbol of cultural persistence for the Indian community. Generally, the new religious system is either added to the traditional Indian religion or acquires syncretic (combined) meanings that blend the Indian with European.[3]

Another aspect of the Protestant missions was the desire to educate and make lay-preachers out of the Indians. By the 1830s, a number of them had been educated and at least one person, George Reed, had become a minister in Reed's Chapel, one of the two Indian churches. George Reed went to mission school and returned at the age of thirteen in 1830. He was the first recognized Indian minister. The first Indian mission school was named Kunshak (apparently for one of the Choctaw clans named *Koonsha*, which means cane or reeds). This was also the name of the Indian mission church that became Reed's Chapel, which was built in a canebrake near a community of Indian people. Before the church was built, the area had brush arbors indicating it was being used for Indian ceremonial activities. In addition, the church was a power institution in the non-Indian society surrounding the Indian Choctaw, so they developed a parallel church system that conveyed to them similar prestige and authority.

Although no formal records of organized churches or missions exist between the 1830s and 1870s, the Indian community constructed temporary shelters and held religious ceremonies at their traditional "stomp" (meeting) grounds. By the 1880s, organized religions resumed their ministry to the Choctaw east of the Mississippi.[4] The first record of Baptist work was by the Reverend Tom Morgan, an independent mission-educated Choctaw from Oklahoma, who helped organize a Baptist church.[5] The Association of the Baptist Church licensed one of the earliest and most beloved preachers, George R. Weaver, as a minister of the Gospel in 1916.[6]

The desire for learning was strong among the Indian people, but they were denied access to formal education. Education provided a means of dealing with affairs in the non-Indian world, and from that time until today, community leaders often have been mission-educated ministers. As a result they valued the educational opportunities afforded by the Protestant Indian missions. The log church, also used for a school, was built in 1850. The school bell, kept there since the log church was built, is located today in the cemetery of Reed's Chapel Church near the Reed's Chapel Indian School. The bell was used as a means of communicating major events to the community. Through a code of rings, the community could be made aware of births, deaths, and emergencies. Today, the bell is a community symbol of the first Indian school and the community that supported its development.

The Indian schools were and are a symbol of community persistence and cultural pride. Early schools were built with the assistance of the Indian community. Families paid the salary of the Indian teachers, provided supplies for the students, and cooked lunches for the children. The food

Present siting of the Reed's Chapel Bell (courtesy of the State of Alabama Historical Commission).

came largely from the school garden, tended by voluntary community labor, and from meat donated by community members. As mentioned above, the Indian children were not permitted in the white schools before the Civil War (there were then no schools for blacks), nor later in the segregated schools provided for either the white or the black races.

At the end of World War I, in 1918, a major flu epidemic swept through the South bringing the plight of the Indian communities in Mobile and Washington counties to the attention of the public and eventually causing religious and state agencies—the Missionary Boards of both the Baptists and Methodists, and the Governor of Alabama—to send representatives, which generated written reports.

In the 1920s, the Alabama Baptists began a mission ministry among "American Indians of Choctaw heritage, under the overall program of missions to American Indians"[7] in Washington County; in the 1930s,

Methodist mission work for "Indian Cajuns" began in Mobile County.[8] Teachers boarded in the homes of tribal members and school was held in churches.

One of the first teachers was Martha Walden. Interviewed in 1994 at age 97, Miss Walden said that upon receiving a teaching certificate from the Southern Baptist Theological Seminary she was sent to Alabama by the Home Mission Board to work with the south Alabama Indians. She lived with

Martha Walden, missionary to south Alabama Indians, 1921.

Cleveland Johnston's family. When she arrived, she said,

"About fifty children were waiting for me under a chinaberry tree in his yard. I taught school six months in the Fairford-Mount Vernon area and six months at McIntosh where Rube Reed lived. I was there three and one half years, from 1921 to 1925. I traveled by foot, horseback, or wagon. The children were very intelligent; they had splendid minds, but they never had any education or opportunity. They were so poor. The poorest Indian I ever knew had only one bed, one house that was a sleeping and eating house. Most had a house for eating and a house for sleeping, but this was the poorest house. They did not have a single lamp or lantern in the place. The only light they had was a fat-wood fire. I left because I was told to leave by Cleveland Johnston. He wanted me to just teach, not preach or minister to the sick, or to talk to outsiders."[9]

Cleveland Johnston's fear of Miss Walden's talking to "outsiders" is understandable given the social forces of the surrounding communities. Although they self-identified as Indian, local citizens scorned anyone who was not "pure white." Because there was no such thing as an Indian school in a society that had only black and white schools, Indian schools received limited state and county assistance only after the missionaries approached the superintendents in Mobile and Washington counties.[10] Deaconess Eva Crenshaw stated in her annual report to the Methodist Women's Missionary Society: "Teaching seven grades in the one-teacher public school is still my most time-consuming job."[11] For Indian children to get a high school education, they had to leave the state. Some went to Oklahoma, where they attended Bacone College in Muskogee; to Laredo, Texas, where they attended Holding Institute; to Sue Bennett College in New London, Kentucky; or to Acadia Baptist Academy in Louisiana.

Despite external pressures and missionary influence, the Indian community retained their own exclusive social connectives. Oral history today records places of Indian gatherings in the past. One of these is near the current MOWA Choctaw tribal building. The traditional stomping

Cleveland Johnston's Old Place.

grounds or dance ground there had been used for many generations. Various events could initiate a local Indian ceremony, one was the communal Fire Hunt for deer. Hunters cut splinters off the pine stumps, especially the stumps that had been struck by lightning, in the belief that thunder spirits would bless the hunt. They lit pieces of the wood and then went to hunt deer. The deer, attracted to the many flames, stopped to stare, and then were killed by the Choctaw hunters. After the hunt, the hunters gathered with other community members at the stomping grounds.

Years after their ancestors had been dispossessed of it, one of the Choctaw families squatted on this traditional land, which legally belonged to a railroad company. W. T. Webb then purchased the land in 1872.[12] His children gave it to Southern University in Greensboro, Alabama, in 1906, which later became Birmingham-Southern College, a Methodist school.[13] When the MOWA Choctaw became a state-recognized American Indian tribe, the tribal council specifically requested the return of their traditional ceremonial gathering area. The college sold the land back to them in 1982 for $16,000.[14] Today, the tribe uses the land for ceremonies, including the annual pow-wow, an event that has become for the MOWA, as for many other tribes, a ceremony of cultural revitalization and ethnic identity. In such gatherings, the MOWA perform traditional dances and songs, tell stories, eat traditional foods, honor their elders, and instruct their children—their future leaders.

MOWA Choctaw tell a story about this ceremonial area as it relates to the prison compound that held the Apache leader Geronimo and his warriors. These Indian prisoners were held near the Choctaw Indian community from 1887 to 1894 at Mt. Vernon, a federal arsenal. The arsenal, site of present-day Searcy Hospital, is less than three miles from the stomping ground on Red Fox Road. In the spring of 1887, Geronimo and about seven hundred Apache were transported in small groups to the Mount Vernon Barracks. "At first they lived in army tents just outside the barracks wall, while they built log cabins to form a village near the gate of the post."[15] During their internment, they were allowed to work for people in the neighborhood and to travel to Mobile. Camp commander "Wotherspoon . . . encouraged them to take employment for wages cutting wood or working on farms. By the following February four of them were working on a farm fifteen miles from the post. They were allowed to take their families along and were prospering."[16] One of the Apache worked for Tom Sullivan and his wife, Nancy, cutting wood. They called him "Rye" because he helped carry the rye (grain) to make whiskey. On cold winter evenings, he stayed with the Sullivans overnight. His descendants are among today's MOWA.[17]

Josiah Rivers and Dan Wilkerson, who identified themselves as Choctaw, ran bars on the Level across from the Indian stomping ground.[18] Peter Rivers said his grandfather, Luke Rivers, told about the Apache who "came to

Gertrude Orso, daughter of Lizzie Sullivan and Jim Orso, granddaughter of Caroline "Callie" Sullivan and Dorsey Weaver.

Josiah's still on the Level, killed a cow and made blood pies. They stayed there until they ate it all and made shoe laces from the hide." This story is supported by Lieutenant W. W. Wotherspoon's report from Mt. Vernon Barracks, July 31, 1890: "The general conduct of the Indians during the month has been good with the exception of two men and two squaws who, whilst under the influence of liquor which they obtained at a saloon in the forest, killed a calf belonging to a poor woman . . ."[19]

"Grandpa" Luke Rivers said [the local Choctaw] would go to the Apache camps at Mount Vernon, take their fiddles and play music. The *Mobile Daily News* reported, "Yesterday was payday at Mt. Vernon . . .

[The Apache] came into Mobile on the Birmingham train and proceeded to spend part of their money in purchasing several violins."[20]

MOWA Choctaw Rosie Byrd Rivers tells the story of the Apache who startled her mother while she was cooking cornmeal mush in a large pot outdoors. In her fright, her mother threw a spoonful of hot mush at the Apache and scared them away. Also, she remembers the story of her mother's sister, Dora, being stolen by an Apache woman because her own little girl had died. They chased after her and got Dora back.[21]

When it was time for the Apache to be returned to the fort, a cannon was fired and soldiers "rounded up" the Indians and drove them back to camp. On one occasion, Mollie Weaver, daughter of Jim Weaver, was picked up and kept for a while.[22] After that, local Choctaw children were hidden to keep them from being captured.

"Daddy" Richard Weaver remembers seeing "the Apache walking up the road. They had a lot of beads they were trying to sell. They would trade them for anything out of the fields, corn or beans, whatever they could get."[23] Although Rosie Rivers has some negative memories of the Apache, Roosevelt Weaver and Daddy Richard reported that Indians recognized one another and helped each other out.

In 1894, Geronimo and his people were shipped to Oklahoma, leaving one prison for another. The story of the Apache relationship with the Mt. Vernon Choctaw is told today by many people. The story itself has two critical elements. First, the Apache prisoners hated non-Indians, but liked the local Choctaw. Second, the Choctaw valued the identification with another Indian people because in the 1890s, generations after relocation, there were no other Indian people around Mobile to identify with.

Prior to the coming of the missionaries, early cemeteries were placed on traditional Indian burial grounds. Although today painted fences neatly bound the cemeteries, oral history records where the earlier Choctaw burials are located and the modern MOWA community continues to protect these areas. Indian Grave Branch is the name of the small creek below Byrd Cemetery, and Grave Rock is a place on High Hill near Reed's Chapel that has other nineteenth-century Indian graves. One Indian cemetery, called the Red Wash Hill Cemetery, is located on the

"Daddy" Richard Weaver, right, son of Virginia Rivers, was 93 when this photo was taken in 1985. His father was John Weaver, whose parents were Jesse and Tobe Weaver. With him in this picture are granddaughter Lela Byrd and great grandson John Leonard Byrd. Inset right, Stella Lofton, daughter of Liza and Jack Lofton, wife of "Daddy" Richard Weaver.

Boykin Game Reserve near the Fairford community. This is an old Indian cemetery that has at least fourteen graves with rock markings and a circle of rock with several more graves inside. Although the Boykin Game Reserve is a private hunting club, MOWA Choctaw surreptitiously enter the area to paint the grave rocks and maintain the area. They lost access to their gravesites—their sacred places—because they did not have deeds to the land where they squatted. The graves are a visible and culturally significant symbol of the modern-day MOWA Choctaw community.[24]

Red Wash Hill Cemetery.

Today the MOWA Choctaw people live in ten kin-based subdistricts. Family-based, these areas were established when a land-holding family distributed parcels of land to children and relatives. Over time the larger of these villages came to have their own small Indian churches, established by the Protestant Indian Missions. These small churches became the center of the subdistrict, as the two larger Indian churches served as the centers of the whole MOWA Choctaw community. Today, the local kin-based subdistricts are largely called after the name of their Indian church. Many of the subdistricts have their own graveyards near the church where their history is engraved in stone.

Contemporary villages of the MOWA cluster around the two core areas—Reed's Chapel and Byrd Church—forming almost continuous occupation along the roads in the area west of Highway 43, from just south of Mt. Vernon to about three miles north of McIntosh. A distance of less than a mile separates the northernmost village in Mobile County from the southernmost in Washington County. They are contiguous and boundaries are often indeterminable. Many of the villages bear the names of community leaders. In the below list each of the twenty-one contemporary villages has been assigned a number. Township, range, and sections identifying geographic location are in endnotes. These abstracts include approximate dates when the villages were established; earliest landowners; founders/namesakes; churches; schools; and names of early leaders and early members of the community.[25]

MOBILE COUNTY

1. 27-MILE-BLUFF — on Mobile River/Cedar Creek area below Mt. Vernon to Cold Creek; Choctaw place name: *Kunsly;*[26] founded ca. 1800. The founders were: Chastang, Fisher, Weaver, Byrd, Laurendine, Bru, and Six Towns Choctaw whose phonetically spelled names make them "unknowable."

Refugee Choctaw lived here after the War of 1812 and were joined by other Creek and Cherokee refugees. During the removal era Six Towns Choctaw joined this established village and lived here from the 1830s until the 1860s waiting to be shipped west of the Mississippi. Several of the Six Towns Choctaw women married mixed-blood Indians who lived here. (See Chapter 3.)

Sancer Byrd said, "Pappy said, seven came from west of Citronelle, didn't have no names. Back yonder Indians had to take the name of the white man, same as niggers. Chastang had a big farm, the Indians had to go in and chop corn to get something to eat. They were so hungry; they would just come there, go to cutting and eat the corn raw. Just a

Henry Joseph Laurendine [a.k.a. Londine & Rondene], Choctaw born in Mississippi 1862, baptized 8 Nov 1899, died 31 Aug 1929. He was the son of Jim Laurendine and Lucy, a Six Towns Choctaw. James "Jim" Laurendine and his third wife, Julie, were "Identified but did not remove" on the Mississippi Choctaw Roll.

Above, Nellie Laurendine Bru, daughter of Margarete Laurendine and Naz Bru, granddaughter of Six Towns Choctaws Polly and Jim Laurendine. Naz Bru was a son of Sally Williams, a Six Towns Choctaw, and Simon Bru. Right, Delia Lofton White, daughter of Nellie Bru Lofton and George Lofton. Delia married John Thomas White. She was the granddaughter of Nellie Rose "Mid" Rivers, daughter of Richard Rivers who was the son of Edy Weaver and Joel Rivers of Monroe County.

world of them came. He [Chastang] took them in; some of them went by Chastang. Some worked for Old Man Laurendine down on the bluff and went by Laurendine."[27]

Six Towns Choctaw Jim[28] and Lucy worked for "Old Man Laurendine." They had a son named Henry Laurendine and a daughter named Margaret. Margaret's daughter was Nellie by Naz Bru, half Choctaw.[29] "Margaret was a full-blood Indian woman. She 'busted' Nellie out in a cornfield one night."[30] Nellie Laurendine Bru married George Lofton, son of Jack Lofton and Delphine Laurendine. Their children married into Byrd, Rivers, and Weaver families.

Sally (also known as Polly) Williams, a Six Towns Choctaw, had children by Simon Bru. Simon Bru married Sally/Polly Williams on his deathbed.[31]

2. THE LEVEL — Red Fox Road, off Highway 43, between Calvert and Mt. Vernon[32]; founded ca. 1840. The founders were: Six Towns Choctaw, Lem Byrd, Dave Weaver, Jerome "Pic" Chastang, Orsos, Brashears, Smiths.

The story of how the Byrds, Weavers, and Rivers moved to the Level is told in Chapter 2. Another refugee who moved here in 1841 was Alexander Brashears, one of the sixty-nine reservees who received land under Article 14 of the Dancing Rabbit Creek Treaty. On the list of Choctaw reservees, he was described as a "half-blood Creek." Alexander sold his reserve and went west for a short time and returned. (Ironically, Alexander Brashears is the only MOWA ancestor the BIA/BAR accepted as a "documented" Choctaw.) After his wife, Emeline Wind, died he moved his family from Sumter County to Mobile County. Alexander was the son of Rachel Durant of Alabama-Creek and Samuel Brashears. Alexander's daughters married brothers: Louisa Jane Brashears married Nathaniel John Smith[33] and Emeline Jane Brashears[34] married Ira Byrd Smith, sons of Oliver Merida Smith and Barbara Ellen Byrd.[35] This family, who considered themselves Choctaw, was living near Mt. Vernon in 1851.[36] Nathaniel John Smith and his family helped found Charity Chapel. (See No. 10 below.)

Jerome "Pic" Chastang, son of Cecile Weatherford, married Cornelia "Molly" Weaver, daughter of Jim Weaver and Peggy Parnell. Pic also had children by Rhoda and Mary "Big Sis" Rivers, daughters of Edy Weaver and Joel Rivers. Apparently, Pic went to Monroe County around 1850 and brought them to Mobile County.[37] Sancer Byrd said "Old Mrs. Rivers came here with a big carriage and riggings, but didn't like it and went back."[38] Edy Rivers's children started the Rivers lineage among the MOWA.

Pic is legendary. In 1856 he bought Section 20, T2N, R1W.[39] He owned a store and brought in supplies by steamboat on the river. Molly

Above left, Medora Chastang Reed, daughter of Jerome "Pic" Chastang and Mollie Weaver, married Early Reed, Sr. Above right, Jerry Chastang, son of Watson Chastang. Below, Tollie and Ida Reed, daughters of Medora Chastang and Early Reed.

was his main wife and when she filled a grocery order for her household, she also filled one for his other wives. They had houses located near each other. Pic left his shoes on the front porch of the house where he spent the night. In addition to these three wives, some say he had as many as eight or ten wives and 144 children. As "Daddy" Richard Weaver said, "Pic Chastang was much a man!"

These families started a village at the Level and with the help of mission-trained Choctaw started a church.[40] Lem Byrd owned land and was a trustee for the local school.[41] His son, William T. "Bill" Byrd helped start a school and taught for several months[42] and handled finances for his father and brother.

Lem, Bill, and Wash Byrd revitalized the Byrd Church in the 1840s. Wash Byrd was head of the church. Tom Smith (son of Josephine Williams, a Six Towns Choctaw),[43] who married Glovine Reed, preached there in the early 1900s. He was followed by Jim Byrd and then by Jim's brother, Tom Byrd. This church was renamed Aldersgate when the Methodist missionaries took it over in the 1930s. Members of the church asked the missionaries to leave when they decided they no longer needed them. Byrd Church-Aldersgate continues to be the "mother" church in Mobile County. The history of the community is engraved in the headstones in the Byrd Cemetery.

3. TASSIE BYRD — settlement founded ca. 1920s by Tassie Byrd, located on County Highway 96 toward Calvert.[44]

Tassie Byrd (1898–1937) is the son of Wash Byrd and Minna Rivers; grandson of Lem and Anna Weaver Byrd and of Edy Weaver Rivers. He was also the half-brother of Clifford Rivers. Tassie married Callie Reed, daughter of Joe Reed (village leader in Washington County). His son Sancer Byrd became a village leader, his son Elvin Byrd is active in church and school, and his daughter, Ruth, married Tom Hopkins, a village leader in Mobile County. Tassie and his family started Cedar Creek Church in 1927. It was Baptist until the Methodist missionaries came in. Members of the village sought out Tassie for advice, and he helped people get jobs. He held prayer meetings on Wednesday night,

Children of Charlie Hopkins: Nancy, who married William Byrd, and Jack Hopkins.

at which time people were told what needed to be done in the church or in the school that was held in the church.

The school was originally called Weaver School but later became Calcedeaver. Weaver School was closed in the mid-1940s because Charlie Hopkins, a student, had spinal meningitis. Because a certain number of students were required to maintain a school, members of the village built a bridge across Cedar Creek so that their children could get to a school. To help the situation Rev. Patillo, the Methodist missionary, consolidated the three missionary-founded schools—Calvert, Cedar Creek, and Weaver—in 1949 to form a public school. Using letters from each of the three schools, he named it Calcedeaver. In 1954, the Indians asked the missionaries to leave because of unauthorized sale of school property to the county. In the 1960s, Mobile County School Board members attempted to send Indians to black schools, but the Indians refused to go.[45] Jack Rivers, Richard Rivers, Ada Rivers, Will Byrd, and Jim Byrd started their own school. They taxed themselves and paid for a teacher. Calcedeaver is now recognized as an Indian School in Mobile County and has an active Indian Education Program.

Other families in the Tassie Byrd village in the 1930s were: Thad Reed, Dan Weaver, Willie Jordan, Lymas Reed, Bill Frazier and sons, Will and Melvin. All lived within a mile or two of each other. Brothers Early Reed and Clifford Reed preached in the church, as did Dud Weaver. Thad Reed, their brother-in-law, owned a store and traded horses but lost his property in a lawsuit.

4. MARVIN RIVERS — settlement founded ca. 1920s by Marvin Rivers at corner of County Highway 96 and Red Fox Road.[46]

Marvin Rivers (b. 1898) was the son of James "Jack" Rivers (son of Mary "Big Sis" and Dick Rivers) and Annie Weaver (daughter of David Crockett Weaver and Penny Parnell). Marvin had three wives, owned a store and bar, and hired men to work for him. His wives were Dinks Weaver, Ella Byrd, and Anna Weaver. He fathered eight children.

5. COON BYRD — settlement founded ca. 1900s by Coon Byrd in Shady Grove off Red Fox Road near Calvert.[47]

Coon Byrd (b. 1870), son of Wash Byrd, grandson of Lem Byrd, married Lena Byrd, daughter of Mollie Starland and Frank "Boy" Byrd, son of Nancy Hopkins and Lem Byrd, Jr. He worked in the turpentine business and hired men to "chip, dip and pull boxes" (cups to catch sap). He was a village leader and saw that people were taken care of by butchering cattle and distributing the meat. Coon was related to Tom Sullivan who worked with him and Dave Taylor to start a church. Their first services were held in a brush arbor and then by working together they built the Shady Grove Church. Reverend Early Reed preached there in the beginning and it was Baptist; after the missionaries came in, it became Methodist. Shady Grove Church was used as a school and called West Calvert School. Only the children of the village attended. Other leaders in the 1920s were Lewis Byrd, Tom and

Mollie Lee Starland, wife of Frank "Boy" Byrd, was a midwife. Mollie came from Houma, Louisiana, to Mobile on a boat with Melton Snow, and his wife Ellen Seals, a Choctaw.

Mollie Starland Byrd, grandmother of Mary Byrd Taylor, driving four yoke of oxen pulling an eight-wheel wagon loaded with stumpwood for Retort Plant at Calvert.

Rob Sullivan, and Jessie Weaver.

WASHINGTON COUNTY

6. TIBBIE (Okatibbaha) — founded ca. 1820s by Rose Gaines and Daniel Reed at crossroads of north-south Choctaw Trading Path to Mobile and the east-west Federal Road extension from St. Stephens to Natchez, today's crossroads of State Highway 17 and County Highway 20.[48]

This was the site of the homeplace, inn, and cowpens established by Rose Gaines and Daniel Reed on the western border of the present MOWA Choctaw community, near the Alabama-Mississippi state line. (See Chapter 2.) As their children reached adulthood, land records show they built homes nearby. The Percy Reed Cemetery, located on Lockwood Road off Highway 17 South, provides additional records.[49] No lasting church building or school was established at this site, although a school was operated in this area in 1872.[50]

Upon Daniel's death in 1844, Rose continued to operate her farm, where she owned cattle, sheep, hogs, and horses, until she became unable to care for the property. Both Daniel and Rose were buried under a chinaberry tree on the farm. Their graves were dug up when the new property owners excavated for a farm pond.[51] MOWA Choctaw no longer occupy this site.

7. REED'S CHAPEL — Choctaw place name: *Kunshak*, founded 1829, "brush arbor" church and ceremonial ground by George Reed, eldest son of Rose Gaines and Daniel Reed. Reed's Chapel is located two miles west of Town of McIntosh on Topton Road.[52]

This village was the nucleus for the development of all other MOWA Choctaw villages in Washington County, and includes the *nanih chaha* or High Hill area, which, although not now occupied, was densely settled prior to and immediately after Choctaw removal in the 1830s. Reed's Chapel Church, cemetery, and school are located in this village.[53] In the 1830s, George Reed exercised both spiritual and cultural leadership here. This is also the site of the longest continuously operated Indian school in Washington County. George's brother William also shared some of the duties of community patriarch.

George Reed had two wives and fathered eleven children. His sons, especially George, Jr., succeeded him in a community leadership role.

During his life, George Reed served as pastor of the church, and although he spent some of the early years of his marriage in Texas with his grandmother, Kalioka, and his uncles, Jerry and Isaac Gaines, he returned to spend his later years in Washington County.

His wives were Maria Colbert, a deaf-mute said to be the granddaughter of General William Colbert, Chickasaw, and Jessie Moniac, Creek, who came to McIntosh Bluff by riverboat, and Ellen Bretina (also known as Fotenay) Weaver, daughter of Cecile Weatherford and Dave Weaver and granddaughter of Nancy Fisher.

George's male children, grandchildren, and the men who married his children tended to assume leadership roles after his death. George's sons were Reuben, Seaborn, Oscar, George Jr., Joseph, William "Coon," and Bill. His daughters were Lucretia (Aunt Creasy), Glovina, Matilda, Alabama, and Louisa.

William's sons were Jim, Seaborn, Alex, Tom, and twins Walter and Wesley. His daughters were Emily, Annie, and Virginia.

This settlement was the site of the church that benefited from the work of Reverend Alfred Wright, the missionary from the Choctaw mission and school at Goshen in Mississippi from 1820–1830. In 1920, the Baptist Home Mission Board entertained a resolution to work among the "South Alabama Indians at Reed's Chapel. Baptist missionaries Reverend Weathers and Martha Walden arrived in 1921."[54]

Van Weaver, son of George "Bob" Weaver, with flivver.

Indian property owners in the village at the turn of the century reflect this leadership tendency, and included Dud Weaver, Isaac Weaver, Sam Johnston, Early Reed, Roen Snow, Tanner Snow, Charlie Stevenson[55], Reuben P. Reed, Jodie Weaver, Melton Snow, and Wesley Johnston.

8. CARETTA–High Hill (*nanih chaha*) — founded by Piamingo Hometah, ca. 1800–1805. Caretta/High Hill is located one to two miles northwest of Reed's Chapel on Topton Road.[56]

High Hill is a major landmark in the area and a site of very early Choctaw presence. The site was occupied by Piamingo Hometah's band, a group of Six Towns Choctaw. (See Chapter 3.)

In 1889, Piamingo Hometah's grandson, Henry "Doc" Eaton, and James Taylor Weaver, son of Jim Weaver and Peggy Parnell, homesteaded land on High Hill, although they had long occupied the area.

This village was abandoned as farm roads were built in the vicinity of McIntosh and as families tended to construct homes nearer their central schools and meeting houses at Reed's Chapel. This process was not accomplished until about two generations ago, and some families continue to live in its environs.

9. ISAACTOWN — FOUNDED in 1870s included Pleasant View (formerly Old Mount Moriah) Church and school. Isaactown is located in Fairford community, which is located on County Highway 4 between Calvert and Sims Chapel. It was founded by Isaac Johnston, son of Cornelia "Molly" Weaver and Powell Bates Johnston.[57]

Isaac Johnston was born to Cornelia "Molly" when she was about thirteen years old. Cornelia, the daughter of Peggy Parnell and Jim Weaver, then married Jerome "Pic" Chastang and had ten children.

Other landowners were Albert Weaver, son of Cecile Weatherford and Dave Weaver, who married Polly Byrd, daughter of Betsy Gibson and William T. "Bill" Byrd. They had twelve children: five married Reeds, three of whom were children of Lorinda Weaver (Albert's sister) and William Reed.

By 1900, landowners were Albert Weaver, Isaac Johnston, Ada Smith Chastang (Cornelia's daughter-in-law; Tom and Glovina Reed Smith's daughter), Oscar Reed (son of Miriah Colbert and George Reed), and Kelly Johnston. These families formed the core of the early village in Isaactown. The group at Isaactown had close ties with the nearby villages: three of Albert's children married cousins from Reed's Chapel. In the early 1880s, Isaac Johnston married Matilda Reed, daughter of Ellen Bretina "Tiny" Weaver and George Reed. George, who was village leader at Reed's Chapel, then had a son-in-law who was also an emergent village leader. Isaac and Matilda had eleven children.

The leaders of the village recognized the need to educate their children, so Isaac Johnston and Albert Weaver hired Mose Smith to teach. Each family was assessed two dollars for their children to attend school. Classes were held in an old house and Mose Smith boarded with families. They also established a church, Mount Moriah,[58] pastored temporarily by William Williams, a Six Towns Choctaw who had attended one of Reverend Alfred Wright's mission schools. His mother was Sally Williams, a Six Towns Choctaw who lived in Mobile County.[59] "R" Weaver (probably Robert Weaver, son of Jim) was listed as a trustee of the church during that same period.

By 1917 the church had been renamed Pleasant View but needed a new building. Pleasant View School was held temporarily in St. Andrews Church where a teacher was provided by the Washington County Board of Education. Sophie Rivers (Lem Byrd's granddaughter) was the teacher. Other teachers were Martha Walden (1921); Estelle Hall (1923); and Quinna Stringer (1926). Apparently, the county did not provide teachers in other years.[60] Cleveland and Kelly Johnston were school trustees. In 1969 the school had 120 students; it was then closed and consolidated.

In 1920, the Alabama State Convention and the Woman's Missionary Union passed resolutions requesting that the Home Mission Board open work among the Indians. Albert Weaver and his wife, Mary Ann Weaver, deeded a parcel of land in Section 22 to the Home Mission Board of the Southern Baptist Convention Church October 2, 1922.[61]

In the early 1920s, Wesley Johnston, Isaac's son, became pastor of the church (then called Pleasant View). Wesley was married to Mary Snow, daughter of Melton Snow, who was the settlement leader in Snow Corner. Their children were Wesley Jr., Ervin, Sherman, Jerry, George, Effie, Dora, and Edna. Although Isaac Johnston lived until the late 1940s, Wesley also emerged as a leader during the early part of the century. The church became Baptist through the aid of missionaries in the 1920s but was known as Wesley Johnston's Church. He died in 1948, the same year as his father.

Pleasant View withdrew from the Mission Board in the 1940s. Chandler Weaver, Travis Johnston, and other leaders felt they did not need the missionaries any more. Descendants of its founders continue to live in this village.

10. CHARITY CHAPEL — founded ca. 1880s by Nathaniel J. Smith and Seaborn Reed. Charity Chapel is located between Sims Chapel and Citronelle on County Highway 35.[62]

This village is spatially separate from the other MOWA villages and is located in the south-central portion of Washington County. Eliza Reed, second daughter of Rose Gaines and Daniel Reed, lived in this general area, although not on the same site. She was married to Peter Cole, the son of Mark Cole and Hannah, a Choctaw. After Daniel's death in 1844, Rose and her remaining children lived next to Eliza, Peter, and their five children. In 1871, Eliza's son Seaborn purchased land within what is now the Charity Chapel community (T2 R2W Sec. 5). He married Georgiann Logan. Ten children were born of this union, five of whom married within this village.

Another early leader was Nathaniel, son of Oliver Smith and Barbara Ellen Byrd; he married Louisa Jane Brashears whose father was Alexander Brashears. Of their twelve children (born between 1852–1872), seven married other local Indians. The children and grandchildren of these two families intermarried and formed the village of Charity Chapel.

Seaborn's daughter, Eliza Reed, married Manson Smith in about 1880. He was the grandson of Alexander Brashears. Barbara Reed, also a daughter of Seaborn, married John Smith (Manson's brother). Their sisters, Emeline and Barbara Smith, married John and Frank Cole (respectively), grandsons of Eliza Reed Cole.

John and Manson Smith founded the Charity Chapel church in 1891. Seaborn gave the land for the church and Nathaniel was the first pastor.[63] Barbara Reed Smith became the head of the church after her husband's death, and she also served as the mid-wife for the community. In 1912, a school was established in the church (it had ninety students in 1969, when it was closed). John Everett, Seaborn's nephew, owned a store across from the church. He and his half-brother, "Mannish" Ryan, (children of Florentine Reed, daughter of Eliza Reed and Francis Pargado), also operated a sawmill and turpentine still. John Everett became a large, and extremely wealthy, landowner in partnership with former Congressman Frank Boykin (First Congressional District), but he lost his fortune to the Boykins prior to his death in 1927. (See Chapter 6.) The families in the village were (and still are) mostly all descended from either Eliza Reed or Nathaniel J. Smith (son-in-law of Alexander Brashears). A jealous suitor blinded the grandson of Manson Smith, Abb Cole,[64] in his youth. That was when he "got religion." He became pastor of the church (now called

Abb Cole and wife, Ola Mae Sanderson. Abb's father was Frank Cole, son of Peter Cole and Eliza Reed. Eliza Reed was daughter of Rose Gaines and Daniel Reed. Abb's mother was Barbara Ellen Smith, daughter of Nathaniel John Smith and Louisa Jane Brashears, who was the daughter of Alexander Brashears and Rachel Durant, Choctaw/Creek.

Jesus Name) and preached until his death in 1996 at age one hundred. For well over a half century he was a leader in the church and village. Members of this village continue to be active in tribal affairs.

11. FAIRFORD — FOUNDED ca.1880s by Daniel Weaver and William Hiwanna Reed. Fairford is located on County Highway 4 between Calvert and Sims Chapel.[65]

The families of Daniel Weaver and William Hiwanna Reed began the village near Poll Bayou Creek. They established a brush arbor church first known as Chukka Hula. This was the forerunner of St. Thomas.[66] Other families who helped were the Chastangs and Sullivans. Ed Chastang (son of Jerome "Pic") owned land in this area in 1889. Around 1884 a lumber company purchased land and built a sawmill at Fairford. The company built a railroad to the Tombigbee River and in 1889 a post office was opened.

Daniel Weaver (ca. 1840–1925), son of Jim Weaver, married Mary Louise Taylor, daughter of Dave Taylor and Jane Byrd. Eleven children were born to this union.

William Reed (1821–1894), son of Rose Gaines and Daniel Reed, married Lorinda, daughter of Cecile Weatherford and Dave Weaver. They had twelve children who included Seaborn, Alex, Walter, and Wesley.

John Goodman married Virginia "Ginny," one of William's daughters. Wesley married one of Daniel Weaver's daughters. Some of the children of these two families intermarried; others found spouses among other Indian families.

The village leaders organized a school and assessed the families two dollars to help pay for a teacher. In 1893, school records list Annie Seals

Above left, Frances Smith, wife of Buddy Smith. Above right, Rilla Smith and husband, Thomas Edward Weaver. Right, Virginia Weaver, wife of Amos Reed, and daughter of Rilla Smith and Thomas E. Weaver.

as the teacher.[67]

12. SNOW CORNER — founded ca. 1880s by Melton Snow, Sr. Snow Corner is located west of McIntosh about 1½ miles from Federal Highway 43 on County Highway 35.[68]

Melton Snow, Sr., (1837–1923) came to McIntosh Bluff on a boat in the 1870s with his two brothers and Mollie Starland (wife of Frank "Boy" Byrd). His mother was Dinah Snow. He and his family migrated west during removal and then he made his way back to Alabama. Along the way he married Ellen Seals, a Choctaw from Texas. Melton and Ellen had twelve children. Ellen's sister, Emma Seals (b. 1857), married William Hiwanna Reed (b. 1838 in Texas), son of George Reed, Sr., and Miriah Colbert).

According to Dinah Snow (Melton's granddaughter, who was named for her great grandmother, Dinah Snow, above), Melton and Ellen spoke to each other in an "Indian language." Dinah also said that Ellen had "long black hair and that when she stood up her hair would touch the

Left, Ellen Snow Reed, wife of Tom Reed; daughter of York Snow and Printella Weaver. Right, Lou Ella Stevenson, daughter of Charlie Stevenson, wife of Frank Snow, mother of George Snow.

ground." Melton was a blacksmith, so he had plenty of work to do and hired other men to help him. People came to him from all around to shoe their horses.[69] He purchased land in 1889 from William H. Reed, who had homesteaded it in 1872. By 1910, Melton Snow owned acreage in Sec. 2 and 3, as did Charlie Echols, Reuben P. Reed, William Weaver, and John Johnston.

Melton Snow's grandchildren founded Memorial Baptist Church after a dispute between Shomo Weaver and Brother R. M. Averitt, a Baptist missionary at Reed's Chapel. Brother Averitt's supporters withdrew from Reed's Chapel and started their own church. Beanie Snow donated one acre of land for the building.

13. HILL SPRINGS — founded ca. 1880s by Joseph Reed, son of Emeline Weaver and Reuben Reed. Hill Springs is located west of Snow Corner on County Highway 35.[70]

This area was first known as the Joe Reed settlement and was populated by the children and grandchildren of Joe Reed and his wives: first, Jane Taylor and second, Molly Newbern. He had twelve children and was the father of Early Reed, who became a preacher and leader in the community. Joe founded Hill Springs Church, an Assembly of God church.[71] He owned a store and hired other men to work for him when he got turpentine and timber contracts. School was held in the church after 1928 and Sallie Johnston was paid by the families to teach the children. Henry Lane taught in the school in the 1930s. By the 1940s, the Washington County School Board paid two teachers, and Mrs. John Reed was the school trustee and bus driver. Sixty students attended the school in 1969 when it was closed and consolidated.

14. MAGNOLIA — founded ca. 1890s by Oscar Reed. Magnolia is located between Hill Springs and Snow Corner.[72]

Oscar Reed (1859–1910), son of Ellen "Tiny" Bretina Weaver and George Reed, grandson of both Cecile Weatherford and Rose Gaines, married Lizzie Logan. Oscar's daughter, Lucretia "Creasy" Reed was the midwife for the community through the 1940s. She could count in

Choctaw and taught her granddaughter, Dolly, songs in the Choctaw language. Creasy married Stewart Reed (b. 1856), son of Joe Reed and Molly Newbern; her sister Lonnie married Clifford Rivers. Brother Early Reed, Stewart's brother, started Magnolia Church. It is now a Holiness church.[73] A two-teacher school was held there for a few years until it was closed in 1969. At that time forty-four students were enrolled.

Early landowners in Section 4 were George Rivers, 1899; Joe Johnston, 1889; Slade Orso, 1904; James Orso, 1896, and Oscar Reed in 1900. Melton Snow and Craney Weaver also owned land in this section.

Above, Lucretia "Creasy" Reed, wife of Stewart Reed and daughter of Oscar and Elizabeth "Liz" Reed. "Aunt Creasy" was born January 1, 1891 and was highly revered as a midwife and healer. She spoke Choctaw and taught songs to her granddaughter, Dollie Weaver, pictured inset in 1983.

15. GEORGE FIELDS — founded ca. 1910s by George Fields and is located on Topton Road four miles west of Reed's Chapel.[74]

George W. Fields (born 1872) was the son of Henry Killam,[75] Creek, and Amanda Fields (a three-fourths Choctaw from Demopolis). George married Daisy Dove Reed, daughter of Bill Reed (son of George Reed and Miriah Colbert).

Mt. Pleasant Baptist Church began in 1923, when George W. Fields and his wife, Daisy conducted prayer with their children, Frank, Mariah, Emma Pearl, George Guy, Lula Mae, Hundove, Spencer, Izola, Lora, and William, in their home. The prayer meetings grew as the children married and started their own families. Membership was limited to family members because few people lived nearby and transportation was by foot or horseback. By the 1930s, they had acquired a building and Reverend R. M. Averitt, Baptist missionary to the Indian communities, was the first pastor.[76] During the 1940s, school was held in the church.

Deacons of the church have included Guy Fields, Dorsey L.

Uria Weaver Reed and Harry "Oscar" Reed.

George Fields

Weaver, and William A. Reed. The Reverend Bennett W. Weaver, son of Dorsey Weaver, was ordained as pastor in 1954 and has continued to serve for more than thirty years. He taught at Reed's Chapel School until his retirement in 1995.

Property owners in Sections 28 include: Lem Reed, 1861; William Reed, 1896; and George Reed, 1883; later owners include George Fields, Bill Reed, Jr., Clifford Reed, Luke Rivers, and Thad Reed.

16. BO REED (Topton) — founded ca. 1920s by Bo Reed and is located on Topton Road where it intersects with Ab Richardson Road.[77]

Bo Reed (born c. 1905) was the son of Will Reed and Eldora Taylor, grandson of Reuben Reed and Emeline Weaver. He and his wife Ida had twelve children. Bo Reed moved his family to the Topton area to work cutting crossties for a sawmill, which was established in 1895 by Seaboard Manufacturing Company.

Other Indian families living in the area were Wash Sullivan, Will Cole, Henry Rivers, Needham Reed, and Joe Reed. Bo Reed and his brother hired a teacher for their children for a few months; later the children went to Hill Springs School. They walked the eight miles to church for special events like Homecoming. Occasionally, Reverend Early Reed would visit and hold prayer meeting.

17. LUKETOWN — founded ca. 1910s by Luke Rivers. Luketown is located in Rivers community in Sims Chapel.[78]

Luke Houma Rivers (1880–1964), son of Dan Reed and Fannie Byrd (daughter of Wash Byrd), and his sister, Edy, took the last name of Rivers, after their maternal grandmother Mary "Big Sis" Rivers. Luke married Texas Reed, daughter of William Hiwanna Reed and Emma Seals. Their ten children were Price, Ethel, Gammage, Marvin, Houma, Matthew, Martha, Lessie, Dan, Oliver, and Elliott. Luke homesteaded Section 20 in 1909. He worked in the timber and logging business. His numerous descendants continue to live in this village and his daughter Lessie occupies his homestead.

18. CHOCTAW RIDGE—founded ca. 1910s by Clifford Rivers. Choctaw Ridge is located in Rivers community in Sims Chapel.[79]

Clifford Rivers (b. 1881) son of "Minna" Rivers, married Lonia Reed (daughter of Oscar Reed). They had eleven children. He is half-brother to Tassie Byrd, father-in-law of Price Rivers. There is a close relationship between the Choctaw Ridge and Tassie Byrd villages.

Clifford Rivers started the Rivers Church for his family. Other charter members were Jim Rivers, Francis Rivers, and Bigee Rivers. The church grew out of home Bible studies and some open-air, brush

Martha "Minna" Rivers married Clifford Rivers; she was the mother of Cherry Mae Rivers, who was married to Price Rivers.

arbor revival meetings in the village, which is located about two miles southeast of the Sims Chapel Post Office. The first organized ministry started in 1937 with the Reverend Patillo, who had earlier started a Methodist ministry among the Choctaw of Mobile County. The early ministry included a native minister, the Reverend Clifford Reed, who served from the early 1940s to 1950. The Reverend Early Reed took over the ministry at that time and remained until 1961. The Reverend Gallasneed Weaver began his ministry in 1961 and is still the pastor.[80] Gallasneed Weaver was the principal for Reed's Chapel Elementary School until his retirement in 1995.

19. PAT LANE CIRCLE — founded ca. 1900s by Early Reed. Pat Lane Circle is located off Topton Road between Federal Highway 43 and Reed's Chapel.[81]

This settlement was named for Pat Lane, son of Nancy (daughter of

George Reed and Miriah Colbert) and Patrick Lane,[82] who helped move the Indians west. Nancy had Pat Lane while in Texas and brought him back to Alabama.

Early Reed (b. ca. 1870) was the son of Joe Reed (grandson of Emeline Weaver and Reuben Reed) and married Medora Chastang, daughter of Jerome "Pic" Chastang and Cornelia "Mollie" Weaver. Their nine children were: Ida; Tolie; Mattie (m. George Chastang); Irvin (m. Effie Johnston); Early Van (m. Ruth Weaver); Eugene; Pellie (m. Lula Reed); John; and Sadie Lane. Dud Weaver lived there in the 1920s and Early Reed deeded land for the church and graveyard. He started the Happy Gospel church in the 1930s. Reverend Early Reed preached in the village churches throughout the entire Indian community.

20. SANCTOWN — founded ca. 1860s by Sancho Weaver. Sanctown is located off Fairford Road west of Calvert.[83]

Alfred Sancho Weaver (b. 1845), son of Cecile Weatherford and Dave Weaver, married Rosa Lee "Mid" Rivers, daughter of "Big Sis." They had seven children, four of whom married Sullivans. This village is extremely isolated—only "pig trails lead to Sanctown." Folklore says that they were the major whiskey producers for the Indians. Sancho's descendants continued this tradition: William Weaver, 1880s; Hal Weaver, 1900s; and Hal Weaver, Jr., 1950s. They kept to themselves and have very little outside contact. A small school, the MOWA Choctaw Friends Academy was established in 1985 under the direction of the Associated Committee of Friends on Indian Affairs. Enrollment is based on Native American heritage and proximity to school. Annual enrollment is forty-five to fifty students. Quaker Lodge houses administrative offices, living quarters and kindergarten class. The Friends Center and Academy continues to expand as resources permit.

21. RUBYVILLE — founded ca. 1920s by Pelham Orso. Rubyville is located off Topton Road toward Citronelle.[84]

Land records do not show early ownership in this area. The only current MOWA owner is John Johnston. The village was named for Ruby

Johnston Orso, wife of Charlie Orso. They had eight children. It is no longer occupied.

Residences of other MOWA are scattered throughout the neighboring communities of Chunchulla (Chunk Chulla is Choctaw for the fox's den), Citronelle, and Saraland, too few in number to be described individually, but for the most part contiguous with MOWA settlements.

During the period between the late 1800s and early 1900s, south Alabama Indian people and their community were not greatly different economically from many of their white and black neighbors. Many people in the region were involved in small-scale farming, subsistence fishing, and hunting in the extensive forests. However, the way of life for the Indians changed dramatically in the 1890s when their forest, their region of refuge behind a green wall, became a national economic asset.

6

SUBSISTENCE — LAND LOSS

1890–1920

"John Everett got hold of the land like this. The land wasn't worth nothing, 50 cents to a dollar an acre was all you paid for it. He kept buying until the first thing he knowed he owned all this country. Frank Boykin went in with him and just took it all when John Everett fell dead in 1929, when the people's bank went broke. They let the people live on the land, farm and raise cows. Some folks farmed up to 40 acres and didn't own nare acre of it. They never even had to pay taxes on it. Mr. Frank let them stay as long as they wanted. He wouldn't move them off." — RICHARD WEAVER, 1983

THE MAJORITY of the Indians in south Alabama lived on public land as "squatters" until after the Civil War because only whites and free people of color were eligible to purchase land. The first villages developed around early leaders who could pass as non-Indian and thus could buy land. For example, in 1836, Lem Byrd, Daniel Reed, and James Johnston purchased land and established villages. These villages then expanded, as their families grew, onto public lands that were occupied without official title. This did not become a problem until the mid-1880s, when the major forests of the northern states had been clear-cut and timber companies were seeking new forests.

Until this time, seasonal day labor, some logging, harvesting corn and cotton, and cattle-raising provided income for the Indian families. Cattle roamed in a common herd, distinguished by the brands of individual owners.[1] Roosevelt Weaver said, "Most all of the older folks raised cows. Why, they had cattle running all the way from [McIntosh] to Calvert, all down to the river; wouldn't nobody tell you that you couldn't run your cows on their land then. Cows were branded. Didn't have it fenced up; stock law come later. You could run cows wide open everywhere. When they got ready to sell, they gathered them up, this man four, that man five, and drove them to Mobile."[2] Zeno Orso and Alexander Hollinger had a cowpen at Water Trough Hill on Red Fox Road and a dip vat near the stomping ground where people would bring their cattle.[3] After the Local Option Stock Law of 1939 was enacted, prohibiting free-range cattle, many Indian people had to sell their cows because they could not afford to pay for fences. Without cattle and with wild game scarce, their food supply was greatly diminished.[4]

Like raising cattle, logging took community cooperation. Men from different families participated in cutting the tall timber, "snaking" it (moving logs to a creek with a team of oxen), and floating it down river to market. Periodically, they would combine their logs into an enormous raft for the trip to Mobile. Roosevelt Weaver describes life at that time:

"Before any sawmills come in, old man Isaac Johnston run logs in the river and took rafts to Mobile. They had all them logs rafted up ready to go, so that when the water got up it would run them logs down to what they called Little River, cause it had plenty of water in it and you could go into Tombigbee out of Little River. It come down in between Bates and Bilbo Creek. You had to hold the raft in that stream and stay on the logs. If it got in the woods they would tear up. They had long paddles, about 15 feet, where they could pull that water and hold that raft out of the woods. My daddy said they always had a tent stretched on the logs, on the front end. That's where they cook and eat going to Mobile. There was a place down there what was called Turbine Slough and the raft would tear up if you couldn't hold it on the other side of the river. If that happened, you done worked the whole year trying to get all them logs in the river and make a payday, you had to be very careful with them. My daddy was on the front end and he said that water wouldn't stop pulling that raft toward the woods. He had to fight that water and keep the raft in that stream. After they passed Turbine Slough, they was long gone on to Mobile. Isaac Johnston catched the train and went down to get paid for his logs and meet the payday. He was pretty well known in Mobile around the banks and could cash checks. He give the men their money and they bought all the whiskey, or whatever, they wanted. Then he would bring them all back home on the train."[5]

The long logs were used for ship spars, which supported rigging on ships. This logging industry was so important that the state enacted legislation in 1867 designating several creeks as "public highways."[6]

Around the turn of the century a local white man who became a powerful political leader joined with a trusted Choctaw Indian community leader to defraud people out of lands they had held since the early 1800s. Oral history accounts tell of horse-drawn wagons and later flat-bed trucks loaded with people who were being taken to the county seat at St. Stephens where they filed homestead papers on property they had held since the 1830s Removal Era. Although the Choctaw people claimed title (the right to remain) to these lands under the Treaty of Dancing Rabbit Creek, the Indian community leader who eventually acquired most of their land felt that without actual deeds to the land, the claims could be disputed. (See Appendix C, Homesteads.)

Without legal title, of course, the Choctaw land could not legally be taken from them. Thus getting clear title to Choctaw lands was necessary before the Choctaw people could be defrauded of these lands. Simply put, the process was to (1) establish a homestead title for every member of the community, (2) have them sign the title over to their community leader who was to protect them and their lands from encroachment, (3) have the leader sign title over to the local white businessman — who would later become a powerful politician by virtue of land ownership, and (4) have the land sold to the northern lumber companies. Other versions of the story tell of the white political boss offering to protect for life the rights of Indian people to live in their homes and farm their land, if only they would sign over their land to him so he could officially protect them from those who would forcibly remove them from the area. This last argument exploited a persistent fear by many Choctaw that they would be forcibly removed to Oklahoma by the federal government because their ancestors had been unable or unwilling to sign up with the federal agent after the Treaty of Dancing Rabbit Creek. Interestingly, the threat of removal would only have been real to people who identified themselves as Choctaw Indians.

Contemporary MOWA Choctaw oral history describing this process of land encroachment is consistent. Roosevelt Weaver worked for Frank Boykin for many years and tells how the Choctaw leader, John Everett, and Boykin got together:

> "Everett and Boykin, that's what they called their business. When they started out, old man Everett run a business before he ever got up with the Boykins. Frank Boykin, before he got with John Everett, worked in a store out there at Fairford Lumber Company, a bunch of Englishmen owned all of that land, about 100,000 acres.
>
> "Frank was mighty smart. If he could do a job and get two pays, well he would do it. One time he was totin' water out there. They said they

From left, W. H. Ryans Jr., James "Jimbo" Patrick, Frank Boykin, child Joseph "Muff" Ryans, John Everett [Reed] Sr., Rob Boykin, W. H. Ryans Sr., 1920s.

was going to have to hire another water boy and they wasn't paying but $1.25 and he said, 'I'll tell ya'll what you do, give me that other $1.25 and I'll carry two buckets. I'll put a harness on it and carry a bucket on each side.' And so he did and they paid him the other $1.25 and he made him $2.50 a day. So, John and Frank bought all the land they could find and got a contract with Taylor Lowenstein to hang it with turpentine [tap trees and collect sap in cups] and folks here worked for them. Dick Boykin ran the store at Calvert and if you worked for Boykin and Everett you could go down to that store and get anything you wanted. He talked to the people and filled their orders. They didn't have a list cause they couldn't write, you know. But when a fellow got in a tight and couldn't pay the grocery bill, well they give him a little money and took the homestead deed. They moved the families out of the woods and give them a few acres along Topton Road. I remember a time when John Everett and Frank Boykin both, back in 1922, they was both recognized to be worth $1 million cash a piece, both was a millionaire. They had 35 turpentine stills running at one time, all in Baldwin County and Mobile and Washington County. In 1933, when all these depression times was, Mr. Frank run for congressman. He was elected and went to Washington, D.C. His brother run the business, Mr. Rob. He worked all of my people in this part of the country. Frank Boykin made the wage for all of them, him and Rob."[7]

Fairford Lumber Company, a forerunner of Tensaw Land & Timber Company, owned by the Boykin family, hired whole families and housed them in camp cars that moved as the timber was cut.

The company built railroads to connect with larger lines or to the river and established a lumber mill at Fairford, near the Mobile-Washington county line. It built a railroad line as far north as Uniform (near Tibbie) at Tiger Branch, the end of the line where the turnaround for the train was located.

The economic cost of being a south Alabama Choctaw Indian increased after 1900. During this time Indian people were heavily in-fluenced ("owned," they say) by Frank Boykin. The extent of influence

Angernell Reed, unmarried son of William "Rube" Reed and Dimpse Taylor, with a load of pulpwood.

Boykin had on the economic lives of the Indian people is illustrated by the following cases.

As described above by Roosevelt Weaver, during the early 1900s the pine forests were again being tapped for sap to make turpentine, a product that had been produced in the Mobile area since French dominion. Initially, the Indian people were all supposed to tap pine trees for their sap and were expected to sell raw sap directly to Boykin, who defined them as "his" Indians. A story is commonly told of a time when the Indians found transportation to Mobile and established independently a wholesale relationship with a turpentine buyer there. When the Indians decreased their sales to Boykin, he found out where they were selling the product. He then went to the person and told him not to buy from the Choctaw because "they are my Indians." The Mobile turpentine buyer quit purchasing their pine sap.

Later Congressman Boykin encouraged a number of national and international chemical companies to establish large plants near McIntosh, Alabama. Some of the plants were built on lands owned by him.

Stories abound that as a part of this arrangement, the chemical company managers were told that they could not hire local Indians because they worked exclusively for Boykin in his forests.[8] For years the chemical companies refused to accept applications from the local Indians. According to Bennett Weaver, an Indian schoolteacher, after the 1965 Civil Rights Act was passed, he wrote letters to the local newspaper trying to raise the issue of the companies' ban against hiring Indians. The companies replied that they only had dressing rooms and water fountains for blacks and whites, so could not accommodate Indian employees. Later, Weaver and Gallasneed Weaver, another Indian schoolteacher, met directly with managers of the Ciba-Geigy chemical plant at McIntosh. The managers responded by claiming the Indians were either black or white and that the real Indians had gone to Oklahoma. The Indian teachers replied, "Someone in the employment office can recognize us because they have certainly kept us out of your plants."[9] When the case was reported to the Federal Equal Opportunity Office in Tennessee, a representative was sent who decided (1) that the south Alabama Indians were real Choctaw Indians and (2) that they were being illegally excluded from these chemical plants. Today, the plants hire "Indians" and there are Indian foremen at both plants.

Whether the events and especially the motives of participants in these events could be proven in a court of law is unimportant. Instead, this body of oral history is important because it establishes the existence of an Indian community in the 1890s and continuing into the twentieth century, illustrates the strong trust and reliance of community members in their leaders at that time, and provides an explanation for why the Indians of Mobile and Washington counties came to be controlled by a powerful local white political leader, U.S. Congressman Frank Boykin.[10] Boykin's actions and statements throughout his life document, as much as any other sources of information, the persistence of this Indian community. By defining them as "his" Indians, the Indian people who worked for him and whom he helped and controlled, Boykin inadvertently made a clear and indisputable case for the persistence of this Indian community through the mid twentieth century.[11]

7

SALOONS IN THE FOREST — CUSTOMS

1920–1950

"The last time I seen Mr. Carl Brill up to that day was that day down on David Lake when he was hunting that fellow by the name of Will Rice. He asked me if I had seen him and I said no sir, and he said, 'yes you do know where he is; you are just a God Damn liar, you know where he is at.' I said, 'don't cuss me that way, Mr. Brill. I try to talk nice and kind to everybody,' and he said 'I will not only cuss you; I will shoot the God Damn hell out of you,' and he punched me in the breast with his pistol and I throwed my hands up at him. I said 'Yes sir, that is all right, there will be another day.' I walked off and he stood there and looked at me. That was the last time I seen Mr. Brill before the killing. We used to deal in the liquor business together. Me and Mr. Brill did. I don't know where he would get it, but he would get it and always situate it in a place where I could get it, and I would sell it and carry him the money, and we divided up, and he would give me my portion of it, and there was one time I got a couple of gallons and sold it and he didn't divide up with me. Yes, I knowed he was a Deputy Sheriff. Yes sir, Mr. Chamberlain [Solicitor for Mobile County] give me a cigar at the time he was talking to me. He told me it would make it more better for me to tell it like it was. I disremember what was the first words he did speak to me. Me and him argued over it for a good while. He was arguing with me that I did do it, and telling where it was done all the time. Yes sir, he told me I was the nerviest fellow he ever saw, because I laughed. He wrote down something. I don't know if it was what I said or not. After he

*finished writing it he read it to me. I told him some of it was right
and some of it was not. I can not read. I can not write. I scratched
my name to that paper the best I could."*— DOSSY RIVERS, ALA-
BAMA SUPREME COURT, *Rivers v. State*, MAY 22, 1922.[1]

I N THE EARLY 1920S a notorious crime brought public attention to
the Indians of south Alabama. No longer were they a hidden
community behind the green wall. Because of the publicity surrounding the murder of a white man by a Choctaw, their region of
refuge—now cut-over timberland—and their way of life were exposed.
Choctaw Dossy Rivers felt insulted and cheated by Deputy Sheriff Brill,
his partner in a moonshine business, and accordingly he sought revenge
according to the Choctaw code of honor. Dossy testified in court, "There
was a wagon road there . . . I was standing out there in the broad open.
I was not hiding in no bushes . . . For big game I used buckshot. I killed
him . . . I just leveled my gun at him and shot his head full of buckshot.
When Mr. Brill fell in his tracks there, I walked out to where he was lay-
ing dead on the ground, I said, 'I told you, you son of a bitch, if I ever
got a chance I would get even with you I would and I have done it.' He
had done me a wrong."[2]

Whiskey-making is a tradition among the south Alabama Indians and
mixed-bloods dating back to colonial times. During the territorial period
they made whiskey on High Hill and transported it to their Choctaw
kinsmen in Mississippi. They made it after the Civil War and shared it
with the Apache. With the timber gone, the whiskey-making continued, borne out of necessity for income; later, production was fueled by
Prohibition. As mentioned before, Josiah Rivers and Bud Wilkerson ran
bars at the Level, across from the "old stompin' ground," where today's
Tribal Office is located. During Prohibition, Indians made moonshine
whiskey in secluded hollows and swamps, a business that led to the
murder of Deputy Carl Brill by Dossy Rivers, a mixed-blood Choctaw.[3]
The murder trial and resulting newspaper accounts revealed to the public
the situation of illiterate Indians living in poverty, making and selling
whiskey in partnership with the local law. For several weeks in 1922,

Dossy Rivers's trial and sentencing made the following front-page headlines in the *Mobile News Item:*

Jan. 5 — Sheriff's Posses Search for Slayer of Deputy at Calvert

Jan. 6 — Sheriff's Forces Seek Clue to Assassination of Deputy; "Shiners" Responsible is Charge

Jan. 7 — Confession Says Two Marked to Die at Calvert; Two Facing Charge of Murder

"He had done me a wrong, says the confessor, and I intended to get even with him and did so. Wash Sullivan was to get Ed Everett and I was to pick off Brill. I fired at Brill's head; he toppled over in the bushes. Sullivan weakened and did not fire."

Ed Everett, [son of John Everett], said, "The still was located on Everett & Boykin's land and he said that Frank told [Brill] he would help him out on anything like that. By Frank, I mean Frank Boykin, and Everett is my father."

Jan. 9 — Set Thursday for Grand Jury; probe into Death of Deputy, Special Day Named for Hearing [Brill is pictured.]

Jan. 11 — Grand Jurors to Hear Eye Witnesses to Brill Killing; Murder Case is set for Thursday

Feb. 8 — Court Room packed as Rivers' Trial for Life Begins; Brill Slayer to Make Plea of Insanity

Certificate of Parole

Dossy Rivers was sentenced for killing a deputy, his partner in a bootlegging enterprise. Relatives say the song "I Shot the Sheriff" was about Rivers.

Left, Wash Sullivan, son of Tom Sullivan and Nancy Chastang, in his WWI uniform. Right, Virginia Rivers, daughter of Nancy Sullivan Rivers and Dossy Rivers.

"Rivers at the time of his confession swore he was not sorry for his actions and *coolly smoked a cigar* [italics mine]. Today in Court he did not appear the least bit nervous and shook hands with numerous relatives who came to the rail."

Feb. 9 — Dossy Rivers fights for life today in Circuit Court; Insanity Plea Made in Defense [Dossy Rivers is pictured].

Feb. 10 — Court Room packed as second day Rivers' Trial Begins; Great Crowd Listens to Testimony

Feb. 11 — Jury in Rivers Case still out; Unable to Reach Verdict; Rumors give stand of Jurymen

"One report Jury nine for hanging and three for life; another eleven for hanging and one for life."

Mar. 6 — Dossy Rivers Faces Second Trial for Life on Wednesday; Murder of Deputy Charged; Special Venire of 100 Jurymen Selected from which Jury Will be Chosen

Mar. 7 — Begins Work Selecting Jury for Rivers' Second Trial;

Faces Court to answer for Killing

Mar. 8 — Rivers' Case Testimony Underway; Second Trial of Man Held for Slaying Deputy Begins after Selection of Jury

[Selected jurors are listed after a venire of 250 jurors was examined.]

Mar. 9 — Rivers Case Expected to go to Jury shortly after Noon; Argument in Murder Case Underway

Mar. 10 — Execution Date will be Fixed by Court Monday, Sullivan to face Court Mar. 21. Second Man in Murder Charge growing out of slaying of Deputy, will be brought to Trial

"Sullivan was accompanied to Court by his young wife, a pretty brunette of just 20 years. He is a World War [I] veteran and served eleven months overseas with the 31st Division. Sullivan denied a confession made by Rivers that he was in the plot to kill Brill and Everett."

Mar. 22 — Sullivan Relates story of Assassination of Deputy Brill; Expect Jury to get case late today

[Jurors listed.]

Finally on April 25, 1923, headlines screamed:

"Condemned Man will know Fate; Chief Executive of State announces he will make Decision on eave [sic] of Execution date"—: "Whether Dossy Rivers will pay with his life on the gallows here Friday or whether his sentence will be commuted to life imprisonment will be known Thursday as Governor W. W. Brandon has announced that he will tomorrow make known his decision which will either send Rivers to the gallows or commit him to a penitentiary.

"The governor is to act on a petition to commute the sentence of the man who was sentenced to die on the gallows for the murder of Deputy Sheriff A. C. Brill who was shot to death at Calvert, Ala., in January of 1922, following a raid on an illicit still.

"Rivers' execution has been set three times, and stays of execution have saved the condemned man. The case has been passed on by the Supreme Court and the sentence confirmed. The board of pardons has reviewed the case and refused to recommend clemency. Now Rivers' fate is in the hands of Governor Brandon, who has given much time and study to the case, has announced that his decision will be made public on Thursday, one day before the execution is set, as Friday morning, April 27, was named as the execution date by the Supreme Court after passing on the appeal from the circuit court of Mobile County.

"Thousands of Mobilians have interested themselves in the Rivers case, including hundreds of women and the Women's League of voters has gone on record asking a commutation of sentence. The case has attracted unusual attention, due to the fact that during the trial it was brought out that Rivers was uneducated and knew only the law of the backwoods where he was raised."[4]

The ongoing publicity caused the first missionary schoolteacher to the south Alabama Indians, Martha Walden, who came to their community in 1921, to be invited to speak to the League of Women Voters in Montgomery and to intervene with the governor of Alabama on Dossy Rivers's behalf. Miss Walden explained:

"A group of women in Montgomery asked me to come and tell them what was going on in the community of Indians. They didn't know that the Indians were hungry; that they were starving. They didn't know that they had a code of laws by which they thought they should work and operate. The Baptist preacher drove me to the railroad junction to catch a train to Montgomery. His little Ford car got stuck in the mud in the swamp between the Rivers and Weavers. I had to get out and help push it out. My blouse and suit got speckled with mud. He offered to go back and get me some clean things, but I didn't have another blouse so I said you haven't time, and we didn't. We just barely made it to the railroad spur (shortline) and caught the car to Montgomery. It had two glasses of water and a stack of folded paper napkins. I made myself as clean as I could with that much. I was met in Montgomery with a limousine and the driver took me to supper—you never saw such a feast—and all these important women and the Governor were there. When the meal was over we went into the auditorium of the First Baptist Church in Montgomery, the biggest church I'd ever been in. At first, I didn't talk to them about Dorsey [sic] Rivers; I talked to them about teaching the children to read. I told them that the Indians didn't have anything the black children had. And I said it is a pity. But unless you give those Indians a chance, you're going to have some more Dorseys and every Dorsey that is executed is a shadow on the fair name of Alabama, I said, so shame — it's a shame that they're not getting what they ought to have and they're not. I told them Dorsey Rivers was sentenced to die because he had committed three crimes according to white man's law. He was living by the Indian code of laws. And according to that, he committed no crime at all. His people were hungry. And according to the Indian code, he was—as every Indian young man was—supposed to support his elders with the work of his hands. He went outside of the Indian area with a group of other men and they made liquor. That was against the white man's law. There was nothing said about it in the Indian code. He sold that liquor for cash to feed the elders of his race. One day, when he was on guard to take care of their product officers of the white race came to arrest him. He shot and killed one. Three crimes: made liquor, sold it, killed a man. And for that he was condemned to die. Well, Dorsey was in the prison when I made that speech to the Montgomery women. I told the women how Dorsey had not had an education. He had not had anything. That hit those women, the richest women in Alabama. The woman who owned the limousine owned a railroad. And you know it got them waked up and they wanted to know what they could do. I said they need something to eat and they need something to do. I said to ask the Governor, he was a businessman and would know what to do. The next morning — on Sunday before Dorsey was to be executed — a man came on a motorcycle from the Governor's office. He asked me to go the prison and interview Dorsey and to call the governor after the interview. So I went to the prison to see Dorsey. I was given five minutes to interview him. He was on death row. Dorsey told me, 'Lady, you're just wasting your breath. There's nothing—I'm just as good as a dead man. They have taken my picture.

This is how I will look Friday in my death mask.' I said, 'Dorsey, have
you a message you want to send to the other young men in your area?'
And he looked at me and smiled. Then the guard came in and said,
'Time's up.' Dorsey just gave me a smile, he had given up, but I think
of it yet—Dorsey's smile and that whole death row business. Then I
called the Governor's office and told him that the only expression I had
from him was hopelessness. I felt that I had utterly failed, failed the
Indians, and failed Dorsey."[5]

About the same time, a contingent of south Alabama Choctaw elders
asked Kate C. Hagan, a social worker in Mobile, to write to Governor
William W. Brandon on Dorsey's behalf. Evidently Hagan wrote the
letter, because Governor Brandon responded to her request.[6] The elders
were Tom Byrd, Henry Davis, Henry "Doc" Eaton, George Lofton, Early
Reed, Luke Rivers, Richard Rivers, and George Weaver. They told her,
"if he [Dossy] is killed we will kill a hundred white people." [7]

On April 25, 1923, Dossy's sentence was commuted from death to
life imprisonment. In 1924 Governor William W. Brandon ordered a
survey made of "The so-called Cajun Settlements in Southern part of
Washington County, Alabama." The investigator, Hilary H. Holmes,
reported: "There was the descendants of the old Choctaw Indians. These
Indians had always been the friends of the white man . . . it was only
fitting that their Chief Pushmataha should have been buried in a soldier's
grave at Arlington. [Pushmataha was not buried at Arlington, but in the
Congressional National Cemetery in Washington, D.C.] Many of their
descendants still remain in these hills. . . .They are tribal in their likes
and dislikes." Holmes completely dispels the Cajun label that has often
and wrongly been attached to the MOWA Choctaw and their ancestors:
"These people are not Arcadians [sic]. They are, therefore, not Cajuns,
which is a corruption of the term Arcadian. They not only do not claim
to be remotely kin to the French but disclaim any such descent. They
claim that they are descended from Indian and Spanish and of course
white or American Ancestry . . . The term [Cajun] was applied to them
by an old gentleman who was in business among them . . . [and] the

term stuck. They are spoken of by that name by all other classes of people who come in contact with them."[8]

After the investigation was completed, Governor Brandon "freed Dossy Rivers, Mobile County 'Cajun' serving life for the murder of Deputy Sheriff A. C. Brill in 1923 . . . and his offense must be borne by the state. Rivers was a member of a backwoods clan called 'Cajuns' and could neither read nor write, because they could not go to white schools and would not attend Negro schools. Brandon's statement said some evidence showed Brill was in the illicit liquor trade with Rivers and that the men quarreled and Brill had threatened his life before the slaying."[9]

With all the newspaper publicity and attention by government officials, Dossy Rivers became a sort of folk hero among his people as he was in and out of prison.

His prison history reflects the last quarter century of his life until his death in 1945:

> "Escaped, 1-1-34, parole violation; recaptured, 9-19-35; paroled P.G.B 3-14-40, Kilby; Delinquent 1-19-42; recaptured and returned to Kilby 4-7-42; Remarks: Sentenced to be hung 5-5-22; appealed and case affirmed: Governor Brandon commuted sentence to life 4-25-23; to 1-15-33 on 12-1-32; to 1-1-34 on 12-20-33. Failed to return on 1-1-34, to 1-14-39 on 1-1-39; returned 1-14-39, revocation dated 4-28-42. Date of death, 11-13-45, Kilby [Prison]; cause of death, coronary occlusion."[10]

Oral history in the Indian community says prison officials beat him to death.

Dossy's encounter with white society—trusting the deputy sheriff, being betrayed by him, and then being punished by white man's law for avenging his honor as was the Choctaw custom—essentially destroyed him.

Despite the efforts of Martha Walden and some initial sympathy generated by her accounts, publicity about this Indian community with no name, its poverty and illiteracy, appear overall to have hardened the hearts and minds of local citizens, further isolating the south Alabama Indians. It was at this time that a horde of journalists, anthropologists, sociologists, and medical, dental, and education students descended on the Indians to "study" them, a practice that continued without their consent through the 1960s.[11]

Mystery and misinformation have surrounded the south Alabama Indians—the so-called "Lost Tribe"—for over a century because few researchers focused on the African-Indian-European frontier society despite the prevalence of this type of society that developed soon after European contact. Such societies were ignored by researchers in the southern United States because biologically mixed peoples threatened to introduce disorder and chaos into the social universe of white people who perceived the three racial categories as "pure" categories, each associated with a distinct stereotype. The south Alabama Indians received differing access to resources depending in part upon whether local whites defined them as "non-white" or "white" in a system lacking an Indian racial category.

Where biologically mixed peoples have been studied, researchers generally follow the *local custom* and define the people as either black or Indian. The major exceptions to this point are to be found in a series of papers called, "The American Isolates." These studies of the south Alabama Indians which represent them as African-American, poor whites, Cajuns, or Creoles have been greatly influenced by the "local custom" of southern Alabama which needed to use these acceptable terms for the Indian people who could not exist. This arbitrary identification became an important problem for the south Alabama Indians and people like them because these written academic accounts often become the "authentic" definition of the people, even to the extent that the accounts override definitions people give of themselves.[12]

In 1929, two students from Scarritt College for Christian Workers, Laura Frances Murphy and Obra Rogers, were assigned to work "in a Cajun community, a people of French with an admixture of Spanish and Indian Blood, forty miles north of Mobile, Alabama."[13] From this first summer's work and for the next ten years, Murphy wrote several articles for missionary magazines and state historical journals and based her master's thesis on her life in the community as a missionary teacher. Her writing reflects her Christian-religious training bias as she strives to explain the tribal, clannish nature of the Indian "Cajuns":

> "The temperament of the Indian Cajan [sic] is too little understood at present to be dealt with by an outsider. By living in Cajan homes one finds the native to be a combination of Indian and Latin characteristics . . . to be accepted as a friend of the Cajan one must first prove himself friendly, for this mixed race has been deceived too much by exploiting whites to permit anything but doubt at the outset of an acquaintance."[14]

Missionaries initially referred to the Indians of Mobile and Washington counties in their reports as "Cajun Indians" and described problems of making changes due to "tribal devotion and tribal barriers."[15] Obviously, the missionaries' intent was to abolish "tribal" and "Indian" characteristics, which they saw as hindering efforts to help the Indians "progress." Later reports dropped the term "Indians" and referred to them according to local custom as "Cajun."

Being ostracized by some, studied by others, and wrongly identified by most, the Indians of south Alabama became even more withdrawn from the mainstream of society and continued to seek each other's company in all aspects of their life, thus reinforcing their own unique culture.

Social isolation fostered distinctive cultural practices. Until the 1970s the people who would become the MOWA Band of Choctaw provided for virtually all their own basic needs. Several individuals who were considered to have special gifts for healing served as part-time medical practitioners. Midwives enjoyed considerable prestige within the community. Mollie Starland Byrd, in Mobile County, and Creasy Reed, Jane Reed, and Clara Echols, in Washington County, are remembered with admiration for their healing powers and for delivering babies. A midwife was supposed to receive payment for her services, but in reality the only ones who paid were those who could afford it.[16]

Medical care relied heavily (and still relies in some households) on herbal and folk remedies, supplemented with rituals aimed at appeasing supernatural forces. In 1986, at the first Elders' Conference (See Appendix E), where the average age of the participants was seventy-five, the following remedies were recorded:

"To cure the mumps, take the marrow out of a hog bone and mix it with spirits of turpentine. Rub the jaw with it and it will cure the mumps."

"For a sore throat or a sore on your foot, use red oak and alum. Go to a red oak tree and cut the bark off from the north side, boil it and make a tea; mix it with alum and gargle it for a sore throat or bathe the sore in it. Also for sore throat, boil pine tops and make a tea."

"For the sore eyes, urinate on a rag and wipe the eyes with it."

"For swelling or a hot fever, go out in the field and look for mullet—great big green bushes, similar to a big collard leaf. Make tea from it, drink it or bathe in it or bind it to your swollen joints."

"For the sore mouth, make a tea from turkey berries or from yellow root."

"Men got swamp fever from working in the swamp. To break the fever, make a tea from boneset."

"For a broken arm, mix clay with vinegar, pack it around broken place and let it harden."

"If a baby has a fever, take a big aspirin, break it in four pieces, give the baby one-fourth every hour for three hours, then throw the last piece away over your shoulder to throw the fever away."

"To cut a cold or cure the croup, take a piece of fat hog meat and a lightwood splinter. Light the splinter and put it to a piece of fat meat and let the lard drip into the tablespoon. Cool it enough to give to the baby and it will cut the cold."

"For whooping cough, drink mare's milk."

"To cure chafe on a baby, go to a rotten pine stump, get out the wood, mash it up like powder and put it on the baby."

"For the baby's navel cord, take an iron and burn it. Scorch a cloth binder and bind it around the baby for nine days until the navel cord comes off."

"To cure the hives, boil an onion and drink the water off the boiled onion."

"Midwife's medicine is asafetida and whiskey mixed with camphor. Black pepper tea would bring on the pains. To prevent miscarriages mix up chalk and water and drink it. This is Aunt Bell's remedy. Flour water is good for stomach trouble and for the diarrhea."

Numerous folk tales, customs, and beliefs regarding illness, death, pregnancy, and so forth are strongly indicative of such influences. To cite a few examples: "I have heard people say that if you suck a sow, you can see the wind. They say the wind is red."[17] Pregnant women were not allowed in gardens or streams for fear their "polluting" condition would kill crops and fish.[18] When a person died, the body was laid out on a cooling board, a saucer of salt was placed under the body and pennies were put on the eyes. Coffins were handmade by special men in the village. Family members and friends sat up with the body all night and a big fire was built in the yard even in hot weather. Smoke from the fire was believed to help carry the person's soul into the spirit world. The dead were (and still are) always buried in an east-west orientation, with the head facing east. Ghosts of dead ancestors were greatly feared, and dreaming of a dead relative when sick was regarded as a sign of impending death. Other beliefs relating to death are:

"If a dog gets down on his belly and crawls he is measuring off a grave. If he howls around your house some of your people is going to die.

"Don't kill no owl because it might be a relative or a good friend that died. If you hear an owl screech, it might be some of your people calling you, because the dead can see through the eyes of the owl."[19]

Still other customs seem to have been invented within the south Alabama group, arising out of its particular circumstances. For example, men working in the woods adopted distinctive "hollers" that they periodically yelled out to let others know of their whereabouts. A person hearing this not only knew that someone else was in the vicinity but knew the identity

Evelyn Hughes, daughter of George C. Weaver and Emma Pardue Weaver, and Nancy Reed, wife of Zadock Weaver, daughter of Ophelia Reed, in Mobile in 1940s.

of that person by his call. Before telephone service was available in the 1970s, runners—usually young boys—were sent from house-to-house to deliver messages.

Naming practices utilized by the MOWA designate generations or relationships. For example: Will "Bob" and Joe "Bob" are the sons of Bob Weaver; Dick "Richard" is the son of Richard Weaver, while Mary "Herbert" Taylor is the wife of Herbert Taylor. Some families have used the same names over and over from generation to generation and in the same generation. Four tribal members living at the same time were named Lem Byrd; then there are George Reed and Little George and Early Reed and Little Early. Usually the eldest person of several with the same name is referred to as "old man," as in Old Man Sancer Byrd. Nicknames are common, further confusing identities for researchers attempting to compile family histories—the first Anna Weaver Byrd's nickname was "Twy"; Ellen Bretina Fotenay Weaver Reed's nickname was "Tiny."

Other traditions incorporated elements from a more common rural Southern background. An important community festivity, the "frolic," featured dancing, ringplay, and fiddle playing. Men formed hunting clubs, loosely organized in the early years and evolved into a more formal dues-paying, membership-only club today. Van Johnston, one of the leading men of the community today, recalls that when he was a boy, "we would just get our guns, call the dogs and start walking up the road. Others would join us, with their guns and dogs, and we would go hunting. Whatever game was killed would be shared among us and with the older people who could no longer hunt. I don't go hunting as much as I used to, so my son and his friends have taken over."[20]

Roosevelt Weaver talked about deer hunting, making small arrow points from barbed wire, and making fish traps from strips of cane. He also said that when young men were preparing to hunt, fight, or engage in other competition they would "harden" themselves by scratching arms and legs with gar's teeth (fish), thorns or knifepoints.[21]

The large timber companies allowed unlimited hunting and all land in the area was considered "open range." About thirty years ago, some of the men began the "Rita Branch Hunting Club," at that time informally on High Hill. After they lost the land, they now have to pay Tensaw Land and Timber Company and Woodyard Timber Company for a lease to hunt on about three thousand acres of land located west of Bilbo Creek off Three-C Road in Washington County. Membership is restricted to MOWA Choctaw, who pay an annual fee and hold regular meetings. Some MOWA own small individual plots that adjoin the timber company land.[22] In Mobile County, Cold Water Hunting Club—named because of a cold stream running through the area—is located between Red Fox Road and Poll Bayou. Membership is determined by invitation from charter MOWA members and meetings are held four times a year. They lease twenty-one hundred acres of pine timber and scrub oak woodlands from Tensaw Land Company located along the Mobile-Washington County line—eighty-five percent of the land is in Washington County and fifteen percent in Mobile County—where they hunt deer, coon, rabbit, and quail.[23] More formal community activities and celebrations continue at the original "stomp ground," the reservation where the tribal complex is located.

In this wooded environ the local sheriff and his deputies were always on the lookout for stills because making whiskey continued as an art and as a source of income, especially during the Great Depression. Before World War II, the Indians met at Charlie Weaver's place. It was a meeting place to play cards, shoot dice, and drink whiskey. One of the elders, Mary Ann "Brown" Weaver, was noted for making high-quality rye whiskey and also for outwitting the law. South Alabama Choctaw, like other Indians, enjoy trickster stories—outwitting the enemy through cleverness.[24] During one interview she said,

> "The law come in there one evening and tore up the still. . . . I'm one of the Indians who made it. I made it myself. I made it to sell and for myself. I could make it better than any sold at the state store. I didn't make it with corn, I used rye. I had a turpentine barrel with copper pipe and a big copper kettle that would hold seven pounds of mash at one time. Each run made about five gallons of whiskey. Tap the barrel and let a stream run out about as big as your finger. Took about twenty

Mary Ann "Aunt Brown" Weaver, at Elders' Conference, 1986.

minutes to fill up a gallon jug. Me and my first husband made it. I run about thirteen gallons by myself of an evening. I would go down there to the still and run it by myself. I would fill up a gallon jug and carry it to my kegs. I had the whiskey hid down in the swamp in five-gallon kegs.

"One evening, I had been down in the swamp tending to my still, cutting my night wood, getting ready to go home and get supper ready. I had two big sweet potatoes cooking in the ashes where I had my fire going under the kettle when the deputy sheriff walked up. He said, 'Good evening.' I said, 'Good evening.' He said, 'Where you fixing to go?'

"'I'm going to the house to fix supper.' He said, 'Do you know where a still is around here, close around?'

"'Let me see — the closest one I know of is in Deer Park. Mr. Odoms got a big turpentine still out there.' He said, 'No, lady, I'm not talking about a turpentine still.'

"'What you talking about?' I asked. He said, 'Whiskey still.'

"'I wouldn't know, I never seed one.'

"He said, 'Well, we found one.' I had my axe and was picking up my night wood and I said, 'Where?' He pointed right down there toward my still. I said, 'Would you mind me looking at it?'

"He said, 'No come on, whose ever it is making hisself at home,' pointing to the sweet potatoes cooking in the ashes. He went right to it and showed me the barrel. Look like maggots in that barrel, rye boiling up there.

"I said, 'What's this?' He told me what it was. I already knowed what it was myself. He picked up my granite cup, pushed that rye [motioned] back that way and dipped him up a cup of beer. I said, 'You drinking that stuff?'

"'Lady this is good, take you a cup of it.' I did. I said, 'Uhm, m-m-m! This sure tastes good. How but another cup of it?' I drank me another cup. He reached down, picked up my two big sweet potatoes and handed them to me. I took them and thanked him.

"I said, 'Someone's been cooking down here; look there's a frying pan down here.' I started on home. He said, 'Well wait a minute it, I'll give you something else before I chop up this still.' He drawed off a gallon of that beer and give it to me. Then he drawed one off for hisself. He knocked the barrel over and started chopping it up. When I seen the barrel turn over, I said so long 'Rough Rider' and took off into the woods.

"Another time I was coming back from Sims Chapel where we had been selling our whiskey. I was dressed like a man with my hair up under my hat. I was walking along and had a pint of whiskey in my back pocket when the deputy sheriff come along and stopped me.

"He said, 'Get in this truck. I'm going to arrest you for boot leg-ging.' He frisked me and took my pint of whiskey. He turned it up, took a drink, smacked his lips and said, 'This is mighty good,' and took another good, long drink. He held the bottle out to me and said, 'Here take a drink.' I said, 'No sir.' He said, 'Here take a drink.'

"So I took the bottle, grabbed him by the back of the neck and poured the whisky down him. He started choking. I jumped out of the truck and took off through the woods to the house.

"Later on, when he sobered up, he come house to house looking for this man he had tried to arrest. When he come to my house, I met him at the door dressed like a woman, hair all fixed, with rouge on and lipstick—bright red. When he asked me if I had seen that man, I said, 'No sir, but if I do I will sure let you know.' He went on; never did know it was me."[25]

AFTER WWII, WHEN ELECTRICITY first became available in rural areas in the 1950s, Nellie Reed put in a jukebox at her place on John Johnson Road. Before Nellie's place, Florence Snow and her sister Edna sold whiskey and played guitar for dancing in a side room of their house. Washington County was and still is a "dry" county, but the law stayed out of the community for the most part; however, just in case the deputy sheriff was snooping around, whiskey was kept off the premises. Former chief Framon Weaver explained, "Beer was kept in a No. 3 washtub, iced down and covered with burlap, down in the woods so if the law came, none was visible in the building. People would go down, get it out of the tub and pay for it. Moonshine whiskey was not kept cold, but was hidden in a hole in the ground covered with leaves. She [Nellie] would move back the leaves, take the jug out, pour it into a pint bottle without spilling a drop."[26]

The whiskey trade provided much-needed income for the south Alabama Indians and an opportunity to put themselves in the role of trickster by outwitting white authorities who flaunted their power for personal gain. Understandably, moonshiners and whiskey runners enjoyed considerable prestige in the community. They had money, cars and notoriety, attributes that legends are made of—like the notorious Dossy Rivers.

4171 2 393 McIntosh Ala
Feb. the. 7. 1918.

Der. Sir. please. hand. thise. to
our. loppers. and. tell. them. to
rite. wes. ant. let. wes. no. what
thay. Downin. as. the. is. loppers. her
wonted. to. Talk. the. case. and. thay
say. thay. will. pull. the. thing
of. at. once. Der. loppers. please
let. wes. heare. from. you. by
return. male. so. we. can. be
contemplated. and. no. what. to
Depend. on. your. Truly

R. P. Reed

8

QUEST FOR RECOGNITION

1887–1997

*"Der Sir Please hand thise to our lawers .and tell them to rite us
and let us no what they Dowin as the is lowers hear wants to take
the case and they Say they will pull the thing of at once. Der lowers
please let us heare from you by return male so we can be contented
and no what to depend on. Your truly*
R. P. REED, McINTOSH, ALABAMA, FEB. 7, 1908"[1]

*"We are Choctaw. We want Congress to do the right thing. My great,
great grandfather petitioned Congress, my great grandfather petitioned Congress, my grandfather petitioned Congress, and my father
petitioned Congress. Now I, Leon Taylor, veteran of the United
States Army, petition Congress for our rights under Dancing Rabbit. "—* HEARING BEFORE THE SELECT COMMITTEE ON INDIAN
AFFAIRS, UNITED STATES SENATE, JUNE 26, 1991.[2]

WHILE SOUTH ALABAMA Indians have always privately self-identified as Choctaw, they did not do so publicly after the Civil War due to restrictive segregation laws. Their parents told them "Not to talk it," because they were afraid they would be sent west or that some harm would come to them. Apparently, memories of stories handed down generation-to-generation kept this fear alive. Perhaps they also remembered a clause in the Treaty of Dancing Rabbit Creek which provided that persons who claimed under it "shall not lose the privilege of a Choctaw citizen, but if they ever remove, are not entitled to any portion of the Choctaw annuity."[3] The elders are still careful to whom they speak about their heritage. The south Alabama Indians are a people apart—a separate community.

Local citizens of Mobile and Washington counties began referring to the south Alabama Indians as "Cajuns," rather than American Indians, around the late 1880s, and continued to view them as a unique, separate community. Sporadic references to Indians/Cajun-Indians in and around Mobile in newspapers, journals, government reports, and books confirm their identity. For example, Edward Palmer, a scientist employed by the Bureau of American Ethnology who made several trips through Alabama between 1882–88, principally looking for mounds and archaeological finds, noted, "These Indians have a few of these mortars [vessels] among them. I met a party in Mobile who informed me they made them."[4]

When the General Allotment Act [the Dawes Act][5] was passed in 1887 allotting reservation land to individual Indians, several Indian families in Mobile and Washington counties signed up—James and Julie Londine [Laurendine];[6] Henry Laurendine and his minor niece, Nellie Bru;[7] and Josephine Bru.[8] An agent of the Commission to the Five Civilized Tribes took applications in Meridian, Mississippi. Applications show that some were identified as Mississippi Choctaw but did not remove; others in the same family were rejected because they had no written documentation to prove their degree of "blood" even though they understood the Choctaw language and some spoke it. Those "identified" were full bloods; their three-quarter and one-half blood relatives were rejected. Their applications list their "identified" grandparents, plus their parents, siblings, and children.[9]

In the early 1900s, John Beck, a self-styled attorney and Indian Agent "on behalf of the Indians in South Alabama enrolled the Eastern Creek, Cherokee and Choctaw Indians in South Alabama and West Florida."[10] Because of the tribe's isolation, someone outside the Indian community who knew where the Indians lived had to act as an intermediary and guide Beck to their remote, nearly inaccessible homes. (An intermediary or "go-between" was still necessary in 1982 when the present author was hired by the MOWA Band of Choctaw to research their history.) In 1909, only footpaths connected their settlements and few wagon trails led to the outside. Encouraged by Beck, the Indians again filed applications for the "Indian money" (as they called it) when enrollment for Eastern Cherokees was opened. The act was approved July 1, 1902 (32 Stat. 726), giving the Court of Claims jurisdiction over claims arising under treaty stipulations that the Cherokee Tribe might have against the United States.[11] Not surprisingly, their applications were rejected under Report of Creek Cases, Creek File No. 1139, which says,

> "There are several hundred persons who have filed applications for participation in the distribution of the Eastern Cherokee fund who for the most part, live in the extreme southern section of Alabama and the western section of Florida, who are not Cherokee Indians at all, and most of whom do not claim to be Cherokee Indians, but are Creeks . . . . Powers of attorneys have been received by the Special Commissioner, which provide for the payment to attorneys of a certain per cent of any money recovered from these claims of 'The Eastern and Emigrant Creeks.'"[12]

Although they were rejected because they were not Cherokee (nor were they Creek), the Indian applications do show four generations of mixed Choctaw-Chickasaw-Creek-Cherokee kinship located in the small south Alabama communities of Malcolm, Fairford, Sims Chapel, Calvert, and Mt. Vernon. Of the seventy-one applications submitted, sixty-three families claimed through Nancy Fisher, "the woman who swam the river with the baby on her back."[13] The others claimed through Alexander Brashears,[14] one of the sixty-nine Choctaw allowed to sign up for a reserve under Article Fourteen of the Treaty of Dancing Rabbit Creek.[15] Some applicants had letters written to the U.S. government for them, signing by mark, for few could read and write. Reuben P. Reed, one of the few who could read and write, wrote to the government in 1908. When he died in 1933, his "color" was listed as Indian on his death certificate.

A few ancestors of the MOWA Choctaw were identified as "Indians" in federal censuses beginning in 1870, but it was not until 1910 that 172 Indians were identified in Washington County. The original identification "Ind" was written over with "mixed," evidently by an official U.S. census taker. Marginal notes designated clusters of families in Fairford and Malcolm precincts as: "These people entered as mixed, are composed of Indian, of Spanish, some of them with French, some with white, and some with negro. The prevailing habits are Indian. Called Cajun." The 1920 census listed only ten Indians in Washington County and twelve in Mobile County. This reflects a nationwide trend as fewer and fewer people identified themselves as Indian in view of the proposed 1924 legislation that made citizens of all Indians. Given the racial tension of that era, with the rebirth of the Ku Klux Klan in the 1920s, it was simpler to keep quiet about one's Indian identity. Nevertheless, in response to the number of Indians counted in the 1930 federal census, the Smithsonian Institution ordered a report on the "Surviving Indian Groups of the Eastern United States" by state. In Alabama: "The 3rd major census of Indians in 1930 was the occasion for the 'discovery' of two more Indian mixed groups . . . These people are centered in the area of heavy woods and hills about Citronelle in upper Mobile and lower Washington Counties, and number 3,000 or more."[16]

In 1935, a U.S. Senate Report, "Claims of Choctaw Indians of Mississippi," stated "The claimants number approximately 1,800 individuals who live in small communities chiefly in Mississippi, Alabama, and Louisiana, following to a large degree their primitive customs, and who had until recent years neither Government nor State aid, educational or otherwise." Also, it defines the term "Choctaw of the Mississippi" to include: ". . . only those persons who on July 1, 1902, were residents in the States of Mississippi, Alabama, and Louisiana having not less than one-eighth Choctaw Indian blood, and their descendants." [17]

Despite federal government reports and MOWA ancestors' self-identification as Indians, local government officials and local citizens continued to discriminate against the Indian community as a separate people—neither black and nor white. A striking record of either extreme prejudice or ignorance can be found in birth and death records filed with the Probate Judge of Washington County between 1921 and 1943. Registration required the attending physician or midwife to provide detailed information as to parents, age, occupation, marital status, residence and "color." When a doctor attended the birth or death of an Indian, he listed a variety of "colors," even for members of the same family: "Octoroon, W?, C, mixed, Cajan, K, Arcadian, or Creole."[18] When the Indian midwives—Creasy Reed, Jane Reed, Mollie Byrd, Alabama Echols, and Clara Echols—attended births or family members reported deaths, they listed "Indian."

Annie Timms Byrd, daughter of Sargent Timms and sister of Chris Timms. She married Nathaniel "Nat" Byrd, son of Mollie Starland and Frank "Boy" Byrd.

Mary Taylor said, "Grandma Mollie Byrd would fill out the form and carry it to Henry Cannon [a Notary Public] at Mt. Vernon, but he wouldn't put that seal on it. He put down whatever nationality he wanted to. She was so mad that she was crying when she come back. Dr. Webb would not write down 'Indian' or 'Indian /White' either. He wasn't what he was supposed to be. He got a baby amongst us, but he wouldn't claim it because he was so prejudiced."[19] Records show that many times "color" was left blank, marked through, or erased and changed by the registrar. Of the 141 births of Washington County Indians recorded between 1928–1943, only twelve were identified as Indian.

Newspaper columnist Hugh Sparrow reported that Indian leaders "tried to get the Legislature to revise the severe legal definition of the white race, written into the statutes, supposedly with Ku Klux Klan influence in the 1920s. At each legislative session for many years, the Cajuns sent a lawyer to Montgomery with a bill to change that definition, but session

The Weaver School is described in the Historic American Buildings Survey, Library of Congress Collection, as "Schoolhouse, Indian, County Rd. 96 (Old Saint Stephens Rd.), Mount Vernon, Mobile County, AL, 1933."

after session the bills died in committee."[20]

During World Wars I and II, Indian men from Mobile and Washington counties served in the military. While most were identified as "white," a few were identified as "Indian." One example, Leon Taylor, father of Chief Wilford "Longhair" Taylor, has kept his identification card marked "Indian" since his discharge at Camp Maxey, Texas, in 1943.

From the 1920s through the 1950s, miscegenation cases and school placement cases tried in the circuit courts of Mobile and Washington counties and the appellate courts of the State of Alabama[21] reflected the racial climate of this era. Washington County School Board Minutes report accommodations made by the school board for a third school system in the county for "Cajun" Indian children. Beginning on November 11, 1917, the Board agreed to pay a teacher for "the Cajan school located at St. Andrews Church, between Malcolm and Fairford, and that Sullivans who live southwest of Fairford be allowed to attend either there or the

Cajan school in Mobile County."[22] In 1887, the minutes of the Mobile County School Board lists the Byrd School as "colored" with W. T. Byrd as the teacher; in 1891 it is listed as a six-month "white" school with W. T. Byrd as the teacher.[23] (William Thomas Byrd was the son of Lemuel and Anna Weaver Byrd). Byrd School was not mentioned again until 1910. From then until 1922 schools in the Mobile Indian community were designated "colored."

On January 25, 1922, the school board secretary excitedly recorded the "CADIAN! Settlement near Citronelle! A deed from Travis Taylor and wife, conveyed an acre of land near Citronelle for school purposes; thanks be extended to Lem Weaver, the donor for his Donation."[24] Other Indian leaders also donated land and/or buildings for schools in their villages: "The Superintendent reported receipt of deed from William Weaver for one acre as a site for the Weaver school"[25] and "deed from Lem Byrd for one acre of land and build-ing."[26] Unfortunately, these "schools were mostly inadequate and housed in ramshackle buildings. For many years, they could not hope to get more than a seventh grade educa-tion; there were no high schools for Ca-juns [Indians]."[27]

In 1934, Mrs. El-vin Byrd wrote to the Commissioner of Indian Affairs at the Indian Service Depart-ment in Washington, D.C., and requested information on Indian

Mary Byrd Taylor and her uncle, Victor Byrd, at Mardi Gras. Her parents were Annie Timms and Nat Byrd.

Service Work. She said, "I am now living among people whose origin is Indian. And because of a lack of pupils to make an average of ten each month they are deprived of a school. There is another settlement of Indian origin about six miles from here that have [sic] sufficient children to make the average, but the county will not send them a teacher. Both the settlements mentioned are in Mobile County West of Mt. Vernon, Alabama."[28] Her letter resulted in a "Report on Alabama Indians visited in October 1934," which described the Indian population, living conditions, and school accommodations in Mobile and Washington counties.

Samuel H. Thompson, Supervisor of Indian Education in charge of Public School Relations, visited in Mt. Vernon where he talked mostly to the white missionaries. He was told that Mr. and Mrs. Elvin Byrd lived "some miles out in the pines in rather rough country and that two or three people said they were of Indian blood." Thompson reported that the missionaries told him there were about two hundred school age Indian children, but no more than fifty were enrolled in school and the others had never been in any school; only two or three percent of the adults were able to read and write. Thompson talked with T. B. Pearson, Superintendent in Washington County, where he learned that only half of the three hundred school-age Indian children were enrolled in school. "The others do not attend any schools as they are so scattered and live in such isolated places that a school cannot be maintained for them because they cannot get the required ten pupils." He concluded "these people called Cajans or Indians, or whatever you want to call them, live in isolated and remote parts of both Mobile and Washington counties . . . it appears that these two counties are doing all that they can for these people."[29]

Local school boards went to great lengths to keep Indians out of white schools. The Mobile County School Board hired A. D. Price, a shop foreman for the L & N Railroad, to keep a list of all known Indian children who were to be barred from attending white schools.[30] (A. D. Price gave his records to anthropologist Susan Greenbaum, Ph.D., who turned them over to the MOWA Band of Choctaw Indians to use in their 1987 petition for federal recognition.) In 1932, descendants of

John Everett were not allowed to attend "white" Turnerville School in Mobile County. When the mother of these children addressed the Board, she was told they could not attend because they were "mixed-blood."[31] One of these children, now age seventy-five, said in a voice filled with emotion that his mother moved their family over to Mississippi so they could get an education.

On May 31, 1929 the Washington County Board of Education unanimously passed a resolution

"with reference to teaching other than White Children in the White Schools of this county, and especially those of what is commonly known as "Cajan" [sic] blood be inforced [sic] in toto . . . no teacher will be recommended or employed by this Board who does not subscribe to said resolution, and who will not refuse to teach such children of "Cajan" [sic] or mixed blood, in the White Schools of Washington County . . . in the event any of such children appear at the White Schools of this County, the teacher thereof be and hereby is instructed to send the pupil back to its home, and not to teach the same in any white school."[32]

Leading attorneys of the county volunteered "their services without cost if action was brought against the Board or any teacher."[33] When children were not allowed to enroll, parents brought suit, unsuccessfully, in both Mobile and Washington counties between 1930 and 1944 against local school boards to get their children admitted.[34] The effect of discrimination was devastating to many a young Indian as can be seen in this letter written June 19, 1991, by Rose Marie Stutts, Ed.D., to U.S. Senator Daniel Inouye, chairman of the Senate Select Committee on Indian Affairs:

"The incident involved a boy in my father's Boy Scout troop in Axis, Alabama. The boy and his sisters went to school at Satsuma High School with me. They were in school for about a week when they disappeared. Several weeks later they returned to school. I asked my friend where he had been because the rest of us had missed him. His face got stony and his eyes sparkled with tears that did not fall from his eyes.

"They took us out of this school and put us in the Negro school because we're not 'white' we're Indian. Then, they took us out of the Negro school because we're not Negro. They put us back here 'till they decide where to send us. I know what they'll do. They'll put us in an Indian school, which means we'll get no education at all. I wanted to be a doctor and now I won't even finish high school,' he said in a voice that was flat and toneless.

"He and his sisters disappeared from our school soon after that and I lost track of him. I will always remember my friend's anger, bitterness, and despair over the loss of his education. At the time I didn't understand what he meant. I do now. During Segregation the Negro schools got the discarded equipment and books from the white schools. The Indian schools got the 'cast offs' from the Negro schools. Teachers in the Negro schools were paid less than the teachers in the white schools. If teachers could be found at all for the Indian schools they were paid less than those of the Negro schools."[35]

In the years just before the civil rights movement, local Indian teachers primarily staffed the Indian schools. A story is told that underlines the severe impact of this two-part society on the "non-existent" Indian school system. After the civil rights movement forced the local school system to recognize the Indian schools, a crisis emerged. It was a state requirement that one day a month all the white teachers from the white schools would meet to talk about school issues. It was also a state requirement that one day a month all the black teachers from the black schools would meet to talk about school issues. When the Indian schools were finally recognized as existing, no state official knew what to do with the Indian teachers from the Indian schools. They could not go to the white meeting, because they were not white. They could not go to the black meeting, because they were not black. So the official in charge dismissed the Indian teachers from the state requirement of meeting one day a month. Later the Indian teachers attended the white teachers' meeting. Eventually racial segregation was eliminated and only one meeting was

Elizabeth Byrd, with a 1931 Model A. Ford.

held for all the teachers. During the 1960s civil rights movement and desegregation of schools, correspondence and court cases show efforts of Indian community leaders to keep schools open as Indian schools.[36]

In the 1950s, American Indians across the South joined Creek Chief Calvin W. McGhee, organizer of "Kinsmen of Indians for Liberty, Reform and Instructions in Civic Affairs" (KILROI). Voting members were required to be of Indian descent. Its purpose was to "encourage and unite the eligible voting strength of the American Indian in active support of causes and candidates for office in matters which the directors deem beneficial to the United States as a whole and to those of Indian blood."

Calvin McGhee came to Mobile and Washington counties several times. He met with the local Choctaw in their churches and signed up members for one dollar. Ruth Weaver Shepard said, "We would load up on a flatbed truck and go to Atmore to sign up for Indian help. I went about three times. Then we had Indian meetings up here at Hill Springs Church. I got a letter about it, but didn't know what to do about it."[37] Newspaper announcements of KILROI festivities scheduled for July 12, 1958, in Atmore included a special invitation to descendants of the Choctaw, Chickasaw, Cherokee, and Seminole tribes to meet with the Creek Nation–East to hear a special report on the progress of the 26-million-acre land claim based on the 1814 Treaty of Fort Jackson. Music for the day was to be furnished by a Choctaw Indian band.

A Washington County Chapter of KILROI was chartered in 1961. The officers were R. A. Reed, president; Camellia Reed, vice president; and Thelma Smith, secretary.[38] Membership in this organization offered hope for the local Choctaw to receive assistance and bring their plight to the attention of the Indian Affairs Commission in Washington. Many of their names, addresses, and the amount of dues paid can be found in the "Register of the Descendants of the Creek Indians, East of the Mississippi River."[39] No south Alabama Choctaw received the "Indian money" from the U.S. government; Creek Indians who did, received $112.13 each.[40]

During this same time period, some of the first south Alabama Choctaw graduated from out-of-state Indian colleges. Some never returned, but those who did became teachers and leaders who brought change to their communities. Among these were sisters Lucile, Nola, and Tempress Reed, Priscilla Lewis, Bennett Weaver, and Gallasneed Weaver, all of whom taught at Reed's Chapel in Washington County; and Hattie Byrd, Calvin Byrd, and Elizabeth Byrd, who taught at Calcedeaver in Mobile County. Gallasneed Weaver later became the principal of Reed's Chapel School, a position he held until he retired in 1994.

Bennett Weaver, now a retired teacher and a member of the Washington County Board of Education, said,

"This [college-trained Indian teachers] was an important step because the Indian pupils had some of their own to identify with. The parents had someone now whom they could trust to read and write letters for them. Now we had people who could organize plans to implement goals for our people, one of which was to vote. Prior to 1956 Indians in Washington County were not allowed to vote and as a result we had no power to bargain for anything. But in 1956 we took up an offering in

Clockwise from lower left, Rev. I. C. Snow, Bennett Weaver, Gallasneed Weaver, and Rev. E. R. Isbell, circa 1950.

the Reed's Chapel Church and the Mount Pleasant Baptist Church to pay the transportation expenses for John L. Isaacs, missionary to the Indians, to go to Montgomery and talk to the attorney general, John Patterson, about voting rights for the Indians. Brother Isaacs undoubtedly put up a good argument because the attorney general sent an executive order instructing Chatom [county seat] to register Indian voters of Washington County, Alabama."[41]

The enactment of civil rights laws in the 1960s represented a turning point for the MOWA Choctaw, offering significant opportunities not available to previous generations. Several reporters who wrote about them in earlier periods speculated that if the color bar were ever dropped, the Choctaw Indians' identity, and indeed the community itself, would soon disappear. These predictions could not have been more wrong. To the contrary, with racial discrimination outlawed, expressions of Indian identity among the Choctaw have intensified rather than declined.[42]

Indian schools are one example. Leaders of the local Choctaw community prevented an attempt in 1970 to close all Indian schools in Mobile and Washington counties because of the special nature of the schools.[43] Through their determination to save their schools, they worked together to gain political strength, thus influencing politicians. When Gallasneed Weaver asked then-U.S. Representative Jack Edwards of Mobile for help in 1965 in securing federal assistance for education, Congressman Edwards responded favorably.[44] The federal courts, under Judge Virgil Pittman, specifically ordered that one Indian school in each county remain in operation. In Washington County, a federally funded Indian education program was started with the help of Larry Tillman, principal of McIntosh High School, under *Title IV, Part A,* which supplements education for Indian pupils. It was through this program that Laretta Weaver began teaching American Indian languages, dances, arts, crafts, history, and culture at Reed's Chapel School.[45]

In Mobile County, John Byrd, president of Calcedeaver Action Committee, expressed concern to the Board of Education in 1981 regarding the moving and closing of Calcedeaver School. Board minutes state:

> "Pointing out that members of the community have not been involved in the planning and the decision making which affect the school and the children and that Calcedeaver School is the community's main resource for maintaining community identity and togetherness, Mr. Byrd said the students in the community are receiving an education as good as could be received in another school. His request is not for a new school, or a new wing, all he is asking is that the School Board maintain Calcedeaver School in the community, he added."[46]

The board agreed not to close Calcedeaver School. Members of the delegation who accompanied Mr. Byrd were: Polly Byrd, Bennett Weaver, Lem Byrd, Buffalo Taylor, Delia Lofton, and Erby Reed. The Indian Education Program at Calcedeaver, originated by Maggie Rivers, continues to thrive. It is the only public school in Mobile County to offer an Indian education curriculum and the curriculum is offered in the regular school year and in the summer.[47]

ALTHOUGH THE INDIAN COMMUNITIES of Mobile and Washington counties made progress during this era to keep their schools, the Indians' economic situation had not improved. Most families worked for the timber companies, with extended families cutting timber and planting pine seedlings after the timber was cut.[48] Local chemical companies constructed in the 1950s did not hire local Choctaw until tribal leaders contacted the Equal Opportunity Commission and started negotiations in the 1960s with the industries in the area to hire Indians. (See Chapter 6.)

As another source of income, extended families also participated in seasonal migrant farm work. A 1978 report on the Alabama Seasonal Farm Workers Council (ASFWC) described conditions in Washington County at that time—the year before the State of Alabama awarded tribal recognition to the people who would be known as the MOWA Choctaw.

Jewel Rivers was the ASFWC coordinator in McIntosh of a program organized to provide child care for migrant workers, help them with travel money and emergency food vouchers, and help train them for other jobs. Holly Wiseman, author of the 1978 report, describes social and economic conditions affecting the Indian community in the late 1970s. She characterizes her visit as a "dusty, backroads odyssey."[49] An abstracted account follows (quoted here at length for its insight into south Alabama Indian life at the time):

"Approximately two thousand Indians, as they prefer to be called, or Cajuns, as they are referred to by the rest of the community live around McIntosh. The town lines of McIntosh are currently drawn so as to include the small white population of roughly three hundred, some of the black population of about the same size, and the Ciba-Geigy and Olin Chemical Plants. The Indian community is almost completely excluded, and virtually disenfranchised by this gerrymandering. There are few paved roads in the Indian community, water must be purchased from the town of McIntosh at exorbitant rates, and Farmers Home Administration loans are unattainable. The Indian community is intensely proud, paranoid, and suspicious about outside attempts to help them, since there has been so much promised by outsiders and so little delivered.

"In the past the only effective aid has come from the Creek Indian nation in Atmore, which has started several programs such as adult education and meals for the elderly. Scholarships are available to the Indian college in Oklahoma, and most of the Indians who go to college attend this institution.

"Few of the Indians were on Food Stamps. Many were discouraged from even applying for them because of the unfriendly reception they encounter at the Food Stamp center in Chatom [county seat]. Few of the women were on ADC [Aid to Dependent Children]; the nuclear family is flourishing in McIntosh. Almost no one is on Medicaid or Medicare, although many people have serious health problems. Once again the attitude of officials in Chatom seems to be largely responsible for this.

"The 120 seasonal workers do not travel in one group but in teams of roughly 25 workers. Dependent children are taken with them. The team leader acts as advance person, traveling ahead to the various areas where they will work, contracting with farmers, as well as arranging housing. Different crews leave at different times, depending on when the farmers harvest. In general, the groups leave around June 1st for the Mobile Bay area, Grand Bay in Mobile County, and Foley and Summerdale in Baldwin County. They stay there four to five weeks and then go north to Henegar and Sand Mountain, near Section, Alabama. In the winter, migrants who are physically able 'go into the woods' to cut pulpwood. This is considered to be much harder work than 'going on the farm,' and women, the disabled and older men are unable to do it. Some women find seasonal work in school cafeterias. Informal surveys show that many Indians have no income at all for much of the year. The Indian Community at large suffers from deprivation of basic needs.

"Lack of political representation underlies most of the Indians' pressing problems. The Mayor-Council government of McIntosh is all white, as is the Board of the Clarke-Washington Electrical Cooperative, the School Board, and the Board of the Farmers Home Administration. Recently, an Indian was hired as a deputy sheriff, but until then the police force had been all white. Whites hold the purse strings and the power, and as long as the town lines are drawn as they are now, there is no hope of the Indians gaining any degree of control, although they represent a majority of the community.

"Electricity for the area is provided not by Alabama Power, but by the Clarke-Washington County Electrical Cooperative, an REA established during the Depression. The REA buys its power from Alabama Power. Whereas the electrical rates for Alabama Power are determined by a regulatory agency, the rates for Clarke-Washington Co-op are not. They are astronomically high. Two-room shanties have no air-conditioning, one refrigerator, lights and a black and white television and electric bills of $250 and $300 per month. The electrical company follows the practice of estimating bills rather than reading meters and the electricity is shut off without notice. There are no Indians on the Co-op board. The Indian community must also buy its water from the town of McIntosh at very high rates. Consumers are required to buy a water meter that costs $225 which the water company will repossess if bills are not paid on time. The Creek Indian nation tried to start an emergency energy program to pay the electric bills of persons who weren't able to, but the program foundered. The white community played on the Indians' paranoia by spreading the rumor that this program was an attempt to steal Indian land. As a result, the Indians refused to sign anything and the program was abandoned.

"About ten years ago [1960s] it was estimated that 85 percent of the Indian communities' housing had no plumbing. Money that might be used for home improvement usually goes to pay electric bills. No loans are available for the Farmers Home Administration. Most of this money is bottlenecked at Chatom, and only two FHA loans have ever been approved for the Indian community.

"Few people were even aware that Medicaid and Medicare programs existed, although all of the older people had major health problems.

Dental care is non-existent.

"Most of the Indians seem to own their own homes. Many live on 'heir property.' This means that they have either lost the deed to their land, or it was never recorded, or they never had one, and the land just passed down to them through the generations. This is a major problem because many of the whites are buying up property for use in pulpwooding, in the hopes of discovering oil, or that new chemical companies will locate in the area. The whites do not bother with the niceties of purchase when they deal with the Indians, but simply take the land through a type of private eminent domain. In particular, the late Frank Boykin gobbled up most of the Indians' property. This is easy to do, since the Indians are so frequently unable to prove ownership."

While some improvements in the status of the Indian community did occur in the 1970s, by far the most important was a report of the American Indian Policy Review Commission describing the four thousand Choctaw in Mobile and Washington counties as a "Non-recognized tribe."[50] In 1975, Congress created the American Indian Policy Review Commission to examine the historical and legal background of federal-Indian relations to determine if policies and programs should be revised. The commission concluded that the results of nonrecognition were devastating for Indian communities, leading frequently to total loss of land and deterioration of cohesive, effective tribal governments and social organizations. Nonrecognized Indians represent a sort of underclass within an underclass. In comparison with members of recognized tribes, they tend to be poorer, less well educated, and suffer greater health problems. Most are landless, or have been reduced to extremely small tribal holdings. While the federal government does not recognize their existence, at the local level they frequently comprise caste-like groups based on the fact that they are not white. This status generally confers recognition of a negative sort, especially in the South. Most tellingly, the commission felt that budgetary considerations, not the framework of law, had frequently determined Indian policy. The commission recommended legislation for establishing criteria for recognizing nonrecognized Indian groups.[51]

Federal regulations developed in 1978 outline a procedure whereby nonfederally recognized Indian tribes can petition the Bureau of Indian Affairs for formal acknowledgment. These regulations require petitioning groups to demonstrate that its members comprise a "community" with internal cohesion, external boundaries, and a distinct Indian identity.[52] Federal acknowledgement, if granted, enhances a tribe's potential for federal assistance in health care, housing, education, and business development. There is also the less tangible, but nonetheless compelling, desire by nonrecognized groups to establish formal legitimacy for their claims of Indian identity. For the south Alabama Choctaw, the latter is the most important because of the discrimination they have been subjected to by "white" Southerners who question their origins. The term "white" often has racist connotations for Indians, but is generally not perceived that way by the European Americans who make up the dominant society. Generally racism tends to disappear as groups gain control of their own destinies. In this sense Indian racism toward members of the dominant group in our society reflects a sense of powerlessness.

Local Indian community leaders, teachers, principals, and ministers fully recognized the impact that federal identification as a "non-recognized tribe" would have in securing status in the local community and in securing funds for services to improve the health, education, and general welfare of their people. Also, at that time, a highly respected, progressive woman of the community, Josephine Rivers, who worked for the Comprehensive Employment Training Act (CETA) Program for the Creek Indians at Atmore, reported that "reservation Indians wanted to tighten up the definition of the word Indian. An Indian group would have to be state-recognized before they would be recognized as an Indian group. We contacted our state representative. He said he would be glad to introduce the bill, so our Indian Commission was created."[53] The group selected the name MOWA (an acronym) to represent the geographic area of their homeland in north Mobile County and south Washington County. In 1979, State Representative J. E. Turner of Citronelle drew up a legislative act that became law, creating the MOWA Band of Choctaw Indians. The act, which established a fourteen-member commission in the two counties, stated: "The purpose of this commission shall be to deal fairly and effectively with Indian affairs to bring local, state and federal resources into focus for the implementation of meaningful programs for Indian citizens."[54] Governor Fob James signed into law the bill recognizing the historical rights to sovereignty of Choctaws of Mobile and Washington counties, Alabama, which rights were confirmed in 1980 by the Attorney General of Alabama. (See Appendix D, Tribal leaders.)

When the State of Alabama formally recognized the MOWA Choctaw as an Indian tribe in 1979 they became eligible for services to improve their living conditions in all areas—education, health, housing, childcare, eldercare—provided by federal programs for American Indians.

The MOWA Choctaw were duly incorporated. Their first tribal office, located in McIntosh, opened in 1980. The original incorporators were: LeBaron Byrd, Frank Johnston, Jr., Mary McWane, Cherry M. Rivers, Hattie Rivers, John Rivers, Shell Rivers, Vordie Jewel Rivers, George Snow, Vernon Snow, Bennett Weaver, Framon Weaver, and Kesler Weaver, Sr.[55] The first board members were: Framon Weaver, Chairman; Kesler Weaver, Sr., Vice-Chairman; Josephine Rivers, Indian Commission District Representative; George Snow, Commissioner at Large; Polly Byrd, Commissioner and Paralegal for Legal Services; Cleve Reed, District Commissioner; John Rivers, Commissioner at Large; Verma Reed, Commissioner; Laretta Weaver, Tribal Council Treasurer; Jack Rivers, Councilman; and Barbara Johnston, Tribal Council Member.[56]

Elder and long-time leader Gallasneed Weaver has served the tribe in many capacities. When the state legislature created the Alabama Indian Affairs Commission in 1984, he was elected the first chairman. Three Alabama governors have appointed him as delegate to national American Indian conferences of the National Indian Education Association, National Congress of American Indians, and National Governors' Interstate Indian Conference.[57] Weaver has dedicated his life to preserving Choctaw Indian history and to achieving federal recognition for his people. His leadership in his community and in the county at large is recognized and appreciated.

In 1980, the MOWA's first annual pow-wow was held, attracting several thousand Indians from all over the United States.[58] Organized by Pat Holm, Barbara Johnston, JoKay Johnston, Lorraine Taylor, Laretta Weaver, and Liz Weaver,[59] the annual celebration provides visibility and interaction with non-Indians in the local area, and with Indians from other tribes. In addition, the pow-wow generates revenue used to support the tribal government. It is an exciting time of year for the thousands of members and guests. Indian dance competitions, arts and crafts, live bands, and an Indian Princess contest are highlights of this event. From its small beginning on the football field at McIntosh High School, this annual extravaganza is now held on the Tribal Grounds on Red Fox Road at Calvert. It continues to be held the third weekend in June, the anniversary of the tribe's state recognition.

In 1982 the MOWA purchased 160 acres of land on Red Fox Road with the aid of a loan from Washington County State Bank. To repay the loan, plans were made to raise money by major fund drives, the sale of timber, and proceeds from the annual pow-wow.[60] The MOWA continued to add acreage to the original purchase and used it for horticultural greenhouses to grow vegetables, fruit, and ornamental shrubs for marketing year round; catfish ponds for commercial catfish farming; alligator ponds to grow alligators for both meat and hides; and cattle-raising. These agricultural projects benefit the entire community.[61]

In 1993, the MOWA applied for a federal grant to provide new family housing and a community center. They received a $2.2 million grant from the U.S. Department of Housing and Urban Development's Office of Indian Programs. Chief Framon Weaver said "the first-ever HUD grant for the reservation would fund building thirty much-needed single-family houses and a large assembly hall, a part of which will contain a branch of the Mobile County Health Department."

Carl Snow, head of the MOWA Choctaw Housing Authority, said "the band has been working toward this and other social and economic projects for fifteen years. We have over five hundred families living below the poverty level, and we already have four hundred applications for the new homes. Visiting HUD officials said they were 'shocked' when they first visited the MOWA reservation and saw the poor housing and road

Mother of the Year, 89-year-old Annie "Shomo" Weaver, led the powwow dancers in 1994 with Sue Orso, left, and Nicole Wilkerson, right. (Photo by Mike Kittrell, courtesy of Mobile Register.)

conditions there."[62] By December, the multi-purpose tribal complex was a reality. It houses the tribal office, housing authority, medical facility, and dining hall/assembly room. The center is named for U.S. Senator Richard Shelby, who has supported legislation for the MOWA to become a federally recognized tribe. Thirty houses were built: fifteen on Topton Road in McIntosh and fifteen on Red Fox Road in Calvert.[63] (The Red Fox Road subdivision, Jacqueline A. Matte Village, is named for the author.) The tribal complex is the central meeting place for all the MOWA's social, economic, and political activity, with its offices, clinic, pow-wow grounds, swimming pool, catfish ponds, and lighted ballpark.

Under the leadership of Chief Framon Weaver, the MOWA applied to the Bureau of Indian Affairs to help them become federally recognized. In 1981, the MOWA were awarded a planning and development grant from the Committee for the Humanities in Alabama (now the Alabama Humanities Foundation) a state program of the National Endowment for the Humanities. This three-month research and development project was the beginning of a long struggle for federal recognition. The following is a summary of the various avenues that have been utilized in seeking recognition for the MOWA. Note that each congressional session required that the recognition bill be reintroduced.

In 1983, the MOWA hired Russell Baker as executive director and grants writer. With Baker's guidance, they successfully applied for a research grant from the Administration for Native Americans, a division of the U.S. Department of Health and Human Services. An organizational meeting for the federal acknowledgment research team was held and a letter of intent to petition was sent to the Bureau of Indian Affairs, Branch of Acknowledgment and Research (BIA/BAR), May 19, 1983. Legal Notice of Receipt of Petition was published November 24, 1983.[64]

Between 1984–87, work to produce a petition was underway. In 1987 Chief Framon Weaver reported that "the arduous process of compiling the genealogical information to satisfy the standards of the Bureau of Indian Affairs is nearly complete. Four years in the making, the documentation derives from all matter of sources, from public records to oral histories as recalled by old-timers. Among the anthropologists and historians, both

*Alice Echols Reed, and son Cleve Reed, MOWA Choctaw Chief,
1984-1988.*

professional and amateur, who substantiated the MOWA claim are Susan
Greenbaum of the University of Florida Department of Anthropology;
Doris Brown, of Chatom, local genealogist; and Jacqueline Matte, of
Birmingham, local historian."[65] Margaret Searcy, retired head of the
Anthropology Department at the University of Alabama, volunteered
her assistance in organizing an Elders' Conference. (See Appendix E.)
Tribal members who contributed to the research and who went with the
researchers into the communities to interview the elders were Reva Lee
Reed, Peter A. Rivers, and Mary Byrd Taylor.

In 1987 U.S. Sen. Richard Shelby introduced legislation to "establish
federal recognition for the MOWA Band of the Choctaw Indian tribe
in north Mobile and Washington counties. The group has been situated
in south Alabama for more than ten generations."[66] On April 28, 1988,
Chief Framon Weaver submitted the Federal Acknowledgment Petition to
the Bureau of Indian Affairs, Branch of Acknowledgement and Research
(BIA/BAR) with an up-to-date tribal roll. In 1989 a bill was introduced
by U.S. Sen. Richard Shelby, which would give federal recognition to

the MOWA Band of Choctaw Indians. Shelby said, "the MOWA Band hopes to preserve its tribal community. Federal recognition would enable the tribe to seek assistance for education, housing, economic development and job training."[67]

After reviewing the petition, the Branch of Acknowledgement and Research sent an Obvious Deficiency letter to the MOWA on February 15, 1990, requesting additional information and written documentation of the social and political history of the tribe. BIA/BAR staff held a technical assistance teleconference with Chief Framon Weaver and staff in September outlining problem areas and suggesting solutions. On March 28, Chief Framon Weaver, accompanied by eighteen tribal members and Doug McCoy, a Mobile attorney representing the MOWA, brought their case for federal recognition to the U.S. Senate once more. Chief Weaver said that the MOWA Choctaw have petitioned the federal

Gallasneed Weaver, John Young, Bill Johnston, Dr. Paul Petcher, Bennett Weaver, Leon Taylor, and U.S. Sen. Richard Shelby, 1989.

From left, Tribal Chairman Verma Reed, author Jacqueline Matte, Tribal Chief Framon Weaver, and Community Services Director Peter Rivers, at the dedication of the new MOWA complex near Calvert December 16, 1993. Rivers is accepting, on behalf of the tribe, a book presented by Matte, who was the featured speaker at the event. She told of her work as a historian helping the MOWA Choctaw research tribal history as a part of their quest to receive federal recognition. (Photo by Mike Breedlove, courtesy of The South Alabamian.*)*

Bureau of Indian Affairs for recognition, but the Bureau is so backlogged that processing an application can take ten years. The three other Indian bands—the Aroostook Band of Micmacs, the Ponca Tribe of Nebraska, and the Jena Band of Choctaws of Louisiana—seeking federal recognition, agreed, based on their experience with the lengthy application process.[68]

In 1991 Sen. Shelby introduced for the third time a bill that would provide federal recognition for the MOWA Choctaw. The Poarch Band of Creeks, Alabama's only federally recognized Indian tribe, opposed the legislation and went so far as to hire historians to refute the MOWA petition,[69] although their chief had encouraged "Indian brotherhood" in 1981 when the Poarch Creeks were seeking federal recognition and needed MOWA support.[70] The Philadelphia, Mississippi, Band of Choctaw who also opposed the legislation hired an anthropologist to refute the MOWA petition.

Nonetheless, the Tunica-Biloxi Indians of Louisiana, being "aware of just how difficult this struggle is, and of the many hours of work that must be put into proving something to others that we feel so natural about," expressed their full support in a letter to U.S. Senator Daniel Inouye, chairman of the Select Committee on Indian Affairs.[71] The *Mobile Register* reported, "A Senate panel approved a bill that would give federal recognition to the MOWA Band of Choctaw. The committee passed the bill 11-2. Senators Don Nickles, R-Okla., and Thad Cochran, R-Miss., voted against the legislation because it circumvents established federal procedures for recognizing Native American tribes."[72] This interpretation may have been influenced by the large Native American populations in Oklahoma and Mississippi who do not want other American Indian tribes recognized for fear of receiving a smaller "piece of the pie" of federal funding.

On November 8, 1991, in response to the Obvious Deficiency letter, MOWA chief Framon Weaver submitted a revised petition with additional documentation. The *Mobile Press Register* reported, "The Senate passed legislation that would give federal recognition to the MOWA Choctaw. The Measure, passed by voice vote, officially recognizes the tribe. The bill must also be approved by the House."[73] Regretfully, it was not introduced before the session ended.

In 1993, Chief Framon Weaver sent BIA/BAR supplementary documentation showing MOWA ancestors' Dawes Roll Applications and supporting evidence as to why they submitted applications for the Eastern Cherokee Roll. Due to the BIA/BAR's numbering system for considering applications, the MOWA, who had been at the top of the list, were bumped back to fifth place.[74] The MOWA were foiled again by bureaucratic red tape. On May 17, 1994, the MOWA Band of Choctaw Indians Recognition Act received another Senate hearing, and on December 16, 1994, the BIA/BAR sent a Proposed Finding Against Federal Acknowledgment of the MOWA Band of Choctaw.

Denial of recognition, after ten years of research, writing, and petitioning the government, took its toll on the MOWA administration. The people lost faith in their leaders and voted them out of office.

In 1994, the MOWA elected a new chief, Wilford "Longhair" Taylor. Chief Taylor requested an extension of time from the BIA/BAR for submitting a response to their negative finding. The MOWA applied for and received a grant from the Administration for Native Americans to complete the federal acknowledgment process. Chief Taylor, the research committee, and the tribal council met with BIA/BAR staff in Washington, D.C., for technical assistance on March 1, 1996. An experienced and highly recommended anthropologist, Richard W. Stoffle, Ph. D., University of Arizona, was hired in 1996 to do a "rapid ethnographic study" of the MOWA community.

Dr. Stoffle explained to the elders and research committee that "the rapid ethnographic study methodology, well established in the academic discipline of applied cultural anthropology, involves seeking information through a variety of sources. Documents are used, original field data are collected, face-to-face observations are made, in-depth and focus group interviews are conducted, and findings are compared to other cases. Key in the use of multiple sources of information is triangulation, a process by which data confidence is strengthened as independent and different sources of information point to the same conclusion."[75] His findings, which were included in "Response of MOWA Band of Choctaw Indians to December 16, 1994 Proposed Finding," firmly established that "the MOWA Choctaw today are a community of Indian people who occupy lands traditionally and aboriginally held by their Choctaw ancestors. It is the firm conclusion of this rapid ethnographic study that the MOWA Choctaw are an extension of the community of Indian people who occupied these lands in the early 1800s, especially in the year 1830 which began the forced relocation of the Choctaw people to the far west, to a place that is now called the state of Oklahoma."[76] Chief Taylor submitted the report on June 27, 1996, with his letter of transmittal explaining:

"I write as chief of the MOWA Choctaw. Since the original filing

Wilford "Longhair" Taylor, MOWA Choctaw Chief, son of Leon and Ella Weaver Taylor, grandson of Viney Taylor, great-grandson of Henry "Doc" Eaton, and great-great-grandson of Piamingo Hometah.

of our Petition for Recognition in 1988, we have responded to the requests of the Bureau in good faith and to the best of our ability with our limited resources. The process has been a long one and continues. Nevertheless, because of the significance of federal recognition to the MOWA Choctaw, we persist in seeking your assistance in recognition. As is demonstrated in the attached material from Dr. Richard W. Stoffle and Ms. Jacqueline Matte, the conclusions reached in the proposed finding dated December 16, 1994, that the MOWA cannot satisfy criteria 83.7(e), must be rejected. The MOWA Choctaw are entitled to a full review of their petition for recognition. The summary denial of that petition on December 16, 1994 was erroneous.

"The attached material fully demonstrates that we are a Choctaw community. We existed before the Europeans came. We were here during the 1830s Treaty Removal era. We did not remove — we remained here — we are here today — we are a persistent people. We believe that judging our Choctaw community on a single criterion, that of genealogy, is unfair. That criterion alone, is particularly unfair when it is based solely on the records of White men. Applying the single criterion puts an undue burden of proof on a people whose most important genealogical source is oral history. The reviewer of the MOWA Choctaw Petition did not consider oral history as proof. In our tradition, oral history is history. Tribal history is not made more legitimate by the fact that it is written. Printed historical accounts originated in the oral tradition. When one takes into account the several languages used by the many peoples involved in our history, for example, Spanish, English, French and the dialects of the so-called five civilized tribes, an objective observer must be understanding of the difficulties inherent in documenting in written form our oral history.

"Ironically enough, we can most persuasively prove our presence by our absence from all writing-based White institutions. We can prove our presence by our absence from all writing-based Black institutions. Finally we can prove our presence by our absence from the local industrial environment prior to 1965. As is Demonstrated in Dr. Stoffle's report, although no names are written down, someone connected with the land harvested millions of barrels of turpentine, millions of cords of timber for the lumber and pulp industries, and developed separate schools and educational systems. We, the MOWA Choctaw, are these absent people. We, the MOWA Choctaw, are these land-connected, persistent people.

"An exchange of correspondence between our MOWA Choctaw leaders and the federal government also establishes that we were located in the Mobile-Washington County geographic area between the Removal Era and the Civil War (1830–1860). While we can trace some of our people to ancestors in the 1830s (these persons had white names), we cannot trace the bulk of our people who had phonetically-spelled Choctaw names. Correspondence and reports as late as 1856 list our Choctaw ancestors in Mobile, Alabama. These same Choctaw ancestors were not listed on the 1850 U.S. Census of Mobile County.

"Our history is not written on paper — it is written in stone. The gravestones of our cemeteries from 1814 to 1996 memorialize our history. We were a Choctaw community in 1814, we are a Choctaw community now, and we will always be a Choctaw community . . . It is time that the MOWA Choctaw should be recognized by the United States government. It is time that the MOWA Choctaw should be legitimized and accorded the respect which is due. Extensive research by Dr. Stoffle, Ms. Matte, and the tribal members firmly establish that we are a Choctaw Indian community and we believe the issue of our Native identity should be finally resolved. The governor of Alabama, state legislators in Alabama, and local officials are once again submitting letters to you supporting our application and petition as they have done in the past when they wrote letters for our ancestors from 1830 to 1860.

"As the elected Chief of the MOWA Choctaw, I can tell you that the most important aspect of seeking federal recognition is that my people should have an identity. The Choctaw identity has been denied my people since 1830 when the United States Government forced our ancestors to sign the Removal Treaty. Since that time we have struggled to merely survive. We have been left out of records, or when included, were wrongly identified. Our Choctaw names became lost after the Civil War. We lived on public land until lumber companies came into the area. Our Choctaw ancestors were told to take White men's names so they could apply for homestead land or leave. Lumber companies clear-cut the forests, our homeland, our subsistence, our means of survival. Now the BAR reviewer uses the same insults to deny us our Indian heritage.

"We want your recognition of our identity so that we can pursue our religious, cultural, and economic practices without suffering the discrimination and unfair treatment our ancestors and even our elders endured. We are a proud, persistent people. We want the right to pass our Choctaw heritage and culture on to our children and grandchildren. We need your help to do that in the most effective way. As for me, Wilford "Longhair" Taylor, federal recognition means that our identity will be preserved."[77]

9

Epilogue

1997–2002

"Today, I am Choctaw. My mother was Choctaw. My grandfather was Choctaw. Tomorrow, I will still be Choctaw."

— Leon Taylor, 1985

As one millenium drew to a close and a new one opened, the MOWA Choctaw remained one of a large number of Native American groups who live more or less collectively, within a framework of their own values and institutions, with their own sense of their special history, without being recognized as Indians by the United States government. This is the same government which currently defines the following "affirmative action race and ethnic categories":

- White (not of Hispanic origin)—a person having origins in any of the original people of Europe, North Africa, or the Middle East.
- Black (not of Hispanic origin)—a person having origin in any of the Black racial groups of Africa.
- American Indian or Alaskan Native—a person having origins in any of the original people of North America, and who maintains cultural identification through tribal affiliation or community recognition.[1]

Of the seven state-recognized tribes in Alabama, the Poarch Creek is the only tribe that is federally recognized.

The MOWA's final petition was sent to the BIA/BAR on June 27, 1996. BIA/BAR sent an employee, Lee Fleming, to Alabama to confirm the tribe's research. Fleming met with Doris Brown, local genealogist, at the Washington County Courthouse where he checked probate records. Fleming then went to the MOWA tribal complex where he met with Chief Wilford "Long Hair" Taylor and other tribal members. Fleming then drove to Birmingham, where he inspected the MOWA files compiled by the author. After phoning Chief Taylor, Fleming was given permission to take copies of audiotaped interviews of MOWA oral history and transcripts. He left all of us on a positive note of good will and with hope for federal recognition.

These hopes were dashed on Christmas Eve of 1997 when the U.S. Department of Interior denied federal recognition. "We were hoping this would be the Merry Christmas of all Christmases," said Gallasneed Weaver, a former chairman of the MOWA Tribal Council, after the department released its sixty-page decision. "But I don't know if we'll ever make it now. I hope and pray that we do."[2]

According to the BIA/BAR, the MOWA could not satisfy the mandatory criteria in 25 C.F.R., 83.7. An expedited review was made based only on the one criteria that "the petitioner has been identified from historical times until the present on a substantially continuous basis as American Indian . . ."[3] The BIA/BAR determined that "the MOWA band lacks documentation for its claim of American Indian ancestry because "most of the records of the known MOWA ancestors did not document them as Indian, but described them racially or ethnically with ambiguous terms, such as 'Black,' 'Cajun,' 'Caucasian,' 'Creole,' 'French,' 'Mulatto,' 'Spanish,' or 'White.'"[4]

The BIA/BAR reviewers conveniently ignored MOWA ancestors found in the Dawes Roll applications, Eastern Cherokee applications, Alabama Supreme Court cases, Methodist and Baptist Missionary records, the 1910 U.S. Census which designated clusters of MOWA families as "Indians," and the 1930 U.S. Census describing the "3,000 Indians around Citronelle in upper Mobile County and lower Washington County." (See Chapter 8.)

Chief Taylor, with the consensus of the tribal council and after consulting U.S. Representative Sonny Callahan, (R-Mobile), appealed the BIA/BAR decision. (Callahan promised to help get a recognition bill through

Congress if the BIA refused to reverse its decision, "if there is substantial evidence that the bureau is just denying [the MOWA petition] because they don't want more Indians to share in the pie . . ."[5]

Chief Taylor's appeal to the Interior Board of Indian Appeals asked for reconsideration because the BIA decision was based primarily on "an unfair and inappropriate requirement that descendancy be proven through the most strict, narrowly-defined genealogical documentation [which] doomed the MOWAs in the final determination."[6]

The MOWA, frustrated and angered by the BIA decision, continued to believe strongly that their petition provided ample evidence through genealogy, cultural anthropology, and oral histories sufficient to establish a reasonable likelihood that the MOWA descended from an historical tribe.

According to the federal government "cultural identification" is necessary for the racial or ethnic identification of Indians, but not for blacks or whites. Such a policy, which allows the federal government and the BIA to practice policies that the government condemns in dealing with other races and people, is understandably seen by the MOWA and other Indian groups as blatant racism. The MOWA self-identify as Indians and are recognized as a separate culture by the dominant society. Why, they ask, should the federal government have a role in determining who or what any person or group is?

An editorial in the *Mobile Register* entitled "Doesn't take government to tell us who we are" encouraged the MOWA:

> "Do not be defeated because some government agency was not compelled to believe that you are Choctaw Indians. You are today what you were yesterday. You are what you will be for the rest of your lives.
>
> "You have not been diminished by this ruling, just as you should not have been exalted by it.
>
> "Go forth into the world as warriors, scholars, doctors, teachers and other common and uncommon men and women, girded by the blood of your mothers and fathers and by your liberating legacy as Americans to be whatever your own abilities and energies allow you to be.

"Do not spend one moment mired in the rut of lamentation over this denial of your legacy. No persons or government can ever deny you that right of citizenship.

"None of us deserves more or less than the truth of that birthright."[7]

In early 1998, Chief Taylor gathered support from federal and state officials for reconsideration. The Alabama Legislature, Governor Fob James, Secretary of State Jim Bennett, U.S. Senator Richard Shelby, U.S. Senator Jeff Sessions, U.S. Congressman Sonny Callahan, State Representative Jeff Dolbare, and State Senator Pat Lindsey all endorsed recognition.[8]

Upon submission of the appeal, the Southern Assistant Secretary of Indian Affairs gave the review panel until July 1998 to study new evidence and review the decision rejecting the tribe's bid for federal recognition.[9]

Unhappily, the MOWA's efforts and hopes again came to no avail. On December 19, 1998, the BIA/BAR denied Chief Taylor's appeal.

But the story does not end there.

Shortly after the final appeal was denied an important event confirmed the MOWA Choctaw's right to their heritage. The Smithsonian Institution returned 400-year-old Choctaw bones to Alabama for reburial. As required by the Repatriation Act, remains of aboriginal people are being returned to their descendants all across the United States and Canada. Eight large crates of bones were returned to Alabama to be buried on federal land along the Alabama River.

The Smithsonian Institution contacted Oklahoma Choctaw Chief Terry Cole to arrange the ceremony. Chief Cole, in a spirit of unity, invited participation from representatives from the MOWA Choctaw of Alabama, Clifton Choctaw of Louisiana, and Mississippi Choctaw.

Chief Wilford "Longhair" Taylor and his wife, Mary; his mother and father, Mr. and Mrs. Leon Taylor; Verma Reed; Kessler Weaver; Wiley Reed, and I participated in the ceremony with the representatives from other states.

As we were standing in drizzling rain among the trees at the edge of the large grave, listening to the songs and words in Choctaw, with thunder rumbling in the distance, a hawk flew to the branches of a nearby tree. Indians believe that the hawk is a messenger. The appearance of this one, at that moment and at that time, added to a mood of spirituality or peace, a sense of eternity, that could be felt within the crowd.

Olin Williams, a Mississippi Choctaw from Oklahoma, delivered the reburial service in Choctaw language from the writings of his ancestor recounting the Trail of Tears. The message was of sorrow in a world where mankind oppresses mankind. But it was also a message from the ancestors that oppression makes a people strong, united in spirit and hope.

After the songs and prayers, each of us picked up a handful of dirt and sprinkled it on the wooden crates of the remains. The storm held off long enough for the grave to be filled.

This reburial service strengthened the resolve of Chief Taylor and other participants to go forward despite setbacks by negative government decrees.

The MOWA resolve was tested again in December 2000. Kevin Gover, director of the BIA under President Clinton, invited Chief Taylor to Washington to present the MOWA case again on the promise that he would push it through before he left office as President Bush and his appointees took over. Chief Taylor had previously given Mr. Gover a copy of the first edition of *They Say the Wind Is Red,* which Mr. Gover had promised to read. Because this book summarizes the MOWA ancestral history and explains how racism and discriminatory policies had contributed to the lack of documentary records, Gover's promise to read it seemed a hopeful sign. Chief Taylor, his wife, Mary, Craig Taylor, and I flew to Washington during the week before Christmas. We had a one p.m. appointment, but were left waiting until four p.m. When the BIA/BAR staff finally met with us, they asked if we had anything new. We attempted to present our new information, but it was tossed aside as insufficient. I asked Mr. Gover if he read my book and he said "No!" The whole meeting was a farce. We were very disappointed and wondered why we were invited to it in the first place.

After leaving office, Kevin Gover was criticized for going from the BIA to a Washington law firm which solicits business from tribes. He went on the offensive. On April 18, 2001, *Indian Country Today* reported that "Gover Admits Leaks in BIA Ranks." In addition to "moles" in the BIA, Gover explains other reasons why tribes like the MOWA are turned down for federal recognition:

> "The real difference between me and the BAR is that they're trying to decide things as historians, anthropologists and genealogists. They want proof that will stand review from other historians, anthropologists and genealogists. I looked at things as a lawyer. A lawyer wants decisions that will hold up in court . . . [He also said that] ". . . trying to plug leaks at the BIA is a fool's errand."[10]

Although Mr. Gover's statement confirms what we have suspected all along about the federal recognition process, perhaps he did have good intentions when he told Chief Taylor that he would help us.

Nevertheless, the MOWA Choctaw are not giving up. Under the leadership of Chief Taylor and the Tribal Council, they have continued to pursue economic and cultural development.

Two industrial plants have located on the reservation and now provide jobs for tribal members. A gymnasium is being added to the already established ballpark. Twelve new houses located in the old peach orchard provide homes for MOWA families.

Reed's Chapel School has been returned to the tribe after being arbitrarily closed by the Washington County School Board. Van and Barbara Johnston, Chief Longhair Taylor, and other tribal leaders worked for more than three years to get this landmark facility turned back over to the MOWA people. It will be renovated for a community center.

The Alabama Historical Commission dedicated a historical marker on the Old Stomping Grounds to commemorate the Choctaw who have historically lived in this area. The marker is located at the cultural center—a work in progress.

The MOWA Choctaw Cultural Center features a museum and

research library. The Alabama Historical Commission renovated this 1855 Creole-style building, the former home of Dr. Wilbur Heard, who was on the staff of Mt. Vernon Arsenal. Apache leader Geronimo was a frequent visitor in Dr. Heard's home between 1887–1894 when the arsenal became a holding ground for several hundred Apache prisoners. Artifacts in the museum are directly related to MOWA Choctaw history from pre-European contact to the present. Reva Reed, the director, is assisted by Monica Lawrence. A board of advisors meets quarterly to help implement the goals of the cultural center.

The anthropology department at the University of Alabama at Birmingham has taken a great interest in the culture of the MOWA Choctaw. Dr. Lori Cormier is gathering information from oral histories and interviews with elders to develop a Native American Ethnobotanical Garden on the cultural center grounds. Her student Rebecca Turley developed two exhibits of Southeastern Native American artifacts for the cultural center and is writing her Master's thesis on ways in which archaeologists and Native Americans can establish successful collaborations. Further collaborative work is planned between the UAB anthropology department and the cultural center in creating a multimedia archival system and interactive exhibit that would serve as a resource for those interested in MOWA Choctaw cultural heritage and as an educational tool for visitors. The final phase of the cultural center will be the construction of a traditional Native American village.

The annual pow-wow that has taken place for the last twenty-two years continues to draw large crowds on the third weekend in June. The pow-wow is well-attended by tribes nationwide and provides spectacular entertainment under the inspired direction of Todd Johnston. A fall heritage festival provides cultural enrichment for school children in surrounding counties.

All of the above activities commemorate the Choctaw culture and act as a bridge between the past and the present. The circle of life continues.

Overall, the MOWA Choctaw are doing well.

SOUTHEASTERN INDIAN GENEALOGICAL RESEARCH RESOURCES

HISTORICAL OVERVIEW

During the period of Indian Removal beginning in 1831 extensive records were generated through the turn of the century when Southeastern Indians were uprooted from their homelands in Georgia, Alabama, Mississippi and Florida. They were taken west of the Mississippi River in what is now Oklahoma. These records relate to treaties, trade, land claims, removal to Oklahoma, allotments, military affairs, military service and pensions, trust funds, and other activities. The following books, available in most libraries, provide the most useful background for understanding the Removal Era:

Cotterill, R. S. *The Southern Indians: The Story of the Civilized Tribes before Removal.* Norman: The University of Oklahoma Press, 1954.
Debo, Angie. *The Rise and Fall of the Choctaw Republic.* Norman: The University of Oklahoma Press, 1934.
Debo, Angie. *A History of the Indians of the United States.* Norman: The University of Oklahoma Press, 1970.
Foreman, Grant. *Indian Removal.* Norman: The University of Oklahoma Press, 1932.
Foreman, Grant. *The Five Civilized Tribes.* Norman: The University of Oklahoma Press, 1934.

BEGINNING YOUR RESEARCH

Research for American Indian ancestors begins just like any other search for ancestors; you have to begin with what you know now. Prepare your ancestor charts beginning with yourself. Include all names, nicknames and any other identifying information on each person. In addition to the sources listed below, be sure to check the more traditional resources: local and state records, census records, land records, court cases, probate records, church and school records. Be sure to check the Internet for

Southeastern Indian sites. Several are listed below.

Check these rolls first:

1. Guion Miller Roll 1906–1909, Eastern Cherokee Applications of the U.S. Court of Claims. RG 123, M-685. Last round up of the Eastern Cherokees; Roll 1 has an Index of names. Use it to get the application number. Rolls 2-6 have cards in numerical order. The cards indicate whether the application was accepted or rejected. If you see a notation on the card to a volume and page reference, that means there will be something in the miscellaneous testimony on Rolls 7-11. Roll 12 has copies of earlier enrollments, from 1850, 1851, and 1884 rolls. The earliest census for the Cherokee is the 1835 Henderson Roll, on T-498. Many of these rolls have been transcribed and are available in most large libraries.

The beauty of the Miller roll is that Native Americans of many tribes applied just after the turn of the century, when many of your grandparents were living. This is especially true for Creeks. A man named John Beck enrolled everyone he could in south Alabama and northwest Florida, for a percentage of the "Indian money." All were rejected under Case No. 1139 because they were not Cherokee. Many Choctaw were rejected for the same reason. The actual applications are in numerical order in microfilm roll M-1104.

The applications usually give you four generations, applicant and children, plus grandparents and great-grandparents, with birth and death dates; place of birth and address.

Also, for Creeks, a roll was taken in the 1950s of the Descendants of the Creek Indians, East of the Mississippi River, called "the Head of Perdido, Friendly Creek Indian Band." The 1833 Census of the Creek Nation lists some names in English, but most are phonetically spelled Creek names. Lists are arranged by towns. Copies of these are in the Mobile Library—Local History Division.

2. Dawes Commission Roll—Index to Final Rolls of the Five Civilized Tribes in Indian Territory. 1898–1914. Contains records on Oklahoma tribes and Mississippi Choctaws who lived in Alabama, Mississippi, and Louisiana. M-1186 Index.

The index is broken down by tribe, and then by categories of relationship (Cherokee by blood, by marriage, minor, etc.). Go to the tribe you are researching and category to look up the name. The index is not strictly alphabetical—there are many instances of names out of order, and whole sections of index are added at the end of a section. Once you have located the name in the index you will see an enrollment number by the name. Go to the second part of Roll 1 for the final roll.

There you will find the same arrangement of tribes and categories. Look for the number. Once you find the number and the name, it will tell you the age and sex of the person, and give another number. This number is for the census card. Look up the census cards on rolls 2-93. They follow the same arrangement of tribe and category, then number. The census card shows all the people in the same family, who applied.

The actual applications are in M-1301. They are filmed here in the same arrangement: by tribe, category, and census card number. You can get many kinds of information from the applications whether they were accepted or rejected.

3. Records Relating to the Choctaw Net Proceeds Case. The Choctaw Net Proceeds Case derived from claims of individual Choctaw Indians arising from their removal to Indian Territory under the provisions of the 1830 Treaty of Dancing Rabbit Creek. The term "net proceeds" refers to money remaining from the sale of the ceded land in the East after necessary expenses had been deducted. Most records are still in individual file folders in the National Archives. Related records are in Court of Claims General Jurisdiction Case File 12742 in Records of the U.S. Court of Claims, Record Group 123. Microfilmed copy of this case is located at Samford University Library, Special Collections.

These records contain testimony taken in 1838 as well as in later years that give the ancestors from whom the claimant descends; some depositions are written in the Choctaw language. Plus, the early testimony tells who attended the treaty of Dancing Rabbit Creek, what village they are from, who their leader was and why they were never registered.

Muster Rolls of Choctaw Indians who fought in the Creek Wars are available at the Alabama Department of Archives & History. They are photocopies from the National Archives. Again, the problem for researchers is that the names are phonetically spelled Choctaw. Some of the captains had English names, so if you know who they fought under, you may be able to determine if your ancestor is listed. (See Public Information Subject File: Alabama at War, 2nd Creek War—SG 13379.)

4. Choctaw Roll of 1830-Armstrong Roll. This is available in Gales & Seaton's *American State Papers, Public Lands*, vol. 7. Indexed. Document No. 1230, 23d Cong:1st Sess. "In Relation to the Location of Reservations under the Choctaw Treaty of the 27th of September, 1830." This gives names, locations, and number in family, some names are in English, most are phonetically spelled Choctaw names.

Books

Baker, Jack D. *Cherokee Emigration Rolls.* (Emigration Rolls, 1817–38) Relates to: (M-685, Roll 12 Records *Relating to Enrollment of Eastern Cherokee by Guion Miller, 1908–1910,* contains Old Settler Roll, 1851, Drennen Roll, 1852, Chapman Roll, 1852, and Hester Roll, 1884.)

Blankenship, Bob. *Cherokee Roots.* Cherokee, NC: the author, 1978. This work contains enrollment Records of the Cherokee Nation, 1834–1924.

Bogle, Dixie. *Cherokee Nation Births and Deaths, 1884–1901.* Owensboro, KY: Cook & McDowell Publications, 1980. Names are abstracted from the newspapers *Indian Chieftain* and *Daily Chieftain.*

_____. *Cherokee Nation Marriages, 1884–1901.* Owensboro, KY: Cook & McDowell Publications, 1980. This is an alphabetical surname list of names abstracted from the newspapers *Indian Chieftain* and *Daily Chieftain.*

Goss, Joe R. ed. *A Complete Roll of All Choctaw Claimants and their Heirs.* Goss reprinted index to the U.S. Court of Claims under the existing treaties between the United States and the Choctaw Nation. In order to be useful, you must know the Indian name and the English name.

Hampton, David Keith. *Cherokee Reservees.* (From NARC M-208: Records of the Cherokee Indian Agency in Tennessee, 1801–1835, 14 rolls. (Birmingham Public Library has microfilm).

Harper, Josephine L. *Guide to the Draper Manuscripts.* Madison: The State Historical Society of Wisconsin, 1983.

Hoskins, Shirley. *Cherokee by Blood.* vol. 1- Chattanooga, TN: The author, 1982-. This is a surname listing of persons who made applications to the U.S. Court of claims, 1906–1909. (Guion Miller Roll)

Kirkham, E. Kay. *Our Native Americans and Their Records of Genealogical Value.* 2 vols. Logan, UT: Everton Publishers, 1980–1986.

Matte, Jacqueline Anderson. *They Say the Wind Is Red: The Alabama Choctaw Lost in their Own Land.* Montgomery: NewSouth Books, 2002.

McClure, Tony Mack. *Cherokee Proud: A Guide for Tracing and Honoring Your Cherokee Ancestors.* Somerville, TN: Chunannee Books, 1997.

Mooney, Thomas G. *Exploring Your Cherokee Ancestry: A Basic Genealogical Research Guide.* Tahlequah, OK: Cherokee National Historical Society, Inc, 1987.

Southerland, Henry deLeon, Jr. and Jerry Elijah Brown. *The Federal Road through Georgia, the Creek nation and Alabama, 1806–1836.* Tuscaloosa, AL: The University of Alabama Press, 1989. Describes locations and people who lived along the Federal Road (Three-notched Way) which divided the Creek nation and includes maps.

Starr, Emmet. *History of the Cherokee Indians and Their Legends and Folk Lore* and *Old Cherokee Families and Their Genealogies.* Oklahoma City, OK: The Warden Company, 1921; reprint, Millwood, NY: Kraus Reprint Company, 1977. This history contains names of Cherokee families and their genealogies.

Strickland, Ben and Jean. *Records of the Choctaw Trading House, 1803–1824.* 2 vols. Moss Point, MS: The authors, 1984–1990. Abstracted and indexed records of NARC microfilm T-500. Contains many names of people who traded skins at the trading houses at St. Stephens until 1816 when it was moved to Demopolis.

Walker, Charles O. Cherokee Footprints, 2 volumes. privately printed, 1989. Copies available from Charles O. Walker, 573 Church Street, Jasper, GA 30143. Maps, ink line drawings and pictures are included in this book to give a view of where and how Cherokees lived. Land evaluation records are reproduced just as the agents wrote them, therefore spelling varies. Occupants names and improvements are listed by lot numbers in specific counties. It is indexed.

Woodward, Thomas S. *Woodward's Reminiscences of the Creek, or Muscogee Indians, contained* in *Letters to Friends in Georgia and Alabama.* Montgomery, AL: 1859. Stories of Indians and events of the Creek Wars. Not indexed, but available in most libraries and worth the time to locate names of early Creeks and inhabitants of south Alabama. (At this writing, a revised, annotated edition of *Woodward's* was scheduled for publication in Fall 2002 by NewSouth Books, Montgomery, Alabama.)

JOURNALS

Chronicles of Oklahoma. Many stories, names, places and general understanding of events can be found in these indexed volumes. They are available in most large libraries.

SouthEastern Native American Exchange (SENA). This is a quarterly publication dedicated to the research of Native American history and genealogy. It is in most libraries and is available for $20 by subscription from Jacqueline Hines, Editor, P.O. Box 161424, Mobile, AL 36616.

Catalogs of Microfilm and Guides Available from National Archives

Hill, Edward E., comp. *Guide to Records in the National Archives of the United States Relating to American Indians*. Washington, DC: 1981 *National Archives Microfilm Resources for Research: A Comprehensive Catalog*. NARC, Washington, DC. To order, call sales department 1-800-553-6847.

American Indians — A select catalog of National Archives Microfilm Publications.

Military Service Records - Records of Volunteer soldiers who Served in the War of 1812. Record Groups 94 & 407, pp. 31–39.

Hill, Edward E., comp. *Preliminary Inventories: Records of the Bureau of Indian Affairs*, Vol. I and II, Washington, DC: 1965, Record Group 75. Describes records generated by Bureau of Indian Affairs, many of which have not been microfilmed and can only be seen at the National Archives.

Yoshpe, Harry P. and Philip P. Brower, comps. *Preliminary Inventory of the Land-Entry Papers of the General Land Office*. No. 22, Washington: 1949. Choctaw Scrip — Certificates issued pursuant to Acts of Aug. 23, 1842, and Mar. 3, 1845, in satisfaction of claims of heads of Choctaw families under the treaty of Sept. 27, 1830, made at Dancing Rabbit Creek.

Lending Libraries

Am. Geneal. Lending Library
593 West 100 North
P.O. Box 244
Bountiful, UT 84011
Phone (801) 298-5358

Nat. Archives Microfilm Rental
Microfilm Rental Program
P.O. Box 30
Annapolis Junction,
MD 20701-0030
(301) 604-3699

ARCHIVES

Alabama

Alabama Archives & History
624 Washington Avenue
Montgomery, AL 36130

Special Collections
Univ. of Alabama Library
Box 870266
Tuscaloosa, AL 35487-0266

Special Collections
Samford University Library
Birmingham, AL 35229

U. of So. Alabama Archives
USA Springhill Ave., Rm. 0722
Mobile, AL 36688

Auburn University Archives
Ralph Brown Draughon Library
Auburn, AL 36849-5606

Cobb Memorial Archives
3419 20th Avenue
Valley, AL 36854

Birmingham Public Library
2100 Park Place
Birmingham, AL 35203

Wallace State College
P.O. Box 2000
Hanceville, Alabama 35077

Arkansas

Arkansas History Commission
One Capitol Mall
Little Rock, AR 72201
(501) 682-6900

Florida

The Native American Research Center
West Florida Regional Library
200 W. Gregory St.
Pensacola, FL 32501-4878

Florida State Archives
R.A. Gray Building (M.S. 9A)
500 South Bronough Street
Tallahassee, FL 3299-0250

University of West Florida
Pensacola, FL 32501

Georgia

Ga. Dept. of Archives & History
330 Capitol Avenue, S.E.
Atlanta, GA 30334

National Archives-SE Region
1557 St. Joseph Avenue
East Point, GA 30344

Louisiana

Governor's Commission on Indian Affairs
P.O. Box 44072
Baton Rouge, LA 70804-4072

Mississippi

U.S. National Park Service
Library & Visitors' Center
RR #1, NT 143
Tupelo, MS 38801

Miss. Dept. of Archives & History
P.O. Box 571
Jackson, MS 39205-0571

Oklahoma

Oklahoma Historical Society
Indian Archives Division
Historical Building
Oklahoma City, OK 73105

University of Oklahoma Libraries
Western History Collection
630 Parrington Oval
Norman, OK 73019

Tennessee

Tennessee State Library & Archives
403 7th Avenue North
Nashville, TN 37234-0312

Texas

Texas State Lib. Archives Div.
P.O. Box 12927
Capitol Station
Austin, TX 78711

National Archives–SW Region
P.O. Box 6216
Fort Worth, TX 76115

MICROFILM

NATIONAL ARCHIVES—*Records of Bureau of Indian Affairs,* RG 75: Can be purchased or rented from National Archives Microfilm Rental Program, P.O. Box 30, Annapolis Junction, Maryland 20701-0030. Check local library before ordering.

M-208 "Records of the Cherokee Indian Agency in Tennessee,1801–1835. 14 rolls. No index. Roll 14 contains a list of tenants under Doublehead; another list appears "intruders on Shoal Creek."

M-4 "Letterbook of the Creek Trading House, 1795–1816." 1 roll.

M-271 "Letters Received by the Secretary of War Relating to Indian, 1800–1823." 4 rolls

M-15 "Letters sent by the Secretary of War Relating to Indian Affairs,

1800–1824." 6 rolls.
M-234 "Letters Received, 1824–1881." 962 rolls. **Bold = most names**
Cherokee Agency, 1824–80:

(Cherokee Agency, East)	Rolls 71-76
(Cherokee Agency, West)	Rolls 77-79
(Cherokee Agency)	Rolls 80-112
(Cherokee Emigration)	Rolls 113-116
(Cherokee Reserves)	Rolls 117-118
Chickasaw Agency, 1824–70:	Rolls 135-142
(Chickasaw Agency Emigration)	Rolls 143-144
(Chickasaw Agency Reserves)	Rolls 145-148
Choctaw Agency, 1824–76:	Rolls 169-183
(Choctaw Agency, West)	Roll 184
(Choctaw Agency Emigration)	Rolls 185-187
(Choctaw Agency Reserves)	Rolls 188-196
Creek Agency, 1824–76:	Rolls 219-235
(Creek Agency, West)	Roll 236
(Creek Agency Emigration)	Rolls 237-240
(Creek Agency Reserves)	Rolls 241-248
Seminole Agency, 1824–76:	Rolls 800-805
(Seminole Agency Emigration)	Rolls 806-807

M-1059 "Selected Letters Received by the Office of Indian Affairs Relating to the Cherokees of North Carolina, 1851–1905," 7 rolls.
M-1011 "Superintendents' Annual Narrative and Statistical Reports from Field Jurisdictions of the Bureau of Indian Affairs, 1907–1938," 174 rolls.

Choctaw (Mississippi)	Roll 20
Seminoles of Florida	Roll 131

M-595 "Indian Census Rolls, 1885–1940," 692 rolls

Cherokee (North Carolina), 1896–99, 1904, 1906, 1909–12, 1914	Rolls 23-26
Choctaw (Mississippi), 1926–39	Rolls 41-42
Seminole (Florida), 1913–40	Rolls 486-487

M-1186 "Enrollment Cards of the Five Civilized Tribes, 1898–1914." 93 rolls

Index and Final Rolls	Roll 1
Cherokee	Rolls 2-38
Choctaw	Rolls 39-55
Choctaw (Mississippi)	Rolls 56-66
Chickasaw	Rolls 67-76
Creek	Rolls 77-91
Seminole	Rolls 92-93

T-985 - Old Settler Payment Roll, 1896

M-1301 - Applications for enrollment on the Final Roll Dawes Applications (Enrollment Packets), 1899–1907, 468 rolls:

Choctaw	Rolls 1-82
MS Choctaws	Rolls 82-171
Cherokee	Rolls 174-399
Seminole	Rolls 400-402
Creek	Rolls 402-434
Chickasaw	Rolls 434-468

M-1314 "Index to Letters Received by the Commission to the Five Civilized Tribes, 1897–1913." 23 rolls

M-1104 "Eastern Cherokee applications of the U.S. Court of Claims, 1906–1908." 348 rolls (Note: Mobile and Birmingham Public Libraries have Rolls 1-12, General Index to Eastern Cherokee Applications.)

M-668 "Ratified Indian Treaties, 1722–1869." 16 rolls

T-494 "Documents Relating to the Negotiation of Ratified and Unratified Treaties with Various Indian Tribes, 1801–1869." 10 rolls

Fort Worth Federal Archives & Records Center
Microfilm available from FWARC is identified by "7RA."
Five Civilized Tribes
7RA-70 Five Civilized Tribes - 1896 Index to applications under the act of June 10, 1896 (29 Stat. 321) and dockets. Rolls 1-2.
Cherokee
7RA-24 1907 Index to Rejected Applicants
7RA-06 - Mullay Roll, 1848 and Siler Roll, 1851
Choctaw
7RA-116 1830 Lists of people who remained in Mississippi. Rolls 1-2.
7RA-09 1855 Payment Roll. Roll 1
7RA-147 1902–1907 Index to Dawes Rejected ("R") Cards. Roll 1
Creek
7RA-23 - Old Settlers Roll, 1857, rolls 1–2.
7RA-44 - Dunn Roll of Citizens and Freedmen with indexes
7RA-43 - Census, roll 1
7RA-68 - Lists of applicants and docket books of the Creek Citizenship Commission, 1888–1896.
7RA-31 Loyal Creek payment roll, 1904. 1 roll

Other
The American Board of Commissioners for Foreign Missions operated schools for the Indian children in the South prior to removal and

afterward in the West. Names of missionaries, Indian children and some relationships are given. Microfilmed records can be obtained from: Research Publications, Inc., 12 Lunar Drive/Drawer AB, Woodbridge, CT 06525; phone 1-800-444-0799; FAX (203) 397-3893. A list is enclosed, but microfilm is $100 per reel! The only place that has it in the Southeast is Shorter College Library, 315 Shorter Avenue, Rome, GA 30165; (706) 291-2121. They also have some BIA records.

Internet sites for Southeastern Indians

Rootsweb has several "lists" available by tribe, administered by individuals. For example you can join this list CHOCTAW-SOUTHEAST-L@ rootsweb.com by putting "subscribe" (without the quotes) in body of message. It is hosted by Dusty who answers queries and does "look-ups" from numerous rolls. The archives of this site is a gold mine for genealogists.

For another useful site try Judy White's NATIVE AMERICAN RESOURCE CENTER at http://www.accessgenealogy.com/native for rolls, newsletters, lookups, articles, etc.

Internet sites change frequently and pages get moved or unlinked without notice. Perhaps the most useful advice I can offer is to use your favorite search engine (my favorite is www.google.com), put in the name of the tribe you are researching, and click search. You will be surprised at the number of resources available.

Good luck with your search for your American Indian ancestors.

APPENDIX A—1851 PETITION

Petition from Choctaw Indians, Mobile, Alabama to the Commission of Indian Affairs, Washington City [D.C.], November 24, 1851.

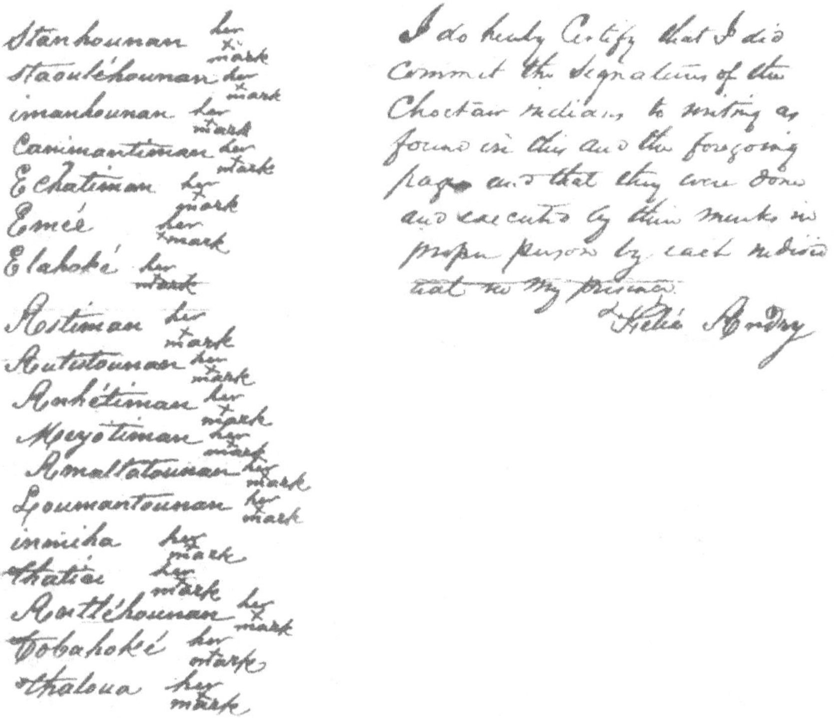

Stanhounan her mark
Staoulehounan her mark
imanhounan her mark
Canimantiman her mark
Echatiman her mark
Emée her mark
Elahoké her mark
Aostiman her mark
Autitounan her mark
Aokétiman her mark
Mayotiman her mark
Amaltatounan her mark
Loumantounan her mark
inmicha her mark
Thatiai her mark
Aottléhounan her mark
Tobahoké her mark
Thaloua her mark

I do hereby Certify that I did Commit the Signatures of the Choctaw indians to writing as found in this and the foregoing page and that they were done and executed by their marks in proper person by each indian ~~in my presence~~
Hélie Andry

[On the Following Page]

Appendix B—1855 Choctaw Census

Census Roll of Choctaw Families, residing East of the Mississippi River and in the State of Mississippi, Louisiana and Alabama made by Douglas H. Cooper, U. S. Agent for Choctaw, in conformity with Order of Commissioner of Indian Affairs, dated May the 23rd 1855.

Census Roll of Choctaw Families, residing East of the Mississippi river and in the States of Mississippi, Louisiana and Alabama; made by Douglas H. Cooper US Agent for Choctaws, in conformity with Order of Commissioner of Indian Affairs dated May the 23rd 1858 —

NARC, RG 75, Entry # 260. Cooper Roll

Heads of Families	Men	Women	Chil	Total	Residences	Remarks
August Charles	1		5	7		
Pow ish tawah homah	1	1	1	3		
Im mu bee	1			1		
E o Nah	1			1		
Pis ti ah	3	2	1	6		
Ye ho to wah		1	1	2		
Lew neah		5		8		
Tish bah he mah	1	2	4	7	St Tammany Parish and Parish of Orleans, La	See Cooper Blank
Ho lo wah	1	4		5		
Eli yo cubbee	1	1	4	6		
Caws fea lubbee	1		1	2		
Po tah	2	3	2	7		
Fillo Kachee	5	2		7		
Ho tah ho mah	2	3	3	8		
Sah ti opah	2	3		5		
On tima hola	2	3	1	6		
Stah nah le tubbee	1	3		4		
Ima ho tubbee	9	2		11		
Ish ti ah		2		2		
Po tah	2	3	1	6		
Ot lo nua	1	6		7		
Oha lis tubbee	2	2		4		
Ow ti emah		1		1		
Ubbe timah		1	1	2		
Wa lee	2	1		3		
Noh o nubbee	1	1	1	3		
Aho fea yo ah	3	2		5		
Ah Kih lo ah	2	1		3		
Wa hi a ho ha	6	1		7		
Hush e no wah	2	3	2	7		
Hoh lo tubbee	2			2		
bene mah tubbee	5	4		9		
Lape ho oho nah	2	5		7		
Yim ma tubbee	3	3	1	7	Jasper and Newton Cos Miss and Mobile Ala	
Ow a hah tubbee	1	1	1	3		
Oh le nas tubbee	2	2		4		
To lo ha chi	2	2	4	8		
Tap fea nam cho tubbee	2	3	5	10		
Forward	68	94	41	193		

184

Appendix C—MOWA Homesteads

MOWA Homesteads by Township, Range, and Section, Date and Certificate Number. Current owners abstracted from 1980 Washington County Tract book. Tensaw Land & Timber Company was established by the Boykin family.

Name	Tn	Rng	Sec	Date	Cert #	Current owner
Byrd, William M.	1N	2W	27	1909	1924	small tracts
Byrd, Sebe	1N	2W	23	1900	18-179	Int'l Paper, Bank
Byrd, Andrew	1N	2W	23	1910	4454	Int'l Paper, Bank
Byrd, George W.	2N	1W	32	1855	14-044	Johnnie Byrd; Bank
Byrd, John	1N	2W	11	1905	20-447	Merchants Bank
Byrd, Thomas E.	1N	2W	13	1907	21-243	Bank; Turner
Byrd, George	2N	2W	35	1902	18-840	Tensaw L&T[1]Byrd Byd
Tom	3N	1W	8	1899	17-620	Tensaw L&T
Byrd, Guy M.	3N	2W	19	1901	18-309	Tensaw L&T
Byrd, Lemuel	2N	1W	18	1899	8305	Tensaw L&T
Byrd, Lemuel Jr.	1N	2W	25	1899	17-232	Turner Sawmill
Chapel, Reed's	4N	1W	34	1850	S&OF	Church & school
Chastang, Joseph	1N	1W	34	1871	546	Woodyard T&L
Chastang, Thomas	3N	1W	8	1896	14-781	Tensaw L&T
Chastang, Jerome	2N	1W	20	1856	14-264	Tensaw L&T
Chastang, Jerome	3N	1W	32	1886	5594	Tensaw L&T
Chastang, Edward	2N	1W	6	1899	8306	Tensaw L&T
Chastang, Francis	2N	2W	1	1899	23-239	Tensaw L&T
Chastang, James	2N	2W	11	1900	17-597	Tensaw L&T
Cole, Mark	2N	2W	3	1899	17-322	Tensaw L&T
Cole, Berry	3N	2W	21	1899	17-389	Tensaw L&T
Cole, Robert	2N	2W	9	1917	8898	Tensaw L&T
Cole, Lucinda	2N	2W	5	1900	18-242	Tensaw L&T
Cole, Dan	2N	2W	12	1899	17-323	Tensaw L&T
Cole, Charles	1N	2W	25	1907	21-307	Turner Sawmill
Davis, Henry	2N	2W	25	1909	2005	Tensaw L&T
Eaton, Henry	4N	1W	22	1889	7887	Tensaw L&T
Evans, George W.	3N	1W	32	1886	5593	Tensaw L&T
Fields, Henry	2N	2W	21	1886	5243	Tensaw L&T
Frazier, William	3N	1W	32	1888	7340	Tensaw L&T
Hopkins, John	2N	1W	30	1901	18-590	Woodyard T&L
Johnson, Samuel	1N	2W	19	1907	21-291	small tracts
Johnson, George W.	4N	2W	34	1889	7828	Tensaw L&T
Johnston, James	4N	1W	24	1825	7598	Tensaw L&T
Johnston, Isaac	3N	1W	34	1900	17-881	Tensaw L&T

Jordan, Rachel	2n	2W	35	1892	11-005	Tensaw L&T
Lofton, Calvin	2N	1W	30	1893	12-485	Byrd Chapel tract
Lofton, Jasper	1N	2W	13	1912	3540	Bank; Turner
Orsaw, Gilbert	2N	2W	33	1874	1714	Tensaw L&T
Orso, Slade	3N	1W	4	1904	19-943	small tracts
Orso, Zeno	2N	1W	26	1840	8981	Shepard Family
Orso, James Mc.	3N	1W	4	1896	14-757	small tracts
Orso, Gilbert, Jr.	2N	1W	18	1899	17-494	Tensaw L&T
Orso, Gilbert	2N	1W	8	1890	9521	Tensaw L&T
Pardue, Hiram A.	4N	3W	24	1895	13-905	Tensaw L&T
Reed, William	3N	2W	14	1894	25-396	Pringle; Dickinson
Reed, James	4N	1W	26	1895	14-667	Tensaw L&T
Reed, George	4N	3W	24	1909	1669	Andrews; Taylor
Reed, Reuben, Sr.	4N	3W	24	1890	9748	Andrews; Taylor
Reed, Joseph R.	4N	2W	36	1899	17-517	Woodyard T&L
Reed, Daniel	6N	2W	28	1836	8144	Jones; Beech, et al.
Reed, Joseph	2N	2W	29	1872	959	Tensaw L&T
Reed, Joseph	4N	1W	5	1899	17-379	Henson, et al.
Reed, William	5N	3W	35	1840	8841	Parnell, et al.
Reed, Daniel	5N	3W	35	1836	7532	Parnell, et al.
Reed, Reuben	3N	1W	4	1876	2472	Reeds, et al.
Reed, Christopher C.	2N	2W	3	1925	11-437	Tensaw L&T
Reed, George W.	3N	2W	22	1896	15-173	Tensaw L&T
Reed, Thomas	3N	2W	24	1897	15-753	Tensaw L&T
Reed, Geo. W., Sr.	3N	2W	2	1897	15-933	Tensaw L&T
Reed, Reuben H.	3N	2W	4	1899	17-343	Tensaw L&T
Reed, Alex	3N	2W	24	1899	17-380	Tensaw L&T
Reed, Seaborn	3N	2W	33	1899	17-502	Tensaw L&T
Reed, Rose	3N	2W	4	1901	18-699	Tensaw L&T
Reed, Christopher	2N	2W	3	1916	986528	Tensaw L&T
Reed, William D.	4N	2W	34	1897	16-061	Tensaw L&T
Reed, Seaborn	2N	2W	5	1871	871	Tensaw L&T
Reed, Eliza	2N	2W	5	1890	9694	Tensaw L&T
Reed, Walter	3N	2W	10	1900	17-773	Tensaw L&T
Reed, Frank	3N	2W	26	1916	15-980	Tensaw L&T
Reed, William	3N	1W	2	1872	917	Tensaw L&T
Reed, Needham	4N	2W	34	1899	17-515	Tensaw L&T
Reed, Lorenda	2N	2W	12	1900	18-226	Tensaw L&T
Reed, Wheeler	3N	2W	27	1912	3365	Tensaw L&T
Reed, Oscar	3N	2W	2	1896	14-900	Tensaw L&T
Reed, Earley	4n	1W	26	1896	15-234	Tensaw L&T
Reed, Mollie	4N	3W	23	1904	19-878	Victor Land Co.
Reed, Miller, Jr.	4N	1W	20	1908	639	Woodyard T&L
Reed, George	4N	1W	28	1883	3177	Woodyard T&L
Reed, William	4N	1W	28	1896	15-071	Woodyard T&L
Reid, Wesley	2N	1W	18	1913	8422	Tensaw L&T

Rivers, Henry	4N	2W	18	1914	4383	Taylor
Rivers, George	3N	1W	4	1899	17-513	Rivers, Reed, et al.
Rivers, Sarah	3N	2W	27	1898	16-564	Tensaw L&T
Rivers, Martha	3N	2W	33	1898	16-664	Tensaw L&T
Rivers, James	2N	2W	25	1893	12-449	Tensaw L&T
Rivers, Luke	4N	1W	20	1901	1886	Woodward T&L
Snow, Milton	3N	1W	2	1889	8050	Tensaw L&T
Sullivan, Geo. W., Jr.	4N	2W	26	1894	25-277	Sullivan, et al.
Sullivan, Mark	2N	1W	10	1891	11-099	Tensaw L&T; MOWA Res.
Weaver, William	2N	1W	30	1898	16-594	Byrd Chapel tract
Weaver, William	1N	2W	27	1909	2077	Small tracts
Weaver, James Taylor	4N	1W	22	1899	7882	Tensaw L&T; Weaver
Weaver, George	3N	1W	18	1896	14-984	Rivers, et al.
Weaver, Josiah	2N	1W	26	1920	9294	Shepard Family
Weaver, David	3N	2W	36	1893	12-059	Tensaw L&T
Weaver, John	2N	2W	25	1894	13-495	Tensaw L&T
Weaver, Daniel	2N	2W	1	1895	13-937	Tensaw L&T
Weaver, Joseph	2N	2W	25	1899	17-285	Tensaw L&T
Weaver, David G.	3N	2W	4	1899	17-400	Tensaw L&T
Weaver, William M.	3N	2W	33	1899	17-497	Tensaw L&T
Weaver, Jessie	3N	2W	36	1893	12-006	Tensaw L&T
Weaver, James A.	3N	1W	8	1894	13-788	Tensaw L&T
Weaver, Filmore W.	2N	1W	6	1894	25-332	Tensaw L&T
Weaver, David C.	3n	1W	24	1890	9049	Tensaw L&T
Weaver, Joseph	3N	1W	8	1890	8894	Tensaw L&T
Weaver, Thomas E.	3N	1W	32	1889	7881	Tensaw L&T
Weaver, David R.	3n	2W	33	1898	16-765	Tensaw L&T
Weaver, George	2N	2W	25	1897	25-932	Tensaw L&T
Weaver, Albert	3N	1W	22	1882	2723	Tensaw L&T
Weaver, Samuel	1n	2W	25	1908	21-479	Turner Sawmill
Weaver, Thomas	1n	1W	31	1901	18-459	Turner Sawmill

[1] Tensaw Land & Timber owns majority of land in sections; small tracts of 5 to 10 acres owned by individuals, some of whom descend from original owners.

Appendix D—MOWA Tribal Leaders, 1979 to Present

Chief:

Framon Weaver—1979–1984; 1988–1995
Cleve Reed—1984–1988
Wilford "Longhair" Taylor—1995–present

Tribal Judge:

John Rivers—1991–1995
Sam Hill—1996–present

Council Chairman:

Verma Reed—1979–1986; 1991–1995
Gallasneed Weaver—1986–1991
Kesler Weaver—1995–present

Council Members:

WASHINGTON COUNTY	MOBILE COUNTY
Prentiss Byrd	Natalie Bruner
Barbara Johnston	Joe Byrd
Frank Johnston	John Bryd
Van Johnston	Lemural Byrd
Cleve Reed	Polly Byrd
Reva Lee Reed	
Jack Rivers	Elizabeth Campbell
Shell Rivers	Viola Campbell
Tommy Rivers	Martha Evans
Vordie Jewel Rivers	Duggar Loften
Charlie Snow	Gertrude Murphy
Daisy Snow	Dale Rivers
Darren Snow	Mary Taylor
George Snow	Prentiss Taylor

Teresa Snow	Mildred Webb
Gallasneed Weaver	
Kesler Weaver	
Laretta Weaver	
Wayne Weaver	

MOWA Choctaw Housing Authority (MCHA)

MCHA was created pursuant to the authority of the Constitution and statutes of the Alabama Legislature, including, particularly, the Code of Alabama H-466, and was duly organized on the 16th day of May 1991. Carl Snow was the Executive Director from 1991–1994. With the election of a new chief, Wilford "Longhair" Taylor in 1995, Craig Thomas Taylor was hired as Executive Director.

Chairmen:

Prentiss Byrd—1991–1994
Verma Reed—1994–1997

Board Members:

Washington County	Mobile County
Prentiss Byrd	Ora Jeanette Allen
Clifton Covington	Natalie Bruner
Grady G. Reed, deceased	John Byrd
Verma Reed	Chris Sullivan
Framon Weaver	Minnie Weaver
Myrtle Weaver	Cathy Wilkerson

Appendix E—Elders' Conference,

15 May 1986, Reed's Chapel Church

Name	Age	Birthdate	County
Bodiford, Nancy	75	11-19-11	MO
Bruner, Joseph	57	12-18-29	MO
Byrd, Amanda	69	6-13-17	MO
Byrd, Lessie	70	3-10-16	WA
Christian, Henry	66	5-21-20	WA
Covington, Annie	59	1927	WA
Douglas, Callie	78	8-28-08	WA
Echols, Alice	64	12-22-22	WA
Howell, Sally D.	74	9-06-12	WA
Johnston, Nancy Weaver	73	9-28-12	WA
Miller, Ethel Reed	81	8-08-05	WA
Orso, Maggie Jane	53	9-11-33	WA
Orso, Minnie	75	12-16-11	WA
Reed, Daisy	72	11-25-14	WA
Reed, Hazel	77	2-15-13	WA
Reed, Ida V.	76	10-24-10	WA
Reed, Lillie	77	3-22-09	WA
Reed, Mauvilla	59	2-19-27	WA
Reed, Nancy	77	1-24-09	WA
Reed, Queenie	63	5-25-23	WA
Reed, Rosie	75	5-29-11	WA
Reed, Ruth	71	4-26-15	WA
Reed, Van	71	8-11-15	WA
Reed, William	74	5-06-12	WA
Rivers, Mary	66	12-16-20	WA
Shepard, Ruth Weaver	74	11-04-12	WA
Snow, Ruth	63	8-28-23	WA
Sullivan, Marie	60	4-03-26	MO
Taylor, Ella Weaver	69	10-22-17	WA
Taylor, Leon	64	8-31-22	WA
Weaver, Annie "Shomo"	81	1-12-05	WA
Weaver, Bennett	57	3-04-29	WA
Weaver, Bufkin	70	5-24-16	WA
Weaver, Margaret	68	6-20-18	WA
Weaver, Margie	73	4-26-13	WA
Weaver, Mary Ann	70	5-1-16	WA
Weaver, Roosevelt	82	11-08-04	WA
Weaver, Shelley Lane	82	8-5-04	WA
Weaver, Willard	69	1917	WA
Wiggin, Emma Byrd	80	5-7-06	MO

NOTES

CHAPTER 1—INTRODUCTION

1   Carl Carmer, *Stars Fell on Alabama* (New York: Farrar & Rinehart, Inc., 1934), pp. 258.

2   Jesse O. McKee and Jon A. Schlenker, *The Choctaws: Cultural Evolution of a Native American Tribe* (Jackson: University Press of Mississippi, 1980), pp. 5–12. Nanih Waiya is located in the southern part of present Winston County, Mississippi.

3   Edward Thomas Price, Jr., "Mixed-Blood Populations of Eastern United States as to Origins, Localizations, and Persistence." (Ph.D. dissertation, University of California, 1950), p. 55.

4   The label "Cajun" is spelled both Cajan and Cajun in records. Cajun, the most common spelling, is used here.

5   Senate Committee on Indian Affairs, *Federal Recognition of MOWA Band of Choctaw Indians*, Sen. Hearing Document 362, 102nd Congress, 1st Sess., 26 June 1991, pp. 246–267, 173–195. Depositions of Kenneth H. Carleton, M.A., Tribal Anthropologist/Ethnohistorian for Mississippi Band of Choctaw Indians, "Comments on the MOWA Band of Choctaw"; Johnnie Andrews, Jr., "Origins of the MOWA Band of Choctaws: A Critique," prepared for the Chief of the Poarch Band of Creek Indians.

6   Richard W. Stoffle, "A Persistent People: Rapid Ethnographic Assessment of MOWA Choctaw Federal Acknowledgement Petition," June 27, 1996. This is a neutral third party report funded by the Association for Native Americans (ANA), an organization which supports the preparation of petitions to the Federal Acknowledgment Division of the Bureau of Indian Affairs.

7   William Armstrong to Commissioner of Indian Affairs, 27 April 1847, National Archives, Record Group 75, Office of Indian Affairs, Letters Received, Choctaw Agency, Emigration M234, Roll 188, frame 226–27 (hereafter cited as RG 75, OIA LR).

8   James Y. Blocker to Commissioner of Indian Affairs, 11 Nov 1851, RG75, OIA LR, M234, roll 171, frame 741–743. See also Caldwell Delaney, *The Story of Mobile* (Mobile: Gill Press, 1962), p. 77; Gordon Baylor Cleveland, "Social Conditions in Alabama as Seen by Travelers, 1840–1850, Part I," *Alabama Review* 2 (January 1949): pp. 3–16.

9   Peter J. Hamilton, *Colonial Mobile* (1910; reprint, with introduction and bibliography by Charles G. Summersell, Tuscaloosa: University of Alabama Press, 1976), p. 58.

CHAPTER 2—KNOWN AND UNKNOWABLE ANCESTORS

1   Gideon Lincecum, "Life of Apushimataha," *Publications of the Mississippi Historical Society*, 9 (1906): p. 479 (hereafter cited PMHS).

2   William S. Coker and Thomas D. Watson, *Indian Trades of the Southeastern Spanish Borderlands: Panton, Leslie & Company and John Forbes & Company, 1783–1847* (Gainesville: University Presses of Florida, 1986), p. 256; Arthur G. DeRosier, Jr., *The Removal of the Choctaw Indians* (Knoxville: University of Tennessee Press, 1970),

pp. 27–28.

[3] Quoted in DeRosier, *The Removal of the Choctaw Indians*, p. 28.

[4] Angie Debo, *The Rise and Fall of the Choctaw Republic* (1934, reprint 2nd ed., Norman: University of Oklahoma Press, 1972), p. 37.

[5] R. S. Cotterill, *The Southern Indians: The Story of the Civilized Tribes Before Removal* (Norman, Okla.: University of Oklahoma Press, 1954), pp. 140–141.

[6] Charles J. Kappler, ed., *Indian Affairs: Laws and Treaties*, 2d ed., 2 vols. (Washington, D.C.: Government Printing Office, 1904), 2: pp. 56–58.

[7] Kappler, ed., *Indian Affairs*, 2: p. 63; Debo, *The Rise and Fall of the Choctaw Republic*, p. 34.

[8] Debo, *The Rise and Fall of the Choctaw Republic*, pp. 40–41.

[9] Kappler, *Indian Affairs*, 2: pp. 69–70.

[10] Ibid., 2: pp. 11, 87.

[11] Samuel J. Wells, "Counting Countrymen on the Tombigbee," *Southern Historian*, 4 (Spring, 1983): p. 9.

[12] Washington County, Alabama Probate Court, *Deed Book A*, pp. 66–67, Piamingo Hometac. See also for varied spelling: Hamilton, *Colonial Mobile*, pp. 247–248, Piamingo Hometah; Horatio B. Cushman, *History of the Choctaw, Chicasaw and Natchez Indians* (Greenville, Tex.: Headlight Printing House, 1899), p. 54, Opiomingo Hesmitta as Hopoamiko Himmittah—the hungry young chief; Kappler, *Indian Affairs*, Opi-a-mingo Henetta, Choctaw Treaty, Aug. 31, 1803; Opiomingo Himeta, Choctaw Treaty, Nov. 16,1805; Piomingo, Opiomingo Hesnitta, Chief on Tombigbee near St. Stephens; *pio* means our; *mingo* means chief.

[13] Interviews with Mary Ann Weaver, 1983 and Lee Weaver, 1984, who were born and reared on High Hill.

[14] Arthur G. DeRosier, Jr., *The Removal of the Choctaw Indians* (Knoxville: University of Tennessee Press, 1970), p. 32.

[15] H. S. Halbert, Manuscript Collection, folder 144, Alabama Department of Archives and History (hereafter cited ADAH).

[16] Jack D. L. Holmes, "Fort Stoddard in 1799: Seven Letters of Captain Bartholomew Schaumburgh," *Alabama Historical Quarterly*, 26 (Fall and Winter, 1964): p. 246.

[17] DeRosier, *Removal of the Choctaw Indians*, 33; "John McKee to Gen. Andrew Jackson, August 9, 1814, and September 9, 1814" and "Capt. James E. Dinkins to Gen. Andrew Jackson, September 18, 1814," Military Records, War of 1812, Choctaw, folder 208, ADAH.

[18] Jacqueline A. Matte, *The History of Washington County: First County in Alabama* (Chatom, Ala.: Washington County Historical Society, 1982), pp. 19–27; George S. Gaines, "Gaines' Reminiscences," *Alabama Historical Quarterly*, 26 (Fall and Winter, 1964): pp. 133–228, gives an account of his tenure as agent.

[19] Debo, *The Rise and Fall of the Choctaw Republic*, p. 37.

[20] RG 75, T500, OIA, Choctaw Trading House Records, St. Stephens, M.T., 1803–1824.

[21] Gaines, *Reminiscences*, pp. 147–148.

[22] Stewart Rafert, *The Miami Indians of Indiana: A Persistent People, 1654–1994* (Indiana Historical Society, 1996), p. 71.

[23] Paula Mitchell Marks, *In a Barren Land: American Indian Dispossession and Survival* (New York: William Morrow and Company, Inc., 1998), pp. 47–48.

24 H. S. Halbert and T. H. Ball, *The Creek War of 1813 and 1814* (1895; reprint, with introduction by Frank L. Owsley, Jr., University: University of Alabama Press, 1969) Albert James Pickett, *History of Alabama* (1851; reprint, Birmingham: Birmingham Book and Magazine Co., 1962), 510–521. Both give detailed accounts of Creek War. (For a 2002 reprint of *Pickett's History,* see Montgomery: NewSouth Books.)

25 Lincecum's narrative is supported by other references to the "disaffected Choctaw" found in "John Pitchlynn, Ocktibbaha to Governor Blount, September 14, 1813," Roll 6; "George Smith, Pitchlands, to A. Jackson, November 23, 1813," Roll 7; John McKee, Fort Smith Mr. Pitchlynns, to A. Jackson, January 6, 1814" and "John McKee, Camp Toote, Massatabbe east bank of the Black Warrior 85 miles above its junction with the Tombigby, to A. Jackson, January 26, 1814," Roll 8, Andrew Jackson Papers, Manuscript Division, Library of Congress; "Narrative, December 5, 1813," John McKee Papers, Manuscript Division, Library of Congress; "David Holmes to Turner Brashears, August 3, 1813," RG 2, Mississippi Territorial Governor's Papers, 6:308, Mississippi Department of Archives and History; "John McKee, Mr. Pitchlynns's, to GS Gaines, January 2, 1814," RG 217, Records of the Accounting Officers of the Department of the Treasurer, Records of the Fifth Auditor, box 1, account 475, National Archives.

26 Debo, *The Rise and Fall of the Choctaw Republic,* p. 41.

27 RG 75, T500, OIA, Choctaw Trading House Records, Daybooks 1808–1813, September 30, 1813.

28 "Capt. James E. Dinkins to Gen. Andrew Jackson, September 18, 1814" and "Thomas Gales, Gen. Jackson's Aide de Camp to Capt. James E. Dinkins, October 3, 1814," Military Records, War of 1812, Choctaw, Folder 208, ADAH.

CHAPTER 3—DISAFFECTED CHOCTAW — THE "LOST TRIBE"

1 Lincecum, "Life of Apushimataha," p. 480.

2 William Warren Rogers, Robert David Ward, Leah Rawls Atkins and Wayne Flynt, *Alabama: The History of a Deep South State* (Tuscaloosa: University of Alabama Press, 1994), p. 54.

3 Jean Strickland and Patricia N. Edwards, *Residents of the Southeastern Mississippi Territory — Three Journals,* Book Four. "Records of the General Land Office, Journal and Report of James Leander Cathcart and James Hutton, agents appointed by the Secretary of the Navy to survey timber resources between the Mermentau and Mobile Rivers, in accordance with an act of March 1, 1817, November 1818-May 1819," pp. 48–49.

4 Lincecum, "Life of Apushimataha," 479–480.

5 Hamilton, *Colonial Mobile,* 138.

6 Will of John Chastang, October 12, 1805, recorded January 18, 1813, Washington County, MT, Ledger 13, 41–42, United States Land Records, Special Collections, University of Alabama Archives.

7 "Some of the People" *The Baldwin County Historical Society Quarterly* (July, 1977): 95.

8 Interview with Ola Irene and Rosie Rivers, sisters of Sancer Byrd, August 23, 1983; interview with Ruth Shepard and Emma Johnston, July 1, 1986. Ruth Shepard repeated this story again to Richard Stoffle, Ph.D., Anthropologist, University of Arizona, on May 8, 1996, at "MOWA Choctaw Elders' Day."

9   "Evidence in the case of Laughlin Durant. Returned to the Treasury; returned to the Commissioner of the GLO, March 10, 1825." Part of this file was sent anonymously to author, without reference. No source has been found for this document; searches were made at the National Archives, General Land Office, Center for Legislative Archives, Bureau of Land Management; ADAH, Baldwin County Probate Records, Monroe County Probate Records, Alabama Supreme Court. Orphans Court Records of Monroe County show that Nancy Oaks was a witness on July 30, 1816 to the will of Josiah Fisher, of Pennsylvania who lived in the Creek Nation, whose wife was Semahoway. Orphans Court Records, Monroe County, LG 217, ADAH.

10   Halbert and Ball, *Creek War*, 143, 157–161.

11   Saustiene Chastang purchased NE frct. NE 1/4, Section 29, T1S, R1E, Mobile County, Cert. No. 9040, Oct. 10, 1843; RG 123, Records of the U. S. Court of Claims, Eastern Cherokee Applications, 1906–1909, M1104, no. 14393 (hereafter cited Eastern Cherokee Applications). Index to applications is in RG 75, Records Relating to Enrollment of Eastern Cherokees by Guion Miller, 1908–1910, M685. Certificate of Death no. 101-14-00080-513 dated August 6, 1914 of Jerome Chastang, lists his mother, Nancy Cecile Chastang and his father, Sostany [sic] Chastang.

12   Eastern Cherokee Applications, no. 43595. Lemuel Weaver, son of David Crockett. Weaver and Ophelia Logan, said, "My grandparents lived in village of Cold Creek. Then my grandparents were living in Mobile County in 1846 at a place called Chastang's. My grandfather was David Weaver and my father is David C. Weaver, born near Chastang's. All of my people have been recognized as half-Indian and half-white."

13   Last will and testament of Philip Chastang, February 23, 1847, *Will Book 3*, 275–277 and Affidavit of James Johnson Sr., *Deed Book 189*, 528, Mobile County, Alabama Probate Court. Fotenay Ellen "Tiny" Bretina was wife of George W. Reed. Certificate of Death no. 101-13-000010-561 dated January 29, 1913 of Ellen Reed, lists her mother, Cecile Weaver and father, Dave Weaver.

14   Interview with James F. Doster, University of Alabama, June 24, 1986. Doster is author of *The Creek Indians and Their Florida Lands, 1740–1823* (New York: Garland Publishing, Inc., 1974).

15   Quoted in Marks, *In A Barren Land*, 78.

16   Land deed and appointment of trustee between Joel T. Rivers and James H. Draughan for the benefit of Edy Weaver, dated August 13, 1844. *Deed Book B*, 401–402, Monroe County, Alabama Probate Records.

17   RG 15, Index to War of 1812 Pension Application Files, M313, no. S.O.25432.

18   Located in southwest side of present-day Mt. Vernon.

19   U. S. Land Records, St. Stephens, Land Certificate no. 7528, June 13, 1836, E 1/2 of SE 1/4, Section 2, T1N, R1W, Mobile County.

20   Interview with Sancer Byrd, August 25, 1983.

21   Edward S. Stone, comp., *The History of Calvert*, (typecript) Mobile Public Library,1977–1978. Red Fox Road, located off U. S. Highway 43 between Calvert and Mount Vernon; Sections 10, 11, 12, 13, 14, 15, 16, 17, 20, T2N, R1W in Mobile County.

22   Interview with Sancer Byrd, August 25, 1983.

23   Peter A. Brannon's Scrapbook, "South Around to Cross Ellicott's Line," LPP6, ADAH.

24   Affidavit stating that Henry Doc Eaton was a full-blood Choctaw Indian, signed

under oath by Creasy Reed, Pat Reed, Harry Hunter Reed, Uria Ann Weaver, Danny B. Reed, and notarized by Comer Pringle, September 26, 1974.

25 Interview with Roosevelt Weaver, August 18, 1983.

26 Interview with Leon Taylor, July 7, 1992.

27 W. Stuart Harris, *Dead Towns of Alabama* (Tuscaloosa: University of Alabama Press, 1977), 13–14.

28 U. S. Land Records, St. Stephens, Land Certificate No. 7598, June 16, 1836, Section 24, T4N, R1W.

29 Interview with Mary Ann Weaver, July 1, 1986.

30 *Book 001, Spanish Land Grants*, 148. Grant was made October 22, 1787; *U. S. Land Records, St. Stephens, Ledger A, Dec. 1806-Mch. 1812, Book 050*, Township 6, Range 1 West, St. Stephens, MT, ADAH.

31 Gaines, *Reminiscences*, 175.

32 Choctaw Trading House Records, "pd. for corn December 1, 1806;" "pd. for cowhides December 31, 1807;" "pd. for beef for Choctaw who fought in Creek War August 14, 1813."

33 Interview with Abb Cole, lineal descendant, July 7, 1986.

34 Gaines Family History File, the *Birmingham News-Age Herald*, Sunday, February 5, 1933, ADAH.

35 Interview with Lee Weaver, June 20, 1988.

36 U. S. Census, Washington County, Alabama, Rose Gaines: 1850, Household #40, 331, mu, [mulatto] age 70, born in Mississippi; 1860, Household 337, 1004, mu, age 80, born in Alabama; 1870, Household 54, age 95, white, born in Mississippi.

37 *Halcyon & Tombeckbe*, March 10, 1819.

38 Letter from Virginia DeMarce, Historian, Acknowledgment and Research Bureau of Indian Affairs, U. S. Department of the Interior, Tribal Services - AR MS:4603-MIB, dated October 18, 1996 to the author; Dale Drake, "Morgan County Yesterday," Morgan County History and Genealogy Association *White River Valley News* (June 7–13, 1997): 7. Other Reeds—Amos, Squire, and Hardy—appear in Mississippi Territorial Records, U.S. Land Office Records at St. Stephens, and Benjamin Hawkins Letters in the same time period.

39 Gary B. Mills, "Backtracking a Cross-Racial Heritage in the Eighteenth and Nineteenth Centuries," *The American Genealogist*, 65 (July 1990): 138.

40 1830 United States Census of Carroll County, Georgia, 214–234.

41 *1803–1816 Washington County, MT Tax Rolls*, 23. Washington County, Alabama Courthouse; Mss Ledger No. 1 "Active and Forfeited land stock of Mississippi Territory, 1815 to 1835 under Act of Congress 23 May 1828." William Stanley Hoole Special Collections Library, University of Alabama.

42 Act passed February 13, 1818 by the First General Assembly of the Alabama Territory in the 42nd year of the American Independence, 1818. No records were found of Rose being bought or sold.

43 U.S. Land Office Records, St. Stephens, October 11, 1836, Certificate No. 8144 (Hobson) Daniel Reed purchased 160 acres in 1817, relinquished all but 40 acres in 1821, which he gained title to in 1836.

44 U.S. Land Office Records, St. Stephens, June 13, 1836, Certificate No. 7532, Section 35, T5N, R3W. (Tibbie)

45 Washington County, Alabama Probate Court, *Will Book B*, 69.

46 Washington County, Alabama Circuit Court, *Book 16, CCS-D-3, 1877–1883*; this is oldest Circuit Court record in basement storage closet of courthouse; no case files exist.

47 *Percy Reed vs. State of Alabama*, October Term, 1921–1922 1st Div. 372–471, Appellate Court Record, Book 270, ADAH.

48 Treaty with the Choctaw, October 14, 1816 (7 Stat., 152. Proclamation, Dec. 30, 1816); Treaty with the Choctaw, October 18, 1820. (7 Stat., 210. Proclamation, Jan. 8, 1821; Treaty with the Choctaw, January 20, 1825. (7 Stat., 234. Proclamation, Feb. 19, 1825.)

49 "Report of the Choctaw Mission School at Goshen, Choctaw Nation, July 1, 1824," Papers of the American Board of Commissioners for Foreign Missions, Houghton Library of Harvard University, microfilm unit 6, reel 757, frame 284.

50 Clara Sue Kidwell, *Choctaws and Missionaries in Mississippi, 1818–1918* (Norman: University of Oklahoma Press, 1995), 144.

CHAPTER 4—REFUGEES — SIX TOWNS CHOCTAW

1   RG 75, Records of the BIA, Records Relating to Indian Removal. Box 6, #267 Misc. Choctaw Records, 1825–58, File: 1830 Choctaws, The President, A. Jackson Talks to Chiefs, Letter to Sec. of War to Comrs. Eaton & Coffee, all autograph.

2   RG 75, Records of the BIA, Case No. 223, Entry 270, Choctaw Removal Records; RG 123, U.S. Court of Claims, *Choctaw Nation vs. United States*, case no. 12742, Evidence File 1837–38 (hereafter cited *Choctaw Nation vs. U.S.*). The two-volume set is in Oklahoma Historical Society; Vol. I is in the General Land Office, Suitland, Maryland.

3   Francis Paul Prucha, ed., *Documents of United States Indian Policy*, 2nd ed. (Lincoln: University of Nebraska Press, 1990), 52; Grant Foreman, *Indian Removal*, (Norman: University of Oklahoma Press, 1972), 21.

4   Kidwell, *Choctaws and Missionaries in Mississippi*, 132.

5   Anthony Winston Dillard, "The Treaty of Dancing Rabbit Creek between the United States and the Choctaw Indians in 1830," *Transactions of the Alabama Historical Society* 3 (1898–99): 99–106.

6   7 Stat. 333, Proclamation, 24 February 1831.

7   No mention was made as to whether head of family was male or female, however in the matrilineal kinship system, children belonged to the mother's family. After Europeans came, this system began to gradually change to patrilineal as mixed-blood families of Indian countrymen increased.

8   *Choctaw Nation vs. U.S.*, 844. Elatubbee, (Elitubbee) was also known as Chief Tom Gibson, a MOWA kinsman.

9   Hilary S. Halbert, "The Last Indian Council on Noxubee River," *PMHS* 4 (1901): 275.

10 *Choctaw Nation vs. U.S.*, 822–828; Halbert, "The Last Indian Council on Noxubee River," 271–280.

11 DeRosier, *Removal of the Choctaw Indians*, 135–36.

12 Ibid., 137.

13 Ibid., 163.

[14] Foreman, *Indian Removal*, 102.

[15] "Muster Rolls of Choctaw Indians," Records of the War Department, Office of the Advocate General, Alabama at War, 2nd Creek War, 1836, SG13379, ADAH.

[16] *Choctaw Nation of Indians vs. U.S.*, 815–817.

[17] DeRosier, *Removal of the Choctaw Indians*, 163.

[18] *Choctaw Nation of Indians vs. U.S.*

[19] Franklin L. Riley, "Choctaw Land Claims" *PMHS* 8 (1904): 345–395. Riley gives a detailed account of this issue.

[20] Charles Hudson, *The Southeastern Indians* (Knoxville: University of Tennessee Press, 1976), 457.

[21] Riley, "Choctaw Land Claims," 366–367.

[22] RG 75, BIA, *Records of the Choctaw Trading House, St. Stephens, M.T. 1803–1824.* T500.

[23] George S. Gaines, Mobile to Gen. Geo. Gibson, Commissary Gen. Of Sub., Washington City, June 30, 1832, Records of the Commissary General of Subsistence, Letters Received, 1831–36, RG 75, entry 201.

[24] "Report of the Committee on Indian Affairs," February 1, 1832, Box 1, envelope 4, folder 1, Doc. 29, Mobile Municipal Archives.

[25] George S. Gaines to Hon. T. Hartley Crawford, September 22, 1844, RG 75, OIA, LR, Choctaw Emigration, M234, roll 1, frame 903–908,

[26] Williaied mstrong to T. Hartley Crawford, November 9, 1845, RG 75, OIA, LR, Choctaw Emigration, M234, roll 185, frame 1088.

[27] William Armstrong to W. Medill, November 26, 1845, RG 75, OIA, LR, Choctaw Emigration, M234, roll 185, frame 1094–1095.

[28] Thomas McAdory Owen. *History of Alabama and Dictionary of Alabama Biography* 3 (Chicago: The S. J. Clarke Publishing Company, 1921), 310.

[29] Chamberlain explained that William Fisher is the brother-in-law of Joseph Krebs, both "worthy citizens." Placide Krebs married a Choctaw woman and went west. Krebs, Oklahoma is named for this family.

[30] One Hundred Red Men to George S. Gaines, December 6, 1849, RG 75, OIA, LR, Choctaw Agency, M234, roll 171, frame 642–648.

[31] William Fisher to the Commissioner of Land East of Pearl River, June 18, 1813, U. S. Land Office Records, Ledger No. 13 (1738–1813): 289, University of Alabama Special Collections; Land Deed from Genevieve Fisher to her children relinquishing her right to the property of her deceased husband, William Fisher, December 17, 1831, Deed Book K:130, Mobile County Probate Records.

[32] Petition in behalf of all the Indians of South Alabama of the Choctaw Nation to Hon. Milliard Fillmore, President of the United States, August 17, 1852. RG 75, OIA, LR, Choctaw Agency West, M234, roll 172, frame 42–47.

[33] J[ohn] Bragg, to Hon. Luke Lea, December 29, 1851, RG 75, OIA, LR, Choctaw Agency, M234, roll 171, frame 755–764.

[34] William Fisher, Mobile, Ala. to Col. P[hilip] Phillips, January 20, 1854, RG 75,OIA, LR, Choctaw Emigration, M234, roll 187, frame 605–606.

[35] "Indians Immigrating," *Mobile Advertiser* (February 24, 1854).

[36] "Off for the Great West," *Mobile Advertiser* (July 1, 1854).

[37] J. W. Zacharia, Hot Springs, Arkansas to Hon. Wm. L. Marcy, Secretary of State,

Washington, D.C., September 8, 1854, RG 75, OIA, LR, Choctaw Emigration, M234, roll 187, frame 609–610.

[38] Douglas H. Cooper to George W. Manypenny, Commissioner of Indian Affairs, May 3, 1856, RG 75, OIA, LR, Choctaw Agency, M234, roll 174, frame 333.

[39] Census Roll, 1856, RG 75, OIA, Choctaw Removal Records, Entry #260, "Mobile, Ala." appears only on handwritten copy; "Mobile" was *not* transcribed on printed copies of the 1856 Census, also called the "Cooper Roll."

[40] Petition submitted by John J. McRae to Hon. J. Thompson, Secretary of Interior, March 11, 1859, RG 75, OIA, LR, Choctaw Agency, M234, roll 175, frame 409–417 and 462–466.

[41] Charles E. Mix, Acting Commissioner, OIA, to Hon. William Barksdale, Columbus, Miss., September 3, 1860, RG 75, OIA, LR, Choctaw Agency, M234, roll 176, frame 13–17 and 165–166.

[42] Charles Lanman, *Adventures in the Wilds: The U.S. and British America*, 2 (Philadelphia: J.W. Moore, 1856), 190–197; James Stuart, *Three Years in North America*, 2 (New York: J & J Harper, 1933), 122–123; Cleveland, "Social Conditions in Alabama as seen by Travelers, 1840–1850," 3–23.

[43] Caldwell Delaney, *The Story of Mobile* (Mobile, Ala.: Gill Printing Company, 1953), 77–78.

[44] Frederica Bremer, *The Homes of the New World: Impressions of America (1849–1851)* (New York, 1853), 11 (New York: A. Hall, Virtue & Co., 1853); copies of sketches of Choctaw in 1851 are in Mobile Public Library-Local History Division.

[45] E. Bryding Adams, ed., *Made in Alabama: A State Legacy* (Birmingham: Birmingham Museum of Art, 1995), 158. "Fig. 164 *Choctaw Belle*, Phillip Romer, 1850. Oil on canvas, 30 x 25 inches. Loaned by Washington and Lee University, Lexington, Virginia, Cat.154."

[46] Halbert Collection, Folder No. 178, ADAH.

[47] Major S. G. Spann, Commander Dabney H. Maury Camp, No. 1312, UCV, Meridian, Miss., "Choctaw Indians as Confederate soldiers," *Confederate Veteran*, 8 (1905): 560–561. Muster Roll of this Choctaw Regiment is in Department of Archives and History, Jackson, Mississippi (cover only, roll missing).

[48] T. H. Ball, *Clarke County, Alabama and its Surroundings, 1540–1877.* (Reprint edition, Clarke County Historical Society, 1973), 95–98.

[49] James M. Glenn, Ph.D., "Indians Still Make Homes in South Alabama Counties: Familiar Figures in Small Towns," 1889, reprinted in *Birmingham News*, (May 15, 1927); also, H. Austill, "White Man's Friend: Choctaw Chief Pushmataha, a Native Great Man," *Mobile Daily Register* (August 21, 1897).

[50] Frances Beverly, "The Red Man in Mobile History," Federal Writers Project, 1930s (typescript).

CHAPTER 5—THE GREEN WALL—HOMELAND

[1] Interview with Roosevelt Weaver, August 18, 1983.

[2] U. S. Department of the Interior. Census Office. Report on Population of the United States at the Eleventh Census: 1890. 1(Washington, D. C.: Government Printing Office, 1895), 132.

[3] Stoffle, "A Persistent People," 10.

[4] Halbert, Folder No. 11, Choctaw Baptist Mission.

5   J. W. Beagle, *People of the Jesus Way* (Atlanta: Home Mission Board, Southern Baptist Convention, 1932) 79.

6   George R. Weaver's original license is in the possession of his daughter, Mrs. Ella Weaver Taylor, McIntosh, AL.

7   The 39th Annual Session of the Mobile Baptist Association, 1919; *Annual Reports of the Southern Baptist Convention,* 1922–1955; Washington County Probate Court, *Deed Book 33,* 1922, "Deed between Albert Weaver and his wife, Mary Ann Weaver and Home Mission Board of the Southern Baptist Convention Church," 436.

8   *Annual Reports of Methodist Mission Work Among the Cajan Communities,* 1931–1966.

9   Interview with Martha Lena Walden, August 12, 1994, Francis N. Sanders Nursing Home, Inc., P.O. Box 130 Gloucester, Virginia 23061. Also, Joan Marble, "Missionary recalls MOWA days, *Daily Press* (October 12, 1994); "Martha Walden Honored," Rappahannock *Times,* (November 3, 1994).

10 Mobile County School Board Minutes, 1854–1950; Washington County School Board Minutes, 1917–1965.

11 "Reports of Cajan Work, Methodist Community House, Mt. Vernon, Ala." *28th Annual Report, Woman's Missionary Society,* 1940, 56.

12 Interview with Mary Taylor, June 30, 1986, whose family lived on the property as squatters and then tenants until 1950s; State of Alabama to W. T. Webb, February 11, 1872, SE 1/4, Sec.10, T2N, R1W, Land Certificate No. 701,11099.

13 Quitclaim Deed from T. A. Webb, Edna M Webb, J. H. Webb, and Mary F. Webb to Southern University, of Greensboro, Alabama, February 6, 1906, SE 1/4, Sec.10, T2N, R1W, Washington County, Alabama, subject to sale of timber thereon to Francis B. Shepard, Washington County Probate Court Records, *Deed Book 9,* 513.

14 Deed from Birmingham-Southern College to MOWA Band of Choctaw Indians, June 17, 1982, SE 1/4, Sec.10, T2N, R1W, Washington County, Alabama, Washington County Probate Court Records, Deed Book 241, 970.

15 Angie Debo, *Geronimo: The Man, His Time, His Place* (Norman: University of Oklahoma Press, 1976), 338.

16 Ibid., 349.

17 Lizzie, oldest daughter of Caroline "Callie" Sullivan (daughter of Tom R. Sullivan and Nancy G. Evans who married Dorsey Weaver) m. 1st Washington Weaver; 2nd Melvin "Jim" Orso.

18 Interview with Mary Taylor and "Bootsie" Byrd, June 30, 1986.

19 RG 94, Records of the Adjutant General's Office, 1780–1917, Consolidated File, Wotherspoon's reports, Mount Vernon Bks., Ala. July 31, 1890.

20 Conversations with Peter A. Rivers, 1983–86; "Geronimo's Indian Orchestra," *Mobile Daily News* (March 11, 1894).

21 Interview with Rosie Byrd Rivers, August 23, 1983.

22 Interview with Ida Reed, July 9, 1985. Mollie was her grandmother and had long black hair.

23 Interview with Richard Weaver, August 22, 1983.

24 Stoffle, "A Persistent People," 10.

25 MOWA tribal members: Viola Campbell, Lola Reed, Virginia Jackson, Leon Taylor, Reva Lee Reed, Ora Jeannette Allen, Mildred Stump, and Barbara Reed reviewed this chapter for accuracy on June 5, 1997.

26 Township 1N, Range 1E, Sec. 43.
27 Interview with Sancer Byrd, August 25, 1983.
28 Jim Laurendine, (also spelled Londine, Rondine) had two known wives, Lucy and Julie. The 1880 U. S. Census, Mobile County, Household 45/51; see RG 75, M1301, Roll 116, MCR, number 2556, Julie Londine.
29 RG 75, M1301, Roll 111 MCR, number 2190, Henry Laurendine.
30 Interview with Richard Weaver, July 28, 1983.
31 RG 75, M1301, Roll 111, MCR number 2189; 1880 U.S. Census, Mobile County, Beat 4, and 1880 U. S. Census, Mobile County, Seals Precinct; Sallie (a.k.a.Polly) is identified as "Indian"; Chancery Court, 13th District, SW Div., Mobile County, Alabama, Henry T. Davis vs. George Brue [Bru], et al., Oct. 2, 1903, *Minute Book "Y"*, 301.
32 Township 2N, Range 1W, Sections 10, 11, 12, 13, 14, 15, 16, 17, 20.
33 RG123, M1104, Easter Cherokee Applications, numbers 43557, 43550,453596, 43548.
34 Native American author and historian, Mary Ann Wells, granddaughter of Emeline Jane Smith Dye, whose grandparents were Emeline Jane Brashears and Ira Byrd Smith, said they considered themselves Choctaw.
35 RG123, M1104, Easter Cherokee Applications, number 9576.
36 1850 U.S. Census, Mobile County: Household 491, Alexander Brashears; Household 500, Lemuel Byrd and William Byrd, age 30; Household 513, Nathan J. Smith; Household 559, David Weaver.
37 1850 U. S. Census, Monroe County.
38 Interview with Sancer Byrd, August 25, 1983.
39 U.S. Land Certificate No. 14-264, November 28, 1856.
40 H. S. Halbert Collection, Folder No. 11, "Choctaw Baptist Mission," ADAH.
41 *Mobile County School Board Minutes*, Mobile Board of Education, Mobile, Alabama.
42 Alabama Board of Education, County Reports, 1870–1910, RC 1-6-25, ADAH.
43 1870 U. S. Census, Mobile County, William's girl; 1880 U. S. Census, Josephine Williams girl, servant to John Smith, with son.
44 Township 2N, Range 1W, 2W Sections 13, 17, 18, 19, 20, 24.
45 *Mobile County School Board Minutes*.
46 Township 2N, Range 1W, Sections 20, 21, 22.
47 Township 2N, Range 1W, Sections 19, 20, 25, 29, 30.
48 Township 5N, Range 3W, Section 35, U. S. Land Certificate No. 7532, June 13, 1836.
49 Barbara Waddell, comp., *The History of Washington County: First County in Alabama* 2 (Chatom, Ala.: Washington County Historical Society, 1989), 331.
50 Washington County School Records, Department of Education, County Reports, 1870–1910, ADAH.
51 In 1983, the new owner, Mrs. Parnell, showed the author buttons and coins retrieved from the graves.
52 Township 4N, Range 1W, Sections 27, 28, 33, 34.
53 Waddell, *History of Washington County 2*, Reed's Chapel Cemetery, 327.
54 Interview with Martha Walden, August 12, 1994, Francis N. Sanders Nursing Home, Gloucester, Virginia; *Royal Service*, May and June 1922; "Missionary recalls MOWA

days," *Daily Press* (October 12, 1994).
55 Charlie Stevenson came from Mississippi. He married Ella Weaver, daughter of James Taylor Weaver.
56 Township 4N, Range 1W.
57 Township 3N, Range 1W, Sections 15, 21, 11, and 28.
58 Waddell, *History of Washington County 2*, Charity Chapel Methodist Church Cemetery, 232.
59 MCR, 2189.
60 *Washington County School Board Minutes.*
61 Washington County Probate Court Records, *Deed Book 33*, 436.
62 Township 3 N, Range 2 W, Sections 4, 5, 7, 8, 27, 28, 32, 33, 34.
63 Waddell, *History of Washington County 2*, Charity Chapel Methodist Church Cemetery, 232.
64 Abb Cole died in 1996 at the age of 100.
65 Township 2 & 3N, Range 1 W, Sections 34, 35, 2, and 3.
66 Waddell, *History of Washington County 2*, St. Thomas Assembly of God Cemetery, 367.
67 Washington County School Board Records, ADAH.
68 Township 3N, Range 1W, Sections 2, 3, 10.
69 Interview with Dinah Snow, October 13, 1983.
70 Township 3N, Range 1W, Sections 5, 6, 7, and 8.
71 Waddell, *History of Washington County 2*, Hill Springs Cemetery Listing, 275.
72 Township 3N, Range 1W, Sections 3, 4, 9.
73 Waddell, *History of Washington County 2*, Magnolia Holiness Church Cemetery Listing, 289.
74 Township 4N, Range 1W, Sections 13, 18, 19, 20, 24,25, 28, 29, 30, 32, 33.
75 RG123, M1104, Eastern Cherokee Applications, number 18402. Henry was son of Easor H. Kellum and Caroline Matilda Weatherford, grandson of John Weatherford and Martha Dyer. (Variations in spelling: Kellum, Killam, Kilian.)
76 Waddell, *History of Washington County 2*, Mt. Pleasant Baptist Church, 120.
77 Township 4N, Range 2W, Sections 22, 23, 24, 26, 27.
78 Township 3N, 4N, Range 1W, Sections 4, 20, 33.
79 Township 3N, Range 1W, Sections 7, 12, 13, 18, 19, 20, 24, 29, 30, 31, 32.
80 Waddell, *History of Washington County 2*, Rivers Baptist Church, 133.
81 Township 4N, Range 1W, Sections 26, 27, 34, 35.
82 Benjamin Hawkins's *Sketch of the Creek Country*, from his diary as he entered Creek nation, December 1796, 3: "Patrick Lane, has a wife among them."
83 Township 3N, Range 1W, Sections 14, 15, 22, 23, 26, 27, 28, 29, 32, 33.
84 Township 3N, Range 1E, IW, Sections, 25, 26, 35.

CHAPTER 6—SUBSISTENCE — LAND LOSS

1 Alabama Legislative Act No. 241, February 7, 1854; Washington County Courthouse Museum, *Record of Marks and Brands*, 1854–1915.
2 Interview with Roosevelt Weaver, August 18, 1983.
3 Edward S. Stone, comp., *History of Calvert* (Typescript, 1977–78), 5, Mobile Public Library, Division of Local History.

4   "Local Option Stock Law," No. 368, *Acts of Alabama*, 1939, 487.

5   Interview with Roosevelt Weaver, July 2, 1986. Isaac Johnston was son of Cornelia "Molly" Weaver and Powell Johnson. Isaac married Matilda Reed, daughter of Rose Gaines Reed.

6   Matte, *History of Washington County*, 100. Frank Parnell listed his occupation as "spar getter" in the 1860 census.

7   Interview with Roosevelt Weaver, August 18, 1983. John Everett was the son of George C.C. Young and Florentine Reed, who was the daughter of Eliza Reed and Francis Pargado. Eliza was the daughter of Rose Gaines Reed, and granddaughter of Kalioka and Young Gaines.

8   *Indian Blood*, prod. and dir. Milton Brown, 58 min., Mobile, Ala.: Bama Boy Productions, 1992, videocassette. WKRG-TV, Mobile, Alabama, aired *Indian Blood* July 4, 1992. Interviews with Daisy Jane Snow, Peter A. Rivers, Gallusneed Weaver, Bennett Weaver, Framon Weaver, and Van Johnston.

9   Matte, *History of Washington County*, 126–127.

10   Ibid., 194–195. Frank W. Boykin (1885–1967) represented the First Congressional District for 27 years.

11   Stoffle, "A Persistent People," 14–15.

Chapter 7—Saloons in the Forest — Customs

1   Alabama Supreme Court: *Rivers v. State*, May 22, 1 Div. 243, Vol. 2741, October 1922 Term, ADAH. (hereafter cited *Rivers v. State*)

2   *Rivers v. State*.

3   Mobile County, Alabama Circuit Court Index 1828–1944, Criminal Court: 1917–1938, Case No. 3745, Dossy Rivers.

4   *Mobile News Item*, Newspaper books: 49–139 and 49–144, ADAH.

5   Walden interview, 1994, 34, 42.

6   Letter to Mrs. Kate C. Hagan, Social Worker, Mobile, Alabama, April 19, 1923 from Governor William W. Brandon re: Dossy Rivers case. Governors' Papers (1923–27: Brandon), RC2:G156, Administrative files, Miscellaneous Correspondence, ADAH. Hagan's letter to Governor Brandon is not in file.

7   Interview with Clasby Rivers, September 20, 1991.

8   Hilary Herbert Holmes, "The so called Cajan Settlements in Southern part of Washington County, Alabama: A Survey made for Governor William W. Brandon, 1924" Governors' Papers (1923–27: Brandon), RC2: G156, Administrative files, folder: "Cajun," ADAH.

9   "'Cajun' Freed; He slew man in 1923." UP, n.p. Montgomery, March 20, n.d. Clipping in vertical file labeled "Cajun" in ADAH.

10   Court History: 745, Board of Pardons, *State Convict Records*, Vol. 10, 984 (SG7466) ADAH.

11   Laura Frances Murphy, "Among the Cajans of Alabama" *Missionary Voice* (November, 1930); Murphy, "Mobile County Cajans" *Alabama Historical Quarterly* (Spring, 1930):76–86; "The Cajans at Home" *Alabama Historical Quarterly* (Winter, 1940): 416–427; Murphy, "The Cajans of Mobile County, Alabama" (master's thesis, Scarritt College for Christian Workers, 1935); R. Clay Bailey, "The Strange Case of the Cajans" *Alabama School Journal* (April, 1931); Horace Mann Bond, "Two Racial Islands in

Alabama" *American Journal of Sociology* 36 (1931): 552–567; Clatis Green, "Some Factors Influencing Cajun Education in Washington County, Alabama" (master's thesis, University of Alabama,1941); Edward Thomas Price, Jr. "Mixed-Blood Populations of Eastern United States as to Origins, Localizations, and Persistence," (Ph.D. diss., University of California,1950); Bibb Bowles Huffstutler, "Oral Anomalies in School Children of an American Triracial Isolate: A Frequency Study" (master's thesis, University of Alabama at Birmingham, 1965); Richard Severo, "The Lost Tribe of Alabama" *Scanlon's* 1 (March 1970): 81–88; B. Eugene Griessman and Curtis T. Henson, Jr. "The History and Social Topography of an Ethnic Island in Alabama" (paper presented at the annual meeting of the Southern Sociological Society, Atlanta, Georgia, 1974); Gary Hinton and B. Eugene Griessman, "The Formation and Development of an Ethnic Group: The 'Cajans' of Alabama" (paper presented at the annual meeting of the American Anthropological Association, Mexico City, November 1974); George Harry Stopp, Jr., "The Impact of the 1964 Civil Rights Act on an Isolated 'Tri-Racial' Group" (master's thesis, University of Alabama, 1971); and others.

12 Stoffle, 18.

13 Laura Frances Murphy, "How Scarritt Students Spend Vacations" *The Trained Lay Worker* 2 (December, 1929): 3.

14 Ibid.

15 *Annual Reports of the Woman's Missionary Council of the Methodist Episcopal Church South.*, 21st *AR*, 386; 22nd *AR*, 348; 25th *AR*, 240.

16 Interview with Mary Taylor and Ruth Shepard, July 1, 1986.

17 Interview with Mary Ann Weaver and Queenie Reed, July 1, 1986.

18 Similar practices are described by William H. Gilbert, Jr., "The Eastern Cherokees" *Bureau of American Ethnology*, Bulletin 133, (1943):168.

19 Interview with Mary Ann Weaver and Queenie Reed, July 1, 1986.

20 Interview with Van Johnston, September 9, 1991.

21 Interview with Roosevelt Weaver, August 18, 1983; also described in Gilbert, 1943, 268; John R. Swanton, *The Indians of the Southeastern United States* (Washington, D.C.: Smithsonian Institution Press; originally published in 1946 as BAE Bulletin 137, 1979), 677.

22 Interview with Framon Weaver, MOWA Tribal Chairman, September 9, 1991.

23 Interview with Kesler Weaver, MOWA and a deputy sheriff for Washington County, September 9, 1991.

24 Dee Brown, *Folktales of the Native American: Retold for Our Times* (New York: Henry Holt and Company, 1993),103.

25 Interview with Mary Ann Weaver, July 1, 1986.

26 Interview with Framon Weaver September 15, 1991.

CHAPTER 8—QUEST FOR RECOGNITION

1 RG 123, M1104, Eastern Cherokee Applications, number 41719.

2 "Hearing before the Select Committee on Indian Affairs United States Senate, 102 Cong:1st Sess., S. 362 "To Provide Federal Recognition of the MOWA Band of Choctaw Indians of Alabama, June 26, 1991" (Washington: U.S. Government Printing Office, 1992), 314.

3 *Brashear v. Williams*, 10 Ala. 630 (1846) and *Wall v. Williams*, 11 Ala. 826 (1847).

4   Papers of Edward Palmer, note dated April 6, 1884, in Mobile, ADAH.

5   General Allotment Act [Dawes Act], February 8, 1887 (U.S. Statutes at Large, 24:388–91) in Francis Paul Prucha, ed. *Documents of United States Indian Policy,* 2nd ed. (Lincoln: University of Nebraska Press, 1990), 171.

6   Applications for Enrollment of the Commission to the Five Civilized Tribes 1898–1914, RG 75, M1301, roll 116, Mississippi Choctaw Roll no. 2556, (Hereafter cited RG 75, M1301, MCR)

7   RG 75, M1301, roll 111, MCR number 2190.

8   RG 75, M1301, roll 111, MCR number 2189.

9   "Proposed Legislation for the Full-Blood and Identified Choctaws of Mississippi, Louisiana, and Alabama with Memorial Evidence, and Brief, 1896–1911," Indian Archives, Oklahoma Historical Society; RG 75, Central Classified Files, 1907–39, 93927-1911-0 53 Choctaw, "Supplement to McKennon Roll, 1899," letter reporting names of Choctaws who were left off approved roll of Mississippi Choctaw Indians; "Enrollment in the Five Civilized Tribes," Hearings before the Subcommittee of the Committee on Indian Affairs, House of Representatives, on the Subject of Enrollment in the Five Civilized Tribes, having under consideration the following bills: 3389, 3390 6537, 7926, 7974, 8007, 10066, 10140, 12586 "The Mississippi Choctaws," 1900–1920s, Library, Oklahoma Historical Society. Contains List of Mississippi Choctaw Indians to whom patents were issued for land under the provisions of article 14 of the Treaty of Sept. 27, 1830 (7 Stat. L, 333–335); List of Mississippi Choctaw Indians in whose behalf scrip was issued under the provisions of the Act of Congress of August 23, 1842 (5 Stat. L., 513) in lieu of land to which they were entitled under Article 14 of the Treaty of September 27, 1830. List of names and testimony of MOWA Ancestors; NARC, Entry 267, Box 4. "List of Persons whose names appear on Identification Roll of Mississippi Choctaws, approved by Act of June 28, 1898 (30 Stat. L., 495), but who were not enrolled on the final rolls of Mississippi Choctaws entitled to allotments in the Choctaw nation under the provisions of the Act of July 1, 1903" (32 Stat. L., 641). On the Dawes Enrollment, the Laurendines (Londines, Rondines) were identified as Mississippi Choctaws, but did not remove.

10 RG 75, OIA, LR, number 10556, John D. Beck, Creek Indian Agent, Cantonment, FL to Secretary of Interior, Office of Indian Affairs, January 25, 1907, "Relative to his final report on the enrollment of Eastern Cherokees and Choctaws." John D. Beck signed MOWA applications.

11 RG 123, M685 Eastern Cherokee Roll, and M1104 Eastern Cherokee Applications.

12 RG 75, M685, "In the Matter of the enrollment of the Eastern Cherokees, Report of Creek Cases, filed with Application number 1139 in case of John Francis McGhee, Atmore, Alabama.

13 RG123, M1104, Eastern Cherokee Applications, numbers 14393, 17390–17395, grandchildren; numbers 41601–41750; 43551–43700, great-grand-children.

14 RG123, M1104, Eastern Cherokee Applications, number 9576, et. al.

15 NARC, RG 75, Entry No. 267, Records Relating to Indian Removal. "Register of Choctaw names as entered by the agent previous to the 24th of August, 1831, who wish to become citizens, according to a provision of the late treaty in 1830;" *American State Papers, Public Lands.* Doc. 1315, 23rd Cong., 2nd Sess. Claims to Choctaw Reservations, "Petition of Alexander Brashears, et al, for claims under Art.

14, Dancing Rabbit Creek Treaty," 648.

[16] William Harlen Gilbert, Jr., "Surviving Indian Groups of the Eastern United States" *Annual Report of the Board of Regents of the Smithsonian Institution for 1948* (1949): 407–438. See No. 18, Alabama.

[17] Senate Report No. 781,Calendar No. 825, 74th Congress, 1st Sess., May 13, 1935; "Choctaw Indians of Mississippi," House of Representatives, Report No. 2415, 74th Congress, 2nd Sess., April 15, 1936; "Claims of Choctaw Indians of Mississippi," House of Representatives, Report 2233, 75th Congress 3rd Sess., April 26, 1948.

[18] Birth and Death Records, Registration No. 651200, Vital Statistics, Records of Washington County, ADAH.

[19] Interview with Mary Taylor, August 9, 1985.

[20] Hugh Sparrow, "White Schools open to Alabama Cajuns," Southwestern Counties *Birmingham News* (November 6, 1967).

[21] *Reed v. State*, Alabama Appellate Reports, Vol. 18:353, 371. Reed testified that his ancestors were of Indian descent; witnesses also testified that Indian ancestry of defendant was proven in an earlier case in 1882: *State v. John Goodman and Jenny Reed*, Circuit Court Book 16, CCS-D-3, 1877–1883, Washington County, Alabama. Defendants were found "not guilty." This is the oldest book of Circuit Court records in courthouse; no case files have been found. John Goodman was Creek Indian, see RG123, M1104, Eastern Cherokee Application, numbers 3392, 18374 and 18382.

[22] *Minutes of Washington County Board of Education*, 1917–1965.

[23] *Mobile County Board of Education Minute Book March 5, 1871- March 9, 1886*, 231.

[24] *Mobile County Board of Education Minute Book November 12, 1919 - November 8, 1922*, 282.

[25] Ibid, 24.

[26] *Mobile County Board of Education Minute Book November 22, 1922- November 10, 1926*, 308.

[27] Hugh Sparrow, "White Schools open to Cajuns" *Birmingham News* (November 11, 1967).

[28] Indian Office File No. 55742-1934; file no. 150. Report on findings was submitted to the Commissioner of Indian Affairs by Dr. W. Carson Ryan, Jr., Director of Indian Education.

[29] Ibid.

[30] Clatis Green, "Some Factors Influencing Cajun Education in Washington County, Alabama." Submitted for degree in Master of Arts in the College of Education in the University of Alabama, 1941.

[31] *Mobile County Board of Education Minute Book November 1930- September 1934*, 701.

[32] *Minutes of Washington County Board of Education*, 1917–1965, 195–196.

[33] Ibid.

[34] *Taylor v. Washington Board of Education, et als,* Circuit Court, Washington County, Alabama, T. J. Bedsole, Judge of the Circuit Court, First Judicial Circuit *Washington County News* (April 3, 1930); *The State of Alabama, Ex Rel Alice Everett v. The Board of School Commissioners of Mobile County et als,* Docket No. 17,750, Circuit Court of Mobile County, Alabama; Also Docket No. 1640, Circuit Court of Mobile County, Alabama, 1941; 244 Ala.467, 1943; 246 Ala. 133, 1944.

35   Letter to Senator Daniel Inouye, Chairman from Rose Marie Stutt, Ed.D., Tuscaloosa, AL in "Hearing before the Select Committee on Indian Affairs, U.S. Senate, 102:1 on S.362 To Provide Federal Recognition of the MOWA Band of Choctaw Indians of Alabama, June 26, 1991." (Washington: Government Printing Office, 1992).

36   Bennett Weaver, "McIntosh Rural News" *Washington County News* (November 16, 1961). Report on PTA meeting at Reed's Chapel School with names listed of leaders and those contributing to fund; Letter from R. A. Boykin to David Scott, Program Associate Education for American Indians Unit, Office of Education, Dept. of Health, Education and Welfare, Washington, D.C, April 24, 1970; Letter from David Scott to R. A. Boykin regarding this issue, June 12, 1970; Letter from Carl Albert, House of Representatives, Congress of the United States, Office of the Majority Leader, to R. A. Boykin stating that he "has received letter from Office for Education for American Indians and that he is referring it to the Office of Civil Rights of the Office of Education to take action responsive to your request." Cc: Bennett Weaver and Gallasneed Weaver, McIntosh, AL.

37   Interviews with Mauvilla Reed, July 29, 1985; Ruth Weaver Shepard, July 1, 1986; Mary Taylor, June 30, 1986; Chandler Weaver, July 10, 1985; Roosevelt Weaver, August 18, 1983;

38   "Indian Descendents Organize Chapter of 'KILROI' In Washington County" *Citronelle-Mt. Vernon Call* (January 11, 1962).

39   Docket 21, Indian Claims Commission, Bureau of Indian Affairs. Copy of Register is in the Mobile County Public Library, Local History Division, entitled "The Head of Perdido Friendly Creek Indian Band," enrolled by Mrs. Roberta Sells, Recording Secretary.

40   "Creeks hold pow-wow" *Mobile Register* (November 26, 1976).

41   Matte, *History of Washington County*, 127.

42   George Pierre Castile and Gilbert Kushner, eds., *Persistent Peoples: Cultural Enclaves in Perspective* (Tucson: University of Arizona Press, 1981), 184. Castile's analysis of the expansion and contraction of ethnicity in "Of the Tarascanness of the Tarascans and the Indianness of the Indians" helps to understand the MOWA Choctaw public resurgence: "While persecution can serve to reduce membership temporarily, it also serves, as many have noted, to increase the strength of the identification of the post-persecution membership. As long as a minimal, 'adequate' mechanism survives, suitable for the transmittal of the symbol sets to new members, the enclave persists, though many of its members may not."

43   Letter from David Scott, Program Associate, Education for American Indians Unit, Department of Health, Education, and Welfare, to R. A. Boykin, Member of Washington County Board of Education, March 27, 1970 and reply from. Boykin to Scott with copies to Gallasneed Weaver and Bennett Weaver, April 24, 1970.

44   "Statement of Jack Edwards, Member of Congress for Alabama 1965–1985" in Testimony in support of S.362 (S.282) Proposed Legislation for Federal Recognition of MOWA Choctaw of Alabama; Sharon Henson, "MOWA Choctaws work hard at economic development" *Mobile Press Register* (January 2–3, 1991).

45   Jeannie Langley, "Weavers Helping preserve Indian culture, language" *Washington County News* (June 4, 1997). Laretta Weaver, Cherokee from Oklahoma, met Gallasneed Weaver at Bacone College. After they married they moved back to his home

in McIntosh.

[46] *Minutes of Mobile County Board of Education*, November 1981, "Delegation No. 3."

[47] Carol Carpenter, "Indian Day held at Calcedeaver" *Mobile Press Register* (August 2–3, 1990).

[48] Interview with Alice Echols, July 26, 1983.

[49] "Memorandum" to Abigail Turner and Ellen Laden from Holly Wise, re: "Migrant Workers in Washington County, June 1, 1978." Stamped "Confidential." Report sent to author anonymously. Searches in ADAH revealed a request for funding for Alabama Migrant and Seasonal Farm Workers Council, 1977, but nothing related to this "Memorandum." Request for further information was made to U.S. Department of Industrial Relations, U. S. Department of Labor and NARC-Southeastern Regional Div. with negative results. Letter to author from Lynda A. Hart, Chief, Workforce Development Division of Alabama Department of Economic and Community Affairs, December 10, 1997 stated, "The records are probably no longer obtainable because CETA had a three-year records-retention requirement."

[50] "Report on Terminated and Nonfederally Recognized Indians," American Indian Policy Review Commission (Washington, D.C.: Government Printing Office, 1976), 468.

[51] "Report on Terminated and Nonfederally Recognized Indians," American Indian Policy Review Commission (Washington, D.C.: Government Printing Office, 1976), 1695–96.

[52] "Regulations, Guidelines and Policies for Federal Acknowledgment as an American Indian Tribe," *Federal Register*, 5 September 1978, 39363. The overall guidelines are 25 *Code of Federal Regulations*, part 81.

[53] "Statement of Bennett Weaver, December 5, 1989" in Testimony in support of S.362 (S.282) Proposed Legislation for Federal Recognition of MOWA Choctaw of Alabama.

[54] Constitution of the MOWA Band of Choctaw Indians of South Alabama.

[55] Articles of Incorporation of the MOWA Band of Choctaw Indians of South Alabama: A non-profit corporation.

[56] Matte, *History of Washington County*, 128.

[57] Connie Baggett, "Indian Educators to Convene this Weekend" *Mobile Press Register*, (November 5, 1993).

[58] Frank Sikora, "Choctaws rekindle council fire to unite red man" *Birmingham News* (September 28, 1980): 2-a.

[59] "Atalwachi," *Newsletter of the MOWA Band of Choctaw Indians*, (June 1980).

[60] "Choctaw Indians Purchase Large Site near Calvert; to Develop It" *Call-News Dispatch* (September 16, 1982).

[61] Sharon Henson, "MOWA Choctaws work hard at Economic Development" *Mobile Press Register* (January 2–3, 1991).

[62] Carol Carpenter, "MOWAs smiling over grant for housing" *Mobile Register* (January 15, 1993).

[63] Gayle Ray, "MOWA Complex Open," *Mobile Register* (December 11, 1993); "MOWA Indians Dedicate New Complex" *Citronelle Call* (December 16, 1993); Mike Breedlove, "Choctaw Indians dedicate $500,000 tribal complex" *The South Alabamian* (December 16, 1993); "Choctaws Dedicate Center, Residential Housing Units" *Washington County News* (December 16, 1993).

64 "Indians Seeking Federal Status" *Call-News Dispatch* (November 11, 1983).
65 Arthur Drago Jr., "MOWA Indians expect federal recognition" *Mobile Press Register* (February 8, 1987).
66 "Shelby introduces MOWA legislation" *Mobile Press Register* (May 7, 1987); Cathy Donelson, "MOWAs Approaching Recognized Tribe Status" *Montgomery Advertiser* (May 8, 1987); S.1142, Shelby; H. R. 3107, Callahan, Nichols, Erdreich.
67 Nan Powers, "Shelby again seeks recognition for MOWAs" *Mobile Register* (February 7, 1991); Brad Clemenson, "Shelby offers bill to recognize Mowas" *Mobile Press* (February 9 1989); S. 381, Shelby, Heflin; H.R. 1562, Callahan.
68 Senate Hearing 101-762.
69 Cathy Donelson, "Creeks object to MOWA recognition; Shelby's bill has local feud brewing" *Mobile Register* (February 15, 1991; Ron Colquitt, "Poarch boss: MOWAs not going by the rules" *Mobile Register* (March 22, 1991); "Tullis said opposing MOWA recognition because of gambling" *Mobile Press Register* (March 23, 1991).
70 Letter from Eddie L. Tullis, Chairman, Poarch Band of Creek Indians to Framon Weaver, Chairman, MOWA Band of Choctaw Indians, June 20, 1981.
71 S. 362 Shelby, Heflin; H.R. 2349, Callahan.
72 "Senate recognizes MOWA Indians" *Mobile Register* (July 19, 1991); S. 362 Shelby, Heflin; H.R. 2349, Callahan.
73 Jeff Hardy, "Senate gives approval to MOWA recognition" *Mobile Press Register* (October 16, 1992).
74 Jeff Hardy, "MOWA recognition on back burner" *Mobile Register* (July 2, 1993); S. 282; Shelby, Heflin, Inouye; H.R. 3605, Hilliard.
75 Stoffle, 1.
76 Ibid.
77 Letter to Ms. Holly Reckord, Bureau of Indian Affairs, Washington, D. C. from Chief Wilford "Longhair" Taylor, Mt. Vernon, Alabama, June 27, 1996.

CHAPTER 9—EPILOGUE

1 Gerald M. Sider, *Lumbee Indian Histories: Race, Ethnicity, and Indian Identity in the Southern United States* (Cambridge University Press, 1993), xvii.
2 "MOWA Band of Choctaws denied U.S. recognition," *Birmingham News* (December 24, 1997).
3 25 *Code of Federal Regulations*, part 81.
4 Jeff Hardy, "MOWAs are denied federal recognition," *Mobile Register* (December 23, 1997).
5 Jeff Hardy, "MOWA Indians seek Callahan's help," *Mobile Register* (January 14, 1998).
6 Samuel M. Hill, Counsel to MOWA Band of Choctaw Indians.
7 "Doesn't take government to tell us who we are," *Mobile Register* (December 26, 1997).
8 Willie Gray, "Governor James supports MOWA tribe," *Citronelle-Call* (May 16, 1996); Larry O'Hara, "Legislature, governor congressmen support recognition of MOWAs," *Washington County News* (April 29, 1998); Resolution HJR 210, April 8, 1998.
9 "MOWAs' appeal must be granted within 120 days," *Washington County News* (May 6, 1998).
10 *Indian County Today*, April 18, 2001, posted on Internet by Jim Adams. Published May 16, 2001, in Special Edition of *Indian Country Today*.

Bibliography

Books

Ball, T. H. *Clarke County, Alabama and its Surroundings, 1540–1877.* 1879. Reprint, Clarke County Historical Society, 1973.

Bremer, Frederika. *The Homes of the New World: Impressions of America, 1847–1851* 11. London: A. Hall, Virtue & Co., 1853.

Brown, Dee. *Folktales of the Native American: Retold for Our Times.* New York: Henry Holt and Company, 1993.

Carmer, Carl. *Stars Fell on Alabama.* New York: Farrar & Rinehart, 1934.

Castile, George Pierre and Gilbert Kushner, eds. *Persistent Peoples: Cultural Enclaves in Perspective.* Tucson: University of Arizona Press, 1981.

Coker, William S. and Thomas D. Watson, *Indian Trades of the Southeastern Spanish Borderlands: Panton, Leslie & Company and John Forbes & Company, 1783–1847.* Gainesville: University Presses of Florida, 1986.

Cotterill, R. S. *The Southern Indians: The Story of the Civilized Tribes Before Removal.* Norman: University of Oklahoma Press, 1954.

Cushman, Horatio B. *History of the Choctaw, Chicasaw and Natchez Indians.* Greenville, Tex.: Headlight Printing House, 1899.

Debo, Angie. *The Rise and Fall of the Choctaw Republic.* 1934. Reprint, Norman: University of Oklahoma Press, 1972.

____ *Geronimo: The Man, His time, His Place.* Norman: University of Oklahoma Press, 1976.

Delaney, Caldwell. *The Story of Mobile.* Mobile, Ala.: Gill Printing Company, 1953.

DeRosier, Jr., Arthur G. *The Removal of the Choctaw Indians.* Knoxville: University of Tennessee Press, 1970.

Doster, James F. *The Creek Indians and their Florida Lands, 1740–1823.* New York: Garland Publishing, Inc., 1974.

Foreman, Grant. *Indian Removal.* Norman: University of Oklahoma Press, 1972.

Halbert, H. S. and T. H. Ball. *The Creek War of 1813 and 1814.* 1895. Reprint, with introduction by Frank L. Owsley, Jr., University: University of Alabama Press, 1969.

Hamilton, Peter J. *Colonial Mobile.* 1897, 1910. Reprint, edited with introduction and annotations by Charles G. Summersell, University: University of Alabama Press, 1976.

Harris, W. Stuart. Dead *Towns of Alabama.* Tuscaloosa: University of Alabama Press, 1977.

Hudson, Charles. *The Southeastern Indians.* Knoxville: University of Tennessee Press, 1976.

Kidwell, Clara Sue. *Choctaws and Missionaries in Mississippi, 1818–1918.* Norman: University of Oklahoma Press, 1995.

Lanman, Charles. *Adventures in the Wilds: the U.S. and British America*, Vol. 2. Philadelphia: J. W. Moore, 1856.

Marks, Paula Mitchell. *In a Barren Land: American Indian Dispossession and Survival.* New York: William Morrow and Company, Inc., 1998.

Matte, Jacqueline A. *The History of Washington County: First County in Alabama.* Vol. 1. Chatom, Ala.: Washington County Historical Society, 1982.

McKee, Jesse O. and Jon A. Schlenker. *The Choctaws: Cultural Evolution of a Native American Tribe.* Jackson: University Press of Mississippi, 1980.

Owen, Thomas McAdory. *History of Alabama and Dictionary of Alabama Biography.* Vol. 3. Chicago: The S. J. Clarke Publishing Company, 1921.

Pickett, Albert James. *History of Alabama.* 1851. Reprint, Birmingham: Birmingham Book and Magazine Co., 1962.

Prucha, Francis Paul, ed. *Documents of United States Indian Policy.* 2nd ed. Lincoln: University of Nebraska Press, 1990.

Rafert, Stewart. *The Miami Indians of Indiana: A Persistent People, 1654–1994.* Indiana Historical Society, 1996.

Rogers, William Warren, Robert David Ward, Leah Rawls Atkins and Wayne Flynt. *Alabama: The History of a Deep South State.* Tuscaloosa: University of Alabama Press, 1994.

Sider, Gerald M. *Lumbee Indian Histories: Race, Ethnicity, and Indian Identity in the Southern United States.* New York: Cambridge University Press, 1993.

Strickland, Jean and Patricia N. Edwards, comps. *Residents of the Southeastern Mississippi Territory - Three Journals, Book Four.* Moss Point, Miss.: Ben Strickland, 1996.

Stuart, James. *Three Years in North America.* Vol. 2. New York: J & J Harper, 1933.

Waddell, Barbara, comp. *The History of Washington County: First County in Alabama.* Vol. 2, Chatom, Ala.: Washington Co. Historical Society, 1989.

JOURNAL ARTICLES

Bailey, R. Clay. "The Strange Case of the Cajans." *Alabama School Journal* (April, 1931).

Beagle, J. W. *People of the Jesus Way.* Atlanta: Home Mission Board, Southern Baptist Convention (1932): 79.

Bond, Horace Mann. "Two Racial Islands in Alabama." *American Journal of Sociology* 36 (1931): 552–567.

Cleveland, Gordon Baylor. "Social Conditions in Alabama as Seen by Travelers, 1840–1850, Part I." *Alabama Review* 2 (January 1949): 3–16.

Dillard, Anthony Winston, "The Treaty of Dancing Rabbit Creek between the United States and the Choctaw Indians in 1830." *Transactions of the Alabama Historical Society* 3 (1898–99): 99–106.

Drake, Dale. "Morgan County Yesterday." Morgan County History and

Genealogy Association. *White River Valley News* (June 7–13, 1997): 7.

Gaines, George S. "Gaines' Reminiscences." *Alabama Historical Quarterly* 26 (Fall and Winter, 1964): 133–228.

Gregg, Rhonda Sessions. "Circle of Life." *UAB Magazine* (Summer, 1995): 12–15.

Halbert, Hilary S. "The Last Indian Council on Noxubee River." *Publications of the Mississippi Historical Society* 4 (1901): 275.

Holmes, Jack D. L. "Fort Stoddard in 1799: Seven Letters of Captain Bartholomew Schaumburgh."
Alabama Historical Quarterly 26 (Fall and Winter, 1964): 246.

Lincecum, Gideon. "Life of Apushimataha." *Publications of the Mississippi Historical Society*, 9 (1906): 479.

Murphy, Laura Frances. "How Scarritt Students Spend Vacations." *The Trained Lay Worker* 2 (December, 1929): 3.

_____ "Byrd Settlement—A New Field of Service" and "Among the Cajans of Alabama." *Missionary Voice* (November, 1930).

_____ "Mobile County Cajans." *Alabama Historical Quarterly* (Spring, 1930): 76–86.

_____ "The Cajans at Home." *Alabama Historical Quarterly* (Winter, 1940): 416–427.

Riley, Franklin L. "Choctaw Land Claims." *Publications of the Mississippi Historical Society* 8 (1904): 345–395.

"Some of the People." *The Baldwin County Historical Society Quarterly* 4 (July, 1977): 95.

Spann, Major S. G., Commander Dabney H. Maury Camp, No. 1312, UCV, Meridian, Miss.,

"Choctaw Indians as Confederate soldiers." *Confederate Veteran* 8 (1905): 560–561.

Wells, Samuel J. "Counting Countrymen on the Tombigbee." *Southern Historian* 4 (Spring, 1983):

NEWSPAPERS

Birmingham News, 1 May 1927; 6 and 11 Nov 1967; 28 Sep 1980.

Birmingham Post Herald, 29 March 1990.

Call-News Dispatch, 16 September 1982; 11 November 1983.

Citronelle Call, 16 December 1993.

Citronelle-Mt. Vernon Call, 11 January 1962.

Gloucester (Virginia) Daily Press, 12 October 1994.

Halcyon & Tombeckbe, 10 March 1819.

Mobile Advertiser, 24 February and 1 July 1854.

Mobile Daily News, 11 March 1894.

Mobile Daily Register, 21 August 1897.

Mobile News Item, 5 January 1922 - 25 April 1923.

Mobile Press, 29 March 1990.

Mobile Press Register, 2–3 August 1990; 2–3 January 1991; 23 March 1991; 16 October 1992; 5 November 1993.

Mobile Register, 26 November 1976; 8 February 1987; 7 May 1987; 29 March 1990; 7 and 15 February 1991; 22 March 1991; 19 July 1991; 15 January 1993; 2 July 1992; 11 December 1993.

Montgomery Advertiser, 8 May 1987.

New York Times, Scanlon's, 1 March 1970.

Rappahannock (Virginia) Times, 3 November 1994.

The South Alabamian, 16 December 1993.

Washington County News, 3 April 1930; 16 November 1961; 16 December 1993; 4 June 1997.

ANNUAL REPORTS

The 39th Annual Session of the Mobile Baptist Association, 1919.

Annual Reports of the Southern Baptist Convention, 1922–1955.

Annual Reports of Methodist Mission Work Among the Cajan Communities, 1931–1966.

Annual Report, Woman's Missionary Society, 1940.

Annual Reports of the Woman's Missionary Council of the Methodist Episcopal Church South.

THESES AND DISSERTATIONS

Green, Clatis. "Some Factors Influencing Cajun Education in Washington County, Alabama." Master's thesis, University of Alabama, 1941.

Huffstutler, Bibb Bowles. "Oral Anomalies in School Children of an American Triracial Isolate: A Frequency Study." Master's thesis, University of Alabama at Birmingham,1965.

Murphy, Laura Frances. "The Cajans of Mobile County, Alabama." Master's thesis, Scarritt College for Christian Workers, 1935.

Price, Edward Thomas Jr. "Mixed-Blood Populations of Eastern United States as to Origins, Localizations, and Persistence." Ph.D. diss., University of California, 1950.

Stopp, Jr., George Harry. "The Impact of the 1964 Civil Rights Act on an Isolated 'Tri-Racial' Group." Master's thesis, University of Alabama, 1971.

PAPERS

Griessman, B. Eugene and Curtis T. Henson, Jr. "The History and Social Topography of an Ethnic Island in Alabama." Paper presented at the annual meeting of the Southern Sociological Society, Atlanta, Georgia, 1974.

Hinton, Gary and B. Eugene Griessman. "The Formation and Development of an Ethnic Group: The 'Cajans' of Alabama." Paper presented at the annual meeting of the American Anthropological Association, Mexico City, November 1974.

REPORTS—GOVERNMENT DOCUMENTS

American State Papers, Public Lands. Doc. 1315, 23rd Cong., 2nd Sess. Claims to Choctaw Reservations, "Petition of Alexander Brashears, et al. for claims under Art. Dancing Rabbit Creek Treaty," 648.

Beverly, Frances. "The Red Man in Mobile History." Federal Writers Project. Typescript in Mobile Public Library, Local History Division.

"Choctaw Indians of Mississippi," House of Representatives, Report No. 2415, 74th Congress, 2nd Sess., April 15, 1936.

"Claims of Choctaw Indians of Mississippi," House of Representatives, Report 2233, 75th Congress 3rd Sess., April 26, 1948.

"Enrollment in the Five Civilized Tribes," Hearings before the Subcommittee of the Committee on Indian Affairs, House of Representatives, on the Subject of Enrollment in the Five Civilized Tribes, having under consideration the following bills: 3389, 3390 6537, 7926, 7974, 8007, 10066, 10140, 12586

"The Mississippi Choctaws," 1900–1920s, Library, Oklahoma Historical Society. Contains List of Mississippi Choctaw Indians to whom patents were issued for land under the provisions of article 14 of the Treaty of Sept. 27, 1830 (7 Stat. L, 333–335).

Gilbert, William Harlen, Jr. "The Eastern Cherokees." Bureau of American Ethnology, Bulletin 133, 1943.

_____ "Surviving Indian Groups of the Eastern United States." *Annual Report of the Board of Regents of the Smithsonian Institution for 1948* (1949): 407–438. See No. 18, Alabama.

"Hearing before the Select Committee on Indian Affairs United States Senate, 102 Cong:1st Sess., S. 362 "To Provide Federal Recognition of the MOWA Band of Choctaw Indians of Alabama, June 26, 1991." (Washington: U.S. Government Printing Office, 1992.

Indian Office File No. 55742-1934; file no. 150. Report on findings was submitted to the Commissioner of Indian Affairs by Dr. W. Carson Ryan, Jr., Director of Indian Education.

Kappler, Charles J., ed., *Indian Affairs: Laws and Treaties*, 2d ed., 2 vols. (Washington, D.C.: Government Printing Office, 1904), 2:56–58.

"List of Mississippi Choctaw Indians in whose behalf scrip was issued under the provisions of the Act of Congress of August 23, 1842 (5 Stat. L., 513) in lieu of land to which they were entitled under Article 14 of the Treaty of September 27, 1830."

McKee, John. Papers. Manuscript Division, Library of Congress.

"Proposed Legislation for the Full-Blood and Identified Choctaws of Mississippi, Louisiana, and Alabama with Memorial Evidence, and Brief, 1896–1911," Indian Archives, Oklahoma Historical Society.

RG 2, Mississippi Territorial Governor's Papers. Mississippi Department of Archives and History.

RG 75, Central Classified Files, 1907–39, 93927-1911-0 53 Choctaw, "Supplement to McKennon Roll, 1899," letter reporting names of Choctaws who were left off approved roll of Mississippi Choctaw Indians.

RG 75, OIA, Choctaw Removal Records, Entry #260, Census Roll, 1856.

RG 75, Records of the BIA, Records Relating to Indian Removal. Box 6, #267 Misc. Choctaw Records, 1825–58, File: 1830 Choctaws, The President, A. Jackson Talks to Chiefs, Letter to Sec. of War to Comrs. Eaton & Coffee, all autograph; Entry 267, Box 4. "List of Persons whose names appear on Identification Roll of Mississippi Choctaws, approved by Act of June 28, 1898 (30 Stat. L., 495), but who were not enrolled on the final rolls of Mississippi Choctaws entitled to allotments in the Choctaw nation under the provisions of the Act of July 1, 1903 (32 Stat. L., 641)."

RG 75, Records of the BIA, Case No. 223, Entry 270, Choctaw Removal Records

RG 75, Records of the Commissary General of Subsistence, Letters Received, 1831–36, entry 201.

RG 123, U.S. Court of Claims, *Choctaw Nation vs. United States*, case no. 12742, Evidence File 1837–38.

RG 217, Records of the Accounting Officers of the Department of the Treasurer, Records of the Fifth Auditor, box 1, account 475, National Archives.

"Regulations, Guidelines and Policies for Federal Acknowledgment as an American Indian Tribe." *Federal Register*, 5 September 1978, 39363. The overall guidelines are 25 *Code of Federal Regulations*, part 81.

"Report on Terminated and Nonfederally Recognized Indians." American Indian Policy Review Commission (Washington, D.C.: Government Printing Office, 1976), 1695–96.

Senate Committee on Indian Affairs, *Federal Recognition of MOWA Band of Choctaw Indians*, Sen. Hearing Document 362, 102nd Cong. 1st Sess., 26 Jun 1991, 246–267, 173–195

Senate Report No. 781,Calendar No. 825, 74th Congress, 1st Sess., May 13, 1935.

Stoffle, Richard W. "A Persistent People: Rapid Ethnographic Assessment of MOWA Choctaw Federal Acknowledgement Petition, " June 27, 1996.

Swanton, John R. *The Indians of the Southeastern United States*. Originally published in 1946 as Bureau of American Ethnology, Bulletin 137. Washington, D. C.: Smithsonian Institution Press, 1979.

7 Stat.333, Proclamation, 24 February 1831.

Treaty with the Choctaw, October 14, 1816 (7 Stat., 152. Proclamation, Dec. 30, 1816)

Treaty with the Choctaw, October 18, 1820. (7 State. 210. Proclamation, Jan. 8, 1821

Treaty with the Choctaw, Jan 20, 1825. (7 Stat., 234. Proclam., Feb. 19, 1825.)

MICROFILM

American Board of Commissioners for Foreign Missions, Houghton Library of Harvard University, microfilm unit 6, reel 757, frame 284.

Jackson, Andrew. Papers. Manuscript Division, Lib of Congress, rolls 6–8.

RG 15, Index to War of 1812 Pension Application Files, M313.

RG 75, Applications for Enrollment of the Commission to the Five Civilized Tribes 1898–1914, M1301.

RG 75, Office of Indian Affairs, Letters Received, April 1847, Choctaw Agency, Emigration, M234.

RG 75, T500, OIA, Choctaw Trading House Records, St. Stephens, M.T., 1803–1824.

RG 75, T500, OIA, Choctaw Trading House Records, Daybooks, St. Stephens, M.T., 1808–1813.

RG 75, Records Relating to Enrollment of Eastern Cherokees by Guion Miller, 1908–1910, M685.

RG 94, Records of the Adjutant General's Office, 1780–1917.

RG 123, Records of the U. S. Court of Claims, Eastern Cherokee Applications, 1906–1909, M1104.

CENSUS

U. S. Census, Mobile County, Alabama; Washington County, Alabama.

U. S. Department of the Interior. Census Office. Report on Population of the United States at the Eleventh Census: 1890.

COUNTY RECORDS

Mobile County, Alabama Circuit Court Index 1828–1944, Criminal Court: 1917–1938.

Mobile County, Alabama Probate Court Records.

Mobile County School Board Minutes, 1854–1950.

"Report of the Committee on Indian Affairs," February 1, 1832, box 1, envelope 4, folder 1, Doc. 29, Mobile Municipal Archives.

State of Alabama, Ex Rel Alice Everett v. The Board of School Commissioners of Mobile County et als, Docket No. 17,750, Circuit Court of Mobile County, Alabama; Also Docket No. 1640, Circuit Court of Mobile County, Alabama, 1941; 244 Ala.467, 1943; 246 Ala. 133, 1944.

Stone, Edward S., comp., *History of Calvert.* 1977–78, typescript. Mobile County Public Library - Local History Division.

Washington County, Alabama Circuit Court Records.

Washington County, Alabama, Probate Court Records.

Washington County Courthouse Museum, *Record of Marks and Brands,* 1854–1915

Washington County School Board Minutes, 1917–1965.

1803–1816 Washington County, MT Tax Rolls. Washington County, Alabama.

State v. John Goodman and Jenny Reed, Circuit Court Book 16, CCS-D-3, 1877–1883, Washington County, Alabama.

Taylor v. Washington Board of Education, et al. Circuit Court, Washington County, Alabama, T. J. Bedsole, Judge of the Circuit Court, First Judicial Circuit.

MISCELLANEOUS DOCUMENTS AT ADAH

Act passed February 13, 1818 by the First General Assembly of the Alabama Territory in the 42nd year of the American Independence, 1818.

Alabama Legislative Act No. 241, February 7, 1854; No. 368, 1939.

Birth and Death Records, Registration No. 651200, Vital Statistics, Records of Washington County.

Brandon, W. W. Governors' Papers (1923–27: Brandon), RC2:G156, Administrative files, Miscellaneous Correspondence.

Brannon, Peter A. Scrapbook, "South Around to Cross Ellicott's Line."

Brashear v. Williams, 10 Ala. 630 (1846).

Gaines Family History File, *Birmingham News-Age Herald*, Sunday, February 5, 1933.

Halbert, H. S. Manuscript Collection, folder 144.

Military Records, War of 1812, Choctaw, Folder 208.

"Muster Rolls of Choctaw Indians," Records of the War Department, Office of the Advocate General, Alabama at War, 2nd Creek War, 1836, SG13379.

Palmer, Edward. Papers. Note dated 6 April 1884 in Mobile*prcy Reed vs. State of Alabama*, October Term, 1921–1922 1st Div. 372–471, Appellate Court Record, Book 270.

Reed v. State, Alabama Appellate Reports, Vol. 18:353, 371

Rivers v. State, May 22, 1 Div. 243, Vol. 2741, October 1922 Term, Alabama Supreme Court.

State Convict Records, Vol. 10, 984 Court History: 745, Board of Pardons (SG7466).

U. S. Land Records, St. Stephens, MT.

Wall v. Williams, 11 Ala. 826 (1847).

HOOLE SPECIAL COLLECTIONS , UNIV. of Alabama

Mss. Ledger No. 1 "Active and Forfeited land stock of Mississippi Territory, 1815 to 1835 under Act of Congress 23 May 1828." Washington County, MT, Ledger 13, United States Land Records.

PERSONAL COMMUNICATION

Letter to author from Virginia DeMarce, Historian, Acknowledgment and Research Bureau of Indian Affairs, U. S. Department of the Interior, Tribal Services - AR MS:4603-MIB, 18 October 1996.

INDEX

www.ingramcontent.com/pod-product-compliance
Lightning Source LLC
Chambersburg PA
CBHW050649270326
41927CB00012B/2936